Kenyan, Christian, Queer

AFRICANA RELIGIONS

Edited by

Sylvester A. Johnson, *Virginia Tech*

Edward E. Curtis IV, *Indiana University–Purdue University, Indianapolis*

Adopting a global vision for the study of Black religions, the Africana Religions book series explores the rich diversity of religious history and life among African and African-descended people. It publishes research on African-derived religions of Orisha devotion, Christianity, Islam, and other religious traditions that are part of the Africana world. The series emphasizes the translocal nature of Africana religions across national, regional, and hemispheric boundaries.

Kenyan, Christian, Queer

Religion, LGBT Activism, and Arts of Resistance in Africa

ADRIAAN VAN KLINKEN

The Pennsylvania State University Press
University Park, Pennsylvania

Library of Congress Cataloging-in-Publication Data

Names: Van Klinken, A. S., author.
Title: Kenyan, Christian, queer : religion, LGBT activism, and arts of resistance in Africa / Adriaan van Klinken.
Other titles: Africana religions.
Description: University Park, Pennsylvania : The Pennsylvania State University Press, [2019] | Series: Africana religions
Summary: "Examines the role of religion in LGBT activism in Kenya. Offers case studies of creative forms of queer visibility through which Kenyan LGBT individuals organize and present themselves in the public domain while critically engaging and appropriating Christian beliefs, symbols, and practices"—Provided by publisher.
Identifiers: LCCN 2019015040 | ISBN 9780271083803 (cloth : alk. paper)
Identifiers: LCCN 2019015040 | ISBN 978027108381-0 (pbk : alk. paper)
Subjects: LCSH: Sexual minorities—Kenya—Religious aspects—Christianity. | Homosexuality—Kenya—Religious aspects—Christianity. | Homophobia—Kenya. | Homosexuality and the arts—Kenya.
Classification: LCC HQ73.3.K4 V36 2019 | DDC 306.76—dc23
LC record available at https://lccn.loc.gov/2019015040

Printed in the United States of America
Published by The Pennsylvania State University Press,
University Park, PA 16802–1003

The Pennsylvania State University Press is a member of the Association of University Presses.

It is the policy of The Pennsylvania State University Press to use acid-free paper. Publications on uncoated stock satisfy the minimum requirements of American National Standard for Information Sciences—Permanence of Paper for Printed Library Material, ANSI Z39.48–1992.

Struggle makes history. Struggle makes us. In struggle is our history, our language and our being. That struggle begins wherever we are; in whatever we do: then we become part of those millions . . . dreaming to change the world.

—NGŨGĨ WA THIONG'O, 1986

Struggle as a *praxis of liberation* has always drawn part of its imaginary resources from Christianity.

—ACHILLE MBEMBE, 2017

Suffering grows a spirituality of persistence
aided by faith in God who enables them to make
a way where there is no way . . .
Suffering sprouts a spirituality of resistance,
refusing to be blamed for the hurts one endures;
refusing to be shamed by the violence on one's self;
telling when the telling itself is taboo,
speaking it out is half of the resistance, for,
it reveals that one is alive to one's full humanity.

—MERCY ODUYOYE, 2001

Contents

Preface

The idea for this book was born during my immediate postdoctoral research, when I was investigating the role of religion in the politics of homosexuality in Africa, specifically in Zambia. I wrote and published several papers, attempting to make sense of religious discourses and politics opposing lesbian, gay, bisexual, and transgender (lgbt) people and campaigning against the recognition of their human rights. I did consider writing a book about this, and without doubt I could have collected enough material. Yet I asked myself: Do I really want to spend several years of my life writing about what, in the end, is religiously inspired social and political homophobia? Do I want to make a serious effort to render such often unintelligible discourse in an intelligible and critical way? What does it do *to me*—personally, emotionally, and intellectually—to engage in such a long-term project concerned with something so negative? I ended up co-editing two book volumes on religion and the politics of homosexuality, but decided that my own major project, what would become this monograph, would approach the subject from a different, more positive and constructive angle—and also from an angle that stayed closer to myself as a gay person who has been exposed to more than enough religiously inspired negative messages about homosexuality and who does not want to voluntarily encounter more.

I developed an interest in the ways in which African lgbt communities organize and empower themselves in a context of religious, social, and political homo-, bi-, and transphobia, and I wanted to foreground emerging lgbt political perspectives and activist narratives on the continent. In particular, I wanted to examine how religion is not only a source of homophobia in Africa but also a source of lgbt activism and queer politics. It turned out that Zambia was not a very fruitful place in which to explore this new direction, and for several reasons I decided to shift the focus of my new line of inquiry to Kenya. This proved to be a stimulating move: researching and writing this book has been an incredibly enriching experience, both personally and intellectually.

Since my first exploratory research trip to Kenya in July–August 2015, I have had the privilege and pleasure of meeting and befriending many lgbt activists and community members. My simple wish for this book is to share their stories as a counternarrative to the well-known narrative of "African homophobia."

The process of researching and writing this book has been a queer one, in various respects: my fieldwork practices, my methodological orientations, my intellectual, emotional, and bodily exposures have all been, in one way or another, transgressive. My second wish for this book is to give an honest account of this process.

A note on the text: in this book, the acronym lgbt (lesbian, gay, bisexual, and transgender) is not capitalized, as an indication of the unstable and unfixed nature of these categories.

Acknowledgments

This book is the result of many interactions with a wide range of people—research participants, academic colleagues, and personal friends—and I gratefully acknowledge their contribution.

First and foremost, I am enormously thankful to all my research participants in Kenya who were willing to share their stories with me. I specifically mention Trust Arinda, George Barasa, John Karari, Erick Keizi, David Ochar, Emmanuel Odhiambo, and Brian Raymond, who in the process of fieldwork have become friends. I acknowledge the leaders and members of Cosmopolitan Affirming Church in Nairobi, who warmly welcomed me into their community and gave me a taste of African Christian queerness. I am also grateful to Binyavanga Wainaina for making time to meet me and discuss issues emerging from my research, first in London in December 2014 and then at his home in Nairobi in July 2015.

This book was largely conceived during a research fellowship at the Stellenbosch Institute for Advanced Study, in Stellenbosch, South Africa, in 2016. I am grateful to the STIAS board and staff members who facilitated my fellowship. My conversations with other STIAS fellows proved to be enormously helpful in shaping the direction of this book. I specifically mention Stella Nyanzi—or Mama Stella, as she is known to many of the Ugandan lgbt refugees I got to know in Nairobi—who helped me feel at home at STIAS, think through questions of queer politics in Africa, and find my own voice in developing this book.

I presented parts of this book, when still works in progress, at research seminars, conferences, and invited lectures. In the United Kingdom, I presented papers at the universities of Cambridge, Durham, Edinburgh, Oxford, and Sheffield, and at my home institution, Leeds. In the Netherlands, I presented my work at VU University Amsterdam and the University of Leiden; in South Africa, at the universities of Cape Town, KwaZulu-Natal, Stellenbosch, and the Western Cape; in Ghana, at the University of Ghana; and in Kenya, at the British Institute in Eastern Africa. I also spoke at conferences of the African Association for the Study of Religions, the African Studies Association (United

States), the African Studies Association (UK), and the American Academy of Religion. I have benefited from the comments, questions, and discussions on each of these occasions, and I am grateful for the opportunities for academic exchange.

At Penn State University Press, I owe a lot to acquisitions editor Kathryn Yahner, who, ever since our first contact, has had faith in this project and understood its rationale and significance. Her enthusiasm has been a steady source of encouragement, especially in the final stage. I appreciate all the editorial and marketing staff at the Press, who have been highly professional and supportive in the process of publishing this book. Suzanne Wolk has done a terrific job in copyediting the manuscript, making the prose flow more smoothly than I ever could. I am also thankful to the anonymous reviewers who provided valuable and constructive feedback on the first full draft of the manuscript, helping me to fine-tune my argument and give a clearer account of my methodology. I further thank the editors of the Africana Religions book series, Sylvester A. Johnson and Edward E. Curtis IV, for accepting my book for publication. I am deeply sympathetic to the series' vision for the global study of black religious experiences, identities, beliefs, aesthetics, ethics, and practices, and am excited to be associated with it.

Since 2013, the University of Leeds has been my academic home base, and I am grateful for the various forms of support I have received there—in particular, from the Faculty of Arts, Humanities and Cultures, the School of Philosophy, Religion and History of Science, and the Leeds Humanities Research Institute—which has helped me establish my career and undertake the research for this book. To my immediate colleagues, both in the Leeds University Centre for African Studies and in the Centre for Religion and Public Life, I am grateful for such a collegial and intellectually inspiring environment. I would especially like to thank Mikel Burley, Rachel Muers, Mel Prideaux, Jo Sadgrove, Tasia Scrutton, Caroline Starkey, Johanna Stiebert, Emma Tomalin, and Kevin Ward, who in various ways have been sources of encouragement and support at critical moments. The same goes for the postgraduate research students in theology and religious studies at Leeds, in particular Kwame Ahaligah, Hollie Gowan, and Tamanda Walker, and to my previous PhD student and current colleague Benjamin Kirby, with whom I have had so many stimulating discussions. I am also grateful to my undergraduate students at Leeds, especially those who took the class "God, Sex, and Gender in Africa," where I tested many of the ideas explored in this book and benefited from student input.

I am grateful to many academic colleagues and friends for being stimulating partners in conversation and collaboration in various areas of interest, especially Rose Mary Amenga-Etego, for her enriching collaboration in exploring the intersections of African, queer, and religious studies; Ezra Chitando, for collaboratively exploring religion and the politics of homosexuality in Africa; Katie Edwards, for encouraging me to engage "hidden perspectives" and to write myself into my work; Martha Frederiks, for inspiring my academic interest in Christianity and theology in contemporary Africa and for encouraging me since the beginning of my academic career; Laura Grillo, for giving me great confidence in my writing skills (whether or not they're driven by juju) and for always reminding me that there's so much more to learn and study about religion, gender, and sexuality in Africa; Nathanael Homewood, for engaging conversations about various queer forms of Christianity in Africa; Anne-Marie Korte, for ongoing academic mentorship and an interest in my intellectual development and personal well-being since my time at Utrecht University; Sarojini Nadar, for constantly reminding me that academic research might be meaningless if it doesn't make a difference in people's lives, and for encouraging me to integrate my academic, political, and embodied selves; Elaine Nogueira-Godsey, for a queer friendship and making such great memories of Cape Town, and for encouraging me in this project (also a group of Elaine's students, for reading and discussing with me a draft chapter of this book via video call); Ebenezer Obadare, for collaboratively thinking through questions of Christianity, sexuality, and citizenship in Africa; Damaris Parsitau, for being a warm supporter of my work, and for helping me understand religion, gender, and sexuality in Kenya; and Martin Zebracki, for sharpening my thinking about queer visibility in various places and spaces. I thank many other academic colleagues and friends as well, including Dianna Bell, Mariecke van den Bergh, Barbara Bompani, Elias Bongmba, Sarah Bracke, Nella van den Brandt, Susannah Cornwall, Marco Derks, Sara Fretheim, Peter Geschiere, Masiiwa Ragies Gunda, Maaike de Haardt, Rosalind Hackett, Sîan Hawthorne, Nina Hoel, Marloes Janson, Stefanie Knauss, Birgit Meyer, Hassan Ndzovu, Kwame Edwin Otu, Hugh Pyper, Teddy Sakupapa, Elizabeth Sperber, Abel Ugba, and Corey Williams, for keeping the little corner of academia where I move a humane space.

I am further grateful to my family members and friends outside academia, who have helped me stay sane in the process of writing this book, particularly Aiwan Obinyan, for being a great conversation partner about anything African and queer, and for allowing her hands to grace the cover of this book. More than he may know, I am indebted to Abenathi Makinana; his friendship and his proud embodiment of black African queerness have been an inspiration and have helped me find the tone, voice, and confidence to write this book. I am grateful to be part of the All Hallows community in Leeds, which offers me such an affirming and enriching social and spiritual home. Thanks also to my parents, Adrie and Annie van Klinken, for being a source of unconditional love, and for giving me a social, political, and religious orientation in life that has influenced my academic interests and the writing of this book (albeit in a different way than they may recognize); and to Linda and Masato Sato, for performing their role as my "English parents" here in Leeds with such great love, care, and cheerfulness. During the process of writing this book I have been in a situation of profound bodily and emotional vulnerability, and I am enormously grateful to everyone who was there to affirm me at critical moments, in particular Dale Carrington, Ben Kirby, Sarojini Nadar, Elaine Nogueira-Godsey, Nienke Pruiksma, and Tasia Scrutton; you've proved invaluable! In this context, last but not least, I express my great thanks to my partner in life and love, Casper Branger, for being a constant source of support in the process of writing this book, and for collaboratively writing the story of our lives.

Portions of this book have been published previously and have been substantially revised and expanded from the following articles: "A Kenyan Queer Prophet: Binyavanga Wainaina's Public Contestation of Pentecostalism and Homophobia," in *Christianity and Controversies over Homosexuality in Contemporary Africa*, edited by Ezra Chitando and Adriaan van Klinken (London: Routledge, 2016), 65–81, © 2016; "Citizenship of Love: The Politics, Ethics, and Aesthetics of Sexual Citizenship in a Kenyan Gay Music Video," *Citizenship Studies* 22, no. 6 (2018): 650–65; "Autobiographical Storytelling and African Narrative Queer Theology," *Exchange: Journal of Contemporary Christianities in Context* 47, no. 3 (2018): 211–29; and "Culture Wars, Race, and Sexuality: A Nascent Pan-African LGBT-Affirming Christian Movement and the Future of Christianity," *Journal of Africana Religions* 5, no. 2 (2017): 217–38.

Introduction

From "African Homophobia" to Queer Arts of Resistance

In July 2015, then U.S. president Barack Obama paid an official visit to Kenya. His visit coincided with my first research trip for the project that resulted in this book. In the weeks preceding Obama's visit, I witnessed the mounting excitement. The reason for this euphoria was twofold. First, Obama was the first sitting American president ever to visit Kenya, which was seen as recognition of the country's rising status as an economic and political power in East Africa, if not on the continent. Second, given Obama's Kenyan ancestry, he was welcomed as a "son of Africa" returning to his ancestral home.

In addition to excitement, however, there also was public anxiety about the visit. This was partly about security risks—understandable in a country that has experienced terrorist attacks. But mainly it was about the question of gay rights, the fear being that Obama would advocate for the rights of sexual minorities. This fear was particularly pertinent because of the ruling of the U.S. Supreme Court, just a month earlier, in favor of equal marriage rights for same-sex couples. In the weeks between this ruling and Obama's arrival, leading Kenyan politicians, including Deputy President William Ruto and National Assembly Majority Leader Aden Duale, spoke out publicly against homosexuality, and they called upon Obama not to raise the issue. Pressured by journalists, Kenyan president Uhuru Kenyatta stated a few days before the state visit that gay rights were "a non-issue for the people of this country" and were not on the agenda for the meeting with his U.S. counterpart.[1] The White House press secretary, on the other hand, stated that "the president will not hesitate to make clear that the protection of basic universal human rights in Kenya is also a priority and consistent with the values that we hold dear here in the United States of America."[2] Unavoidably, during the joint press conference, the question of gay rights came up and the difference in opinion between the two presidents was exposed. Kenyatta repeated his statement that, "for Kenyans today, the issue of gay rights really is a non-issue," while Obama underlined his belief "that the state should not discriminate against people on the basis of their sexual orientation."[3]

This incident can be seen as yet another example of the clash between African countries and "the West" about the human rights of sexual minorities. But there are some interesting twists in this particular controversy. One of them is that because of Obama's Kenyan ancestry, his pro-gay argument could not be as easily dismissed as exogenous and imperialistic by Kenyan political leaders (as similar arguments by other Western leaders have been in the past). Another, more hilarious, twist was that a rather marginal Kenyan political party, the Republican Liberty Party, seized the controversy as an opportunity to promote itself, announcing a "peaceful procession" to protest Obama's "open and aggressive support of homosexuality." This received global headlines, specifically because the RLP said that the procession would be carried out by "approximately 5,000 naked men and women" so that Obama "could see and understand the difference between a man and a woman."[4] The march was supposed to commence from Freedom Corner in Uhuru Park in central Nairobi. On the day of the protest, July 22, I found my way to the park. I did not want to miss out on this paradoxical public performance of nudity that aimed to protect public morality. But there were no nude protesters. Apparently, the organizers had already reached their aim: they had received enormous media attention, and Kenyatta had been forced to declare publicly that Kenya was not going to recognize gay rights.

In a surprising turn of events, while walking through the park looking for nude protesters, I saw two young men seated on a bench adjacent to the Nyayo Monument. As I passed, they turned to look at me, and I glanced back. It felt like I was cruising in the park. I decided to take another path to get closer to them. As they kept stealing glances, one of them greeted me with an elongated "Hi," and with a warm smile he invited me to sit down. In the conversation that unfolded, they initially were vague about what they were doing in the park. When I told them jokingly that I had come to see the nude protesters and was disappointed not to find a single one, they laughed and opened up. It turned out that they were part of a small group of gay men meeting in the park every week—not to cruise for sex, but to support one another in their entrepreneurial activities, for which they had set up a system of savings and loans. In fact, they were waiting for other group members to arrive, and they invited me to attend their meeting. One by one, other folks joined, till there were seven of us. The meeting was opened with prayer, after which the leader welcomed me and asked us to briefly introduce ourselves. This was followed by sharing and discussion, mainly about entrepreneurial activities that members were involved in and small business opportunities they had identified. Clearly, this was an economic empowerment group *avant la lettre*. It also was a social support group, as before, during, and after the meeting, members talked about their challenges and struggles. Moreover, although not a religious group as such, the men naturally opened the meeting with prayer, asking God to bless their deliberations, and they closed with an intercessory prayer for individual group members and friends. Out of sight of the media, these men gathered every week in a highly symbolic spot in Nairobi's public space: the park of independence (Uhuru), under trees planted by political activist Wangari Maathai in an area she baptized "Freedom Corner" in opposition to the oppressive regime of Daniel arap Moi. The park is also "at the religious core of the capital," as it is surrounded by various prominent church buildings of Kenya's major Christian denominations.[5]

It occurred to me that this small, informal support group of gay men was perhaps more significant than the nude mass protest that had received so much media attention. Whereas the protest was supposed to show Obama the difference between a man and a woman, this unpretentious group of gay men showed me the difference between publicly stirred up homophobia and the way in which queer folk go on with their daily lives. Their simple presence in the park challenged the dominant narrative, presented by Kenya's political and religious elites, that homosexuality is "un-Kenyan" and that there is no place for gay people in the country. The natural way in which they prayed during their meeting and integrated faith into their group further challenged the popular narrative of homosexuality as being "un-Christian," and of gay people as sinners removed from God.

This story illustrates the dynamics that this book seeks to explore: dynamics relating to the creative ways in which gay men and other lgbt (lesbian, gay, bisexual, and transgender) people in Kenya make themselves visible despite sociopolitical homophobia; the implicit and explicit ways in which they counter this homophobia and challenge popular religious and political narratives; the agential ways in which they negotiate the politics of religion, sexuality, and citizenship; and the subversive ways in which they mobilize and empower themselves, creating space in a society where their existence and rights are considered, at best, a non-issue. This book is particularly interested in the role of religious belief and practice in what I call Kenyan queer "arts of resistance," and it presents four case studies that analyze how religion, specifically Christianity, is drawn upon in lgbt activism in contemporary Kenya.

BEYOND "AFRICAN HOMOPHOBIA"

In the early twenty-first century, sub-Saharan Africa has become widely associated with homophobia. Admittedly, the idea of homosexuality as "un-African," "unnatural," and "un-Christian" was prevalent throughout the twentieth century, reinforced by European colonial administrators and Christian missionaries, and in recent decades by HIV-prevention strategies.[6] Yet in the past twenty years, many African heads of state, politicians, legislators, and religious leaders have invested tremendous energies and resources in popularizing this belief, entrenching it among their populations, and making it a key issue in the politics of African authenticity, identity, and citizenship—a process that Patrick Awondo has described as the "politicization of homosexuality" in contemporary Africa.[7] This has not been merely symbolic: public and political rhetoric against homosexuality has reinforced the experiences of social discrimination and marginalization of gay and lesbian people; existing colonial antisodomy laws were dusted off and implemented to prosecute people accused of same-sex activity; new anti-homosexual legislation was debated in the parliaments of several countries and was signed into law in Uganda, Nigeria, and The Gambia. One consequence of this development was that Africa, in the Western media and public mind, has become almost synonymous with homophobia, as demonstrated, for instance, in the BBC documentary depicting Uganda—with its infamous Anti-Homosexuality Act, which caused an international outcry—as possibly "the world's worst place to be gay."[8] Such depictions are problematic for various reasons: they tend to give an essentializing and homogenizing account of homophobia as an ahistorical phenomenon driven by African culture, religion, and morality; they reinforce the tradition of othering Africa as a backward and conservative continent, allowing the West to profile itself as liberal and progressive; they overlook the complex political economies and the dynamics of globalization and postcolonialism in which local expressions of sociopolitical homophobia in Africa are embedded; and they fail to grasp the complexity of developments on the ground, which often are more multifarious than they appear at first sight.[9]

The emphasis on homophobia in Africa risks obscuring the other side of contemporary dynamics. Alongside waves of homophobia, but less well documented in Western media and scholarship, increasing levels of lesbian, gay, bisexual, and transgender (*i* for intersex is sometimes added to this acronym: lgbti) community organization, social mobilization, and political activism can be observed in different parts of the continent. Urban spaces and popular culture in particular appear to allow for significant levels of queer visibility. It has been observed that in Kinshasa, in the Democratic Republic of the Congo, "despite its often moralistic and sometimes violent messages, popular culture is itself always already queer,"[10] while in Nairobi, it has been noted that "despite virulent attacks by the political and religious section of the country against queer sexual expression, there is a visible queer existence that is predicated on embodied lived experiences and spatial subjectivity."[11] Sokari Ekine captures these dynamics more generally when she writes, "Over the past 10 years, many African countries have witnessed the transformation of LGBTI Africans out of unseen closets into visible broken glass cabinets, and the replacement of silences by an active and assertive engagement with the state, civil society, queer communities and international NGOs."[12] This development has been informed by broader activism in the areas of HIV and AIDS, women's rights, and human rights, as well as by international discourses of lgbt identities and rights. Various studies have begun to document and examine the forms and strategies adopted by lgbt activists fighting for sexual diversity, especially in the context of southern Africa but also in other parts of the continent.[13] In these mostly social-scientific studies, the phrase "sexual diversity struggles" usually refers to "strategic efforts to defend gender and sexual dissidence and to promote laws and policies that affirm gender and sexual diversity."[14] Such efforts are typically concerned with social advocacy, legal support, political lobbying, and (inter)national networking, and are aimed at community building, creating public and political support, propagating gender and sexual minority rights as human rights, and changing current legislation and policies. Through these strategic efforts, African lgbt activists have made significant advances. For instance, several countries have now included sexual minorities in their governmental sexual health strategies (specifically, HIV treatment); in 2015–16, the High Courts of Botswana and Kenya affirmed the freedom of association for lgbt advocacy groups and instructed the government to allow the registration of these groups as NGOs; in 2015, Mozambique officially decriminalized same-sex practices; in 2014, the African Commission on Human and Peoples' Rights adopted a resolution calling on African states to end the violence and human rights violations against people on the basis of their sexual orientation or gender identity. These developments provide grounds for realistic optimism about the struggle for sexual diversity in sub-Saharan Africa.[15]

As Ashley Currier and Thérèse Migraine-George point out, in addition to "more traditional strategies of mobilization and intervention" (such as the social, political, and legal efforts mentioned above), "African activists have been displaying incredible agility and resorting to inventiveness and creativity, to a kind of political bricolage that draws from new forms of technological productions and artifacts—the 'instant archives' created by websites, social media, blogs, and YouTube videos."[16] The focus of this book is on such creative and inventive expressions of lgbt activism. In other words, this book examines Kenyan lgbt activism as "arts of resistance," that is, as informal modes of civic agency through the use of various artistic expressions.[17] To describe this approach, we might also use the term *artivism*, which is "a hybrid neologism that signifies work created by individuals who see an organic relationship between art and activism."[18] The artivist, in the words of Molefi Asante, "uses her artistic talents to fight and struggle against injustice and oppression—by any *medium* necessary," and "merges commitment to freedom and justice with the pen, the lens, the brush, the voice, the body, and the imagination."[19] In fact, this artivist dimension applies to each of the case studies featured in this book, as they represent various forms of engagement with the arts for the purpose of activism. Thus the case studies are part of the same increasing visibility of lgbt actors in African societies, and they reflect the growing salience of sexual diversity struggles in Africa. Clearly, the methods and strategies employed in these struggles are becoming increasingly diverse.

This book examines recent artistic and sociocultural expressions of lgbt activism, specifically in the context of Kenya. My interest here is in the ways in which these creative expressions interrogate and introduce nuance into several dominant narratives: first, the Western narrative of "African homophobia" and the related stories of lgbt African victimhood; second, the narrative that has become popular in Africa of homosexuality and lgbt identities as "un-African"; and third, the narrative that religion is a dominant force fueling homophobia in Africa. Although I do not deny that religion plays an important role in politics opposing homosexuality and lgbt rights in contemporary Africa, I am more interested in the other side of this coin: in how lgbt activism in Africa also uses and relies on religious language and symbols. In the words of Joseph Hellweg, religion is "neither necessarily a burden nor a boon" to African lgbt dynamics, "but a terrain rich for re-negotiation."[20] A rich terrain indeed, but one that so far has been little explored. This book demonstrates that Kenyan lgbt activists have critically and creatively engaged with religion, specifically with Christian traditions, for African queer world-making purposes. Through a detailed analysis of their strategies, it provides insight into the ways in which Christianity can be employed as a key factor in African queer politics, and it thus interrogates the secular underpinning of Western queer studies. I argue that queer studies, in order to be relevant in African contexts, requires both a decolonizing and a postsecular intervention, and must acknowledge and understand religion as a site and source not only of oppression but also of creative resistance, empowerment, and agency.

INTERSECTING AFRICAN, RELIGIOUS, AND QUEER STUDIES

In developing this argument, I aim to make an innovative contribution to three fields of study: African studies, religious studies, and queer studies. My goal in this section is to position the book within these fields and explore some of their intersections, first crosscutting African and queer studies, then African and religious studies, and third, queer and religious studies.

Queer–African Studies

The current use of the term *queer* has its origins in the activism, politics, and theorizing about sexuality and gender that emerged in the United States in the 1990s. It has been used in a twofold way: first, as an umbrella term for a variety of dissident or nonnormative categories of sexual and gender identification, such as lesbian, gay, bisexual, and transgender, and second, as the name of a theory, or a way of theorizing, that emerged out of lesbian and gay studies, feminist theory, and poststructuralist thought. *Queer* in the latter sense, as referring to queer theory, seeks to interrupt and destabilize the implicit and explicit norms and assumptions that underlie much sexual and gender identification and categorization. From this perspective, *queer* is a critical conceptual and analytical tool, the great political promise of which resides in "its broad critique of multiple social antagonisms, including race, gender, class, nationality, and religion, in addition to sexuality."[21] In the field of queer studies, as in the present book, the two senses of the term *queer* are not always clearly distinguished and can blur into each other.

It has been observed that "the relationship between queer studies and African studies has been ambivalent since the emergence of queer studies as a 'field' in the early 1990s."[22] Even the basic question whether queer theoretical perspectives can or should be applied to the study of African sexualities is contested. For instance, Marc Epprecht has become increasingly skeptical about the relevance and potential of queer theory for African sexuality studies. Referring to queer theory's heavy dependence on Western theoretical frameworks and empirical evidence, Epprecht argues that queer theory "awaits a rigorously theorized indigenous term or terms grounded in African culture and contemporary struggles, sensitive to lessons learned through decades of Marxist, feminist, and postcolonial critiques of power and the sociology of science." However, he himself does not appear keen on contributing to a more rigorous theoretical framework, stating that "it is important to acknowledge but not to promote queer theory as a research strategy in Africa."[23]

Epprecht's hesitation echoes a broader debate about the problem of "traveling theories"—theories developed in the so-called global North, informed by Western epistemologies and traditions of thought, that are being introduced and applied to contexts in the so-called global South. A similar debate occurred a few decades ago concerning feminism and feminist theory. In the 1980s, postcolonial scholars such as Chandra Mohanty presented a strong critique of Western feminist studies, especially its homogenizing representation of women in the so-called Third World, and the West-centric but universalized assumptions underlying such representation.[24] In Africa, such a postcolonial feminist critique was developed, for example, by Oyèrónkẹ́ Oyěwùmí, who in her book *The Invention of Women* interrogates the Western concept of gender and its applicability to Yoruba society. As critical as postcolonial scholars have been of Western feminist theory, they do not generally reject the term *feminist* but rather have sought to decolonize feminist scholarship and to develop postcolonial feminist theories.

A similar development has taken place in queer studies. Epprecht's suggestion that African scholars and activists are "extremely reluctant to embrace the term queer" has been surpassed by history.[25] In fact, as part of "the global trajectories of queerness,"[26] the term has been quite widely adopted in Africa in recent years, as demonstrated by collections of academic and activist writings.[27] Moreover, some recent collections of African literary texts have embraced the term.[28] Although the center of gravity of queer African studies may still be in South Africa—a country where "queer politics has long infused the domestic political agenda"[29]—contributors to such collections come from all over the continent. Indeed, in East Africa, leading scholars such as Stella Nyanzi (Uganda) and Keguro Macharia (Kenya) have made significant contributions to the field. There is thus a broader trend in Africa to adopt *queer* as a label for scholarship, writing, and activism on sexual and gender diversity, though certainly not uncritically. Sokari Ekine and Hakima Abbas acknowledge the limitations of queer terminology in relation to African neocolonial realities, yet they adopt the term to denote a political framework: "We use queer to underscore a perspective that embraces gender and sexual plurality and seeks to transform, overhaul and revolutionise African order rather than seek to assimilate into oppressive hetero-patriarchal-capitalist frameworks."[30] The trend among African scholars and writers of adopting the term *queer* as a political and intellectual framework comes alongside a similar trend among Africanist scholars researching issues of sexual and gender diversity. Together, these trends have given rise to a new, interdisciplinary body of scholarship called queer African studies.[31] At the heart of this scholarship are questions of postcolonialism and decolonization, which I engage in several ways.

First, as Ekine and Abbas's reference to "oppressive hetero-patriarchal-capitalist frameworks" suggests, in queer African studies, the critical analysis of normative frameworks of sexuality and gender is combined with an interrogation of economic structures. This yields a critical focus on colonialism, neoliberal capitalism, and globalization, in addition to the political economies of (homo)sexuality and lgbt rights, both within Africa and globally. I employ this focus as a framework within which to critically examine how such issues are addressed and dealt with in the case studies discussed in this book.

Second, acknowledging the Western origins and hegemonies of queer scholarship, William Spurlin has made a methodological innovation, proposing to intersect queer studies with postcolonial theory in order to "decolonize assumptions in queer scholarship about sexual identities, politics, and cultural practices outside the West." He is concerned that "cross-cultural variations of the expression and representation of same-sex desire" get obscured when they are studied "through the imperialist gaze of Euro-American queer identity politics [or are] appropriated through the economies of the West."[32] Acknowledging this risk, I attend critically to the ways in which African queer subjects themselves adopt and navigate an originally Western and now globalized narrative of lgbt identities and rights, and to the tensions and fissures that the adoption of this narrative frequently creates. My use of lowercase for the acronym lgbt acknowledges that the "certainty, stability or essential nature" of these categories, which capitalization implies, cannot be taken for granted vis-à-vis contemporary African queer realities and thus needs to be interrogated.[33] As Chantal Zabus points out, "African 'homosexualities' can never be comfortably slotted within identity politics carved out of 'gay' and 'lesbian' liberation struggles, and display queer and even post-queer characteristics."[34] Although it is not clear what Zabus means here by "post-queer," in this book I demonstrate how some instances of African queer politics call into question certain hegemonic understandings of "queerness" in Western queer theory, especially as they relate to radical transgression, antinormativity, and antireligiosity.

Third, Ashley Currier and Thérèse Migraine-George put questions of representation at the heart of queer African studies. In view of these questions, they suggest, the intersection of African studies and queer studies becomes particularly productive, because both fields are concerned with crises in and representation of hegemonic structures. "If African studies as area studies problematizes the geopolitical place of African subjects whose national and ethnic identities are caught up in a messy network of global politics," they write, "then queer African studies further questions the location of queer African subjects who live and strategize in liminal spaces as the moving junction of visibility and invisibility." Thus they imagine queer African studies as "the space in which the contours of cultural and sexual identities become questioned and blurred—a space that may allow for the forging of new forms of alliance, sociality, and kinship but also transcends limited assumptions about location, belonging, and identity."[35] This book unfolds within this space, specifically examining the ways in which lgbt or queer subjects themselves negotiate the relationship between cultural and sexual identities and develop new forms of African queerness and queer Africanness. Like Keguro Macharia, I am interested in a form of queer African studies that "centres on Africa-based archives and methods, African thinkers and artists"; such a focus is important not only as a gesture toward the decolonization of the field, but also as a move to decenter what Macharia refers to as "African homophobes," and as an attempt to render African queers visible and foreground their agency.[36]

African–Religious Studies

The second intersection this book addresses is of religion and Africa. More established than the field of queer African studies, African religious studies is an interdisciplinary field examining the historical and contemporary manifestations and dynamics of religion in Africa. With regard to the present study, two key issues stand out: the public role of religion in contemporary African societies, and the question of religion and agency. I explore these issues with particular reference to Christianity, the tradition this book focuses on—which allows us to interrogate how homosexuality in popular discourses, in Kenya and other parts of Africa, is often opposed because it would be "un-African" and "un-Christian."

A recurrent argument in much recent scholarship is that religion in contemporary Africa is very much a public affair. This argument fits in with a wider body of literature concerned with the "public resurgence of religion" and the renewed "power of religion in the public sphere" in societies worldwide.[37] This literature has emerged as a correction to the long-standing assumption in the social sciences that when societies modernize they become more secular, with religion retreating to the private sphere and becoming marginalized. This secularization thesis has been questioned, for instance, by José Casanova, who has drawn attention to "the fact that religious traditions throughout the world are refusing to accept the marginal and privatized role which theories of modernity as well as theories of secularization had reserved for them." Offering case studies from a range of countries, Casanova argues that in all these different contexts, religious institutions and movements claim public space and influence, and do not limit themselves to dealing with strictly religious issues but instead "continue to raise questions about the interconnections of private and public morality and to challenge the claims of the subsystems, particularly states and markets, to be exempt from extraneous normative considerations."[38]

Casanova has acknowledged that his thesis about the deprivatization of religion is characterized by a certain West-centrism.[39] The abundance of scholarship on religion in Africa makes it clear that in Africa (as in many other parts of the world), religion has never been merely a private affair but has generally been an integral component of public and political life.[40] This applies to African indigenous religions—where "religion" cannot even be separated from "politics" because both are rooted in a concept of spiritual power—as well as to Christianity and Islam, which have become the dominant religions on the African continent in recent decades. Yet even though the notion of religious deprivatization is not necessarily relevant, the notion of public religion does still speak to African contexts. This is not only because religious movements and organizations in Africa present and profile themselves publicly and compete for public space—through their use of the media, their engagement with politics, and so on. More interestingly, in doing so, these public religions engage in dynamic and complex ways with secular regimes of knowledge, power, and politics at both the national and the global level.[41] Referring to the vitality and significance of religion in postcolonial African societies, Achille Mbembe has stated that "there is no doubt that most of the religious and healing movements proliferating in Africa today constitute visible, if ambiguous, sites where new normative systems, new common languages, and the constitution of new authorities are being negotiated."[42] This applies to revivalist Pentecostal-charismatic Christian movements as much as to reformist Islamic movements in Africa. In the postcolonial era of uncertainty—culturally, economically, socially, and politically—both Christianity and Islam have grown dramatically in Africa, offering people new senses of belonging, community, and identity while navigating the intersection of local cosmologies with global narratives. In particular, Pentecostalism and reformist Islam "can be seen as two new kinds of social imaginaries which thrive on religion's ability to render meaningful the unstable and often depressing flux of life in Africa," as Brian Larkin and Birgit Meyer put it.[43] These religions have, moreover, made strategic use of the new opportunities opened up by political and economic liberalization and by the privatization of the media, through which they advertise themselves, contest each other, and compete for public space and political influence.

Against this background of the renewed public prominence of religion, the role of religion in the recent politicization of homosexuality in African contexts can also be understood. Both Christian and Muslim actors in many countries have actively mobilized against homosexuality and lgbt rights, expressing concern with public morality and with the purity of the nation. In this regard, as Shobana Shankar observes, it is true that religious leaders and institutions "have become closely aligned to states to the degree that they have become facilitators of discrimination and violence against citizens."[44] An interesting dynamic has been observed in the context of South Africa by Marian Burchardt, who notes that there is a "concomitant rise" of the public presence of sexual minorities, on the one hand, and of the public visibility of religion, on the other, which are often "fashioned antagonistically." Overcoming this antagonistic representation, he argues that "resistance against the progressive institutionalization of equality before the law of same-sex partnerships can even be viewed as a key motif of the emergence of particular kinds of public religion. In other words, both religious and sexual rights mobilizations may depend on and thrive in reaction to one another, sometimes entering a symbiotic social existence."[45] Of course, South Africa is unique on the continent for its laws against discrimination on the basis of sexual orientation and its legalization of same-sex civil unions. Yet in other African contexts, somewhat similar processes can be observed, with "public religion" and "public sexuality" entering into a symbiotic relationship owing to the increased visibility of local lgbt communities and globalized discourses of lgbt rights, and the countermobilization of religious groups in response. Precisely because of its public prominence, lgbt communities cannot ignore religion as a factor in society but must engage with it, critically, strategically, and creatively. Whereas Burchardt appears to conceive of the relationship between public religion and public lgbt identities as one-dimensional—as a relationship simply of opposition—I am interested in the different ways in which public religion is engaged and drawn upon in the context of African lgbt activism and queer politics. Beyond simple opposition, how are religious beliefs and practices negotiated, appropriated, and transformed?

Without falling into the trap of African essentialism, according to which "Africans are notoriously religious,"[46] we can observe that the vast majority of Africans today hold religious beliefs and engage in religious practices. Moreover, according to Stephen Ellis and Gerrie ter Haar, "it is largely through religious ideas that Africans think about the world today, and . . . religious ideas provide them with means of becoming social and political actors."[47] The latter assertion offers a particularly important insight for the study presented here, with its interest in lgbt individuals and communities and their engagement in queer politics. How might religion shape the ways in which African lgbt people think about the world, and provide them with the means of becoming queer political actors? Of course, it cannot be taken for granted that religion plays such a role. As Shobana Shankar has pointed out, "'pulling away' from religion . . . has not been much studied as a conscious political strategy" in Africa.[48] Especially for lgbt Africans, pulling away from institutionalized religion might very well be a desirable option. This book thus examines the different and possibly conflicting ways in which religion, specifically Christianity, is engaged in the context of lgbt activism and queer politics in Africa, from critique and opposition to negotiating, appropriating, and transforming Christian beliefs and practices. My main interest, however, is in the complex ways in which religion serves as a source of African queer creativity and inventiveness.

Queer–Religious Studies

The third intersection to be explored here is, like the first one, contested. In her overview of the relationship between queer studies and religious studies, Melissa Wilcox observes that "many queer theorists, like many queer activists and perhaps many LGBT people in general, regard religion as so inimical to their purposes and lives that it is not even worthy of critique; references to religion in queer theory, queer studies, and even LGBT studies are usually sparse, brief, and generally derogatory."[49] Wilcox is referring here to the context of North America, which has been the center of the development of queer studies since its emergence in the early 1990s. In this context, the gay liberation movement, and its successors in the form of lgbt movements and queer activism, have, historically speaking, emerged largely in opposition to established religion; its successes have been enabled by processes of sociocultural change, such as secularization and the privatization of religion. Embracing an lgbt identity or engaging in queer activism has often meant leaving religion behind—"for many, the two identities are so dissimilar as to have no continuity at all."[50] Against this background, queer theorists and scholars in the field of queer studies have generally not seen the need for, or demonstrated an interest in, thinking about religion. According to Wilcox, in the foundational texts of queer theory there are only "a small handful of passing references to religion," which generally "address only Christianity and brand religion as a stultifying, oppressive institution of a heteronormative, sexist social order."[51] Likewise, it has been observed that Anglo-American queer cultures are often characterized by a "militantly secular" outlook in which religion is perceived as "intrinsically conservative and repressive."[52] As a result, religion has hardly received detailed critical attention from queer theorists, who thus have failed to grasp the potential of religious traditions not only to reinforce but also to subvert heteronormativity. In the words of Wilcox, again, "the analysis of religion's discursive power and the potential for performative resistance to that power has not been of interest in queer theory to date."[53] This may be problematic in Western contexts, where religion is not simply fading away but continues to be a relevant factor in society in general and also in some lgbt people's lives. Yet the secular and often antireligious edge of queer studies is even more problematic in African contexts, where religion is a highly significant locus of social, cultural, and political power.

Postcolonial interventions in queer theory, such as Spurlin's, have emphasized the need to "decolonize assumptions in queer scholarship about sexual identities, politics, and cultural practices outside the West."[54] Obviously, decolonization must also address the secular assumption that underlies much of queer studies. In other words, a postcolonial intervention in queer studies vis-à-vis African contexts also entails a postsecular intervention. By this I mean an interrogation of the Western secular epistemological assumptions underlying much of queer studies, in which religion is often assumed to be conservative and therefore is antagonistically opposed to progressive, emancipatory politics.

A postsecular turn, in the words of Erin Wilson, is a crucial tool in enabling "alternative frameworks for thinking about how questions of the transcendent, the spiritual and the metaphysical are entangled with and impact on various different aspects of human existence in the contemporary age."[55] In other words, postsecularism allows us to think of religion as a site of power, not only for oppression and exclusion but also for empowerment and agency. As Wilcox has suggested, "perhaps religious discourse is the secret that queer theory has hidden (in plain sight) from itself."[56] Thus religion should be taken into account not only as a site of discursive power that (re)produces heteronormativity and homophobia in contemporary African societies, but also as a site of African queer subjectivity and agency.

While queer theorists have generally dismissed or ignored religion, the field of religious studies has engaged lgbt issues and queer theory quite seriously. The emerging body of queer studies in religion is highly diverse in nature, first because it includes the different methodological approaches encompassed by religious studies—theology, anthropology, sociology, the study of sacred texts, and historical studies—and second because of the different uses of the term *queer* outlined earlier, as an umbrella term for lgbt identities and politics, and as referring to queer theory with its radical, anti-essentialist, and deconstructive edge. If studies in this field have something in common, it may be the idea that religion itself, in the words of Elizabeth Stuart's poignant book title, is "a queer thing." It is not reducible to one essence but is open to multiple interpretations, and it is therefore potentially disruptive of any established hegemony or normativity. As much as religion can be a site of contestation over lgbt sexualities, religious beliefs, texts, and practices can also be employed to subvert heteronormativity and to affirm, reclaim, and celebrate queer sexualities.[57]

Like queer studies in general, queer studies in religion have generally focused on Western contexts and traditions. The emerging field of queer African studies, by contrast, tends to reflect the tradition of overlooking religion that is typical of Western queer scholarship. Although it has been observed that many African lgbt people, in Epprecht's words, are "proudly, happily and deeply religious," and often identify with the same religious traditions that are mobilized against them, Western scholars and activists typically perceive this religiosity as an "apparent contradiction" rather than as a force that may challenge secular assumptions about lgbt identities and queer politics. Epprecht himself, significantly, admits that the three major faith traditions in Africa—indigenous religions, Islam, and Christianity—have historically been, and remain, "more amenable to accepting sexual difference than is generally understood."[58]

Yet we need to explore and understand, in much more detail, the complexity of religion in relation to queer identities and politics in Africa. Historically, as Nyanzi reminds us, African indigenous religions present a rich lexicon of queerness, with "understandings of gendered spirits of ancestors who may possess individuals [that] offer socially appropriate notions of handling fluid, transient gender identities."[59] This contemporary appropriation can be seen in the phenomenon of self-identifying lesbian *sangomas* (traditional healers) in South Africa who explain their sexual attraction to other women with reference to male ancestral possession.[60] Many other lgbt Africans engage in Christian or Islamic religious practices and find ways to assert and acknowledge their nonnormative sexual and gender identities within those traditions, and to claim those traditions as sites of lgbt activism and queer politics. These intricate connections between religion and lgbt sexualities in contemporary Africa are beginning to be studied, mainly in the context of grassroots negotiation of religious and sexual identities.[61] The present book contributes to this emerging body of scholarship by focusing on a different, so far understudied, level of publicly visible forms of lgbt activism and queer politics.

READING CREATIVE TEXTS OF LGBT ACTIVISM

With its focus on creative arts of resistance, this book engages a trend in African cultural studies that is concerned with the sociopolitical dimensions of African artistic expression. Moradewun Adejunmobi has proposed that we conceptualize African cultural productions as provocations. To that end, she builds on the general point that "creativity involves originality, and originality is always provocative," in the sense of challenging local norms and cultural conventions. She argues that in contemporary Africa, "the arts manifested in a wide range of expressive and representational practices constitute one of the few areas where a limited or expansive degree of provocation is tolerated in all societies."[62] Applying this model to issues of sexuality, Frieda Ekotto and Kenneth Harrow have suggested that forms of African cultural production that address sexual diversity in a positive way can "mediate the legally and culturally sanctioned violence that LGBTQI individuals are subject to in many African countries and to dispel notions that homosexuality is a Western phenomenon and inherently un-African."[63] Although Ekotto and Harrow, like Adejunmobi, appear to be thinking primarily of particular art forms, such as African literature and cinema, in this book I adopt a broader notion of cultural production that includes a wide range of artistic and creative expressions. Moreover, as interested as I am in the sociopolitical aspects of these expressions, I acknowledge that creative resistance can come in various guises, not always necessarily as bold provocations but also in the form of more subtle negotiations and transformations. My analysis is particularly informed by the notion of "queer aesthetic" as described by queer theorist José Esteban Muñoz, which is centered on the idea that "art manifest[s] itself in such a way that the political imagination can spark new ways of perceiving and acting on a reality that is itself potentially changeable."[64]

This book presents four case studies of creative expressions through which Kenyan lgbt actors have recently claimed visibility. The case studies are quite diverse, reflecting the differing sociocultural forms that lgbt activism takes, and the various queer sociopolitical orientations and imaginations that underlie them. Each case study presents a relatively high-profile case of lgbt activism in Kenya, with visibility and impact on the wider East African region, the African continent, and in some cases beyond. Although independent of one another, the four studies have interesting interconnections, with several symbols of and references to Kenyan history, culture, and society appearing more than once. In keeping with the book's focus on the relationship between Christianity and lgbt activism in Africa, the case studies represent different ways of relating to and engaging with Christian beliefs, texts, and symbols.

Although the four case studies originate in Kenya, they speak to broader lgbt realities on the African continent and contribute to African queer politics more generally. They respond to social and political homophobia in different parts of the continent in various ways, presenting a range of lgbt activist strategies and opening up alternative queer imaginations. The case studies thus transcend the Kenyan context and take on continental relevance and significance. It is my assertion that they contribute to what Macharia has called "queer African archives," and embody forms of African queer politics emerging from Kenyan soil.[65] Claiming that the four case studies are not just "Kenyan" but also "African" does not mean that I draw on an essentialized or reified notion of Africa. My interest is in the ways in which notions of African culture, identity, and history are invoked, deployed, and negotiated in the case studies, while acknowledging the complex and multiple ways in which Africa is part of a globalized world—culturally, politically, and religiously. This interest allows me to explore queer African imaginations and their relation to globalized discourses of lgbt activism and queer politics.

METHODOLOGY

The use of case studies allows for an in-depth examination of specific cases of creative Kenyan lgbt activism. The first case study is of the openly gay Kenyan writer and social critic Binyavanga Wainaina. It offers a reading of selected literary, film, and social media texts that Wainaina produced in the period around and after his coming out in January 2014. I analyze both the content and the form of Wainaina's critique of religion, especially of Pentecostal Christianity, and homophobia, and his alternative narrative of African queer identity.

Case study 2 focuses on the "Same Love" music video released by the Kenyan hip-hop group Art Attack in 2016 and produced by the openly gay gospel musician and activist George Barasa. I examine how the song represents African queer identities, addresses issues of religion and homophobia, and reclaims a Christian notion of love.

The third case study is about the anthology *Stories of Our Lives*, compiled by the Kenyan art collective The Nest. The project built an archive of life stories of 250 lgbt Kenyans, which have been published as a queer anthology. I analyze the intersections between sexual, cultural, and religious identities as creatively narrated in these stories, and explore the political and theological significance of queer storytelling.

Case study 4 is an ethnography of Cosmopolitan Affirming Church, an lgbt-affirming church community founded in Nairobi in 2013, which has become an important hub for lgbt Christian activism in East Africa. Based on participant observations and interviews, I investigate how this church is a space of queer empowerment through faith. The study specifically focuses on the creative religious texts and practices—prayer, preaching, ritual, and worship—employed in the church, and how they embody a grassroots African queer theology.

I began collecting material for this book during my first research trip to Kenya in July–August 2015. During that visit, I did exploratory research on lgbt activism and religion in the country and met with representatives of relevant organizations and with individual lgbt activists and community members. Building on that initial exploration, I decided to focus on these four case studies, and I managed to meet with key people involved: Binyavanga Wainaina (case study 1), the producer of the "Same Love" video, George Barasa (case study 2), staff members of The Nest who were involved in the *Stories of Our Lives* anthology (case study 3), and some of the church leaders at Cosmopolitan Affirming Church (case study 4). During subsequent visits, in

February–March and December 2016, I refined my method of collecting data, and I conducted a total of thirty formal interviews (in addition to many informal conversations), mostly in the Kenyan capital Nairobi but also in Mombasa (on the coast) and Kisumu (in the western part of Kenya). Between and after my visits to Kenya, I continued my fieldwork from a distance, using online resources and social media tools to follow developments in Kenya and to stay in touch with research participants. With some exceptions, where informants gave explicit permission for the use of their names (and in cases where their names are already in the public domain owing to their lgbt activism), the identity of interviewees and other primary data sources is anonymous, and most interviewees are referred to by pseudonyms. Ethnographic methods of data collection such as interviews and participant observation were used primarily in the study of Cosmopolitan Affirming Church, making chapter 4 the most fieldwork-heavy chapter in the book. But, where relevant, I have included ethnographic data in the other chapters based on different methods; more generally, my observations during fieldwork have informed the overall story and argument presented in this book.

Given the varied nature of the source material, or "data," in the case studies, my analytical and interpretive methodology is necessarily highly interdisciplinary. Instead of attempting to develop a systematic methodology according to the conventions of a particular discipline, I have allowed myself a considerable level of freedom and creativity, unabashedly embracing Judith Halberstam's point that "queer methodology, in a way, is a scavenger methodology": it "attempts to combine methods that are often cast as being at odds with each other, and it refuses the academic compulsion towards disciplinary coherence."[66] The particular combination of methods is informed partly by the material I work with in the case studies and partly by my own interests and curiosity (and the limitations thereof). Thus the methodological queerness of this book lies both in its somewhat eclectic array of "data" or source material—literary texts, visual media, social media texts, autobiographical stories, and church-based practices of community building, preaching, and worship—and in the somewhat eclectic combination of methods from different traditions, ranging from empirical and ethnographic social science–informed methods, to methods of literary and media analysis derived from cultural studies and methods of theological and ethical analysis, interpretation, and reflection.

Broadly speaking, I have adopted Donald Hall's hermeneutical methodology of "reading sexualities." Developed in cultural studies, this methodology focuses on the representation of sexuality at the intersection of other relevant categories—in this book, specifically religion but also gender, race, and class. The method is critically sensitive to questions of power and is characterized by a commitment to social change. Following this methodology, I read the four case studies as social and cultural texts.

This reading takes place in three steps: first, a critical and detailed reading of the case studies as such, specifically exploring the complex representation of, and intersections between, queer sexualities, Kenyan and African identities, and Christian symbols, beliefs, and practices; second, an intertextual reading of the case studies with the writings of selected African postcolonial theologians on Christianity, gender, and sexuality in Africa; and third, inspired by and in interaction with the Kenyan lgbt sociocultural texts under discussion, an autoethnographical mode that allows me to reflect upon my own embodied experiences. The first of these steps is informed by and builds on the debates outlined above that explore the intersections of African, queer, and religious studies. These debates and the issues they raise critically inform my reading of the case studies. The second and third steps in my methodology require more detailed consideration.

Queering African Theology

One of the aims of this book is to engage in a dialogue with African theologians about questions of sexual diversity, and to contribute to the development of African queer theology. My motivation for this is twofold. First, I acknowledge that African theologians make a distinct contribution to the study of religion in Africa—distinct because of their insider status in terms of their political self-identification as African, their epistemological privileging of African perspectives, and their religious self-positioning within the traditions and communities they write about, which gives an engaged, sometimes explicitly activist flavor to their work. The value of this contribution has not always been recognized by European and American scholars of religion in Africa, who often come from intellectual traditions committed to detached forms of scholarship, strictly separating religious studies from, and privileging it over, theology. A postsecular and decolonizing intervention challenges this strict separation, which is based on secular principles of Western academia that do not necessarily make sense in African contexts.[67] Such an intervention allows for a stronger engagement with African theology within the broader interdisciplinary field of the study of religion in Africa. I use the term *African theology* here to refer to a particular body of writing and scholarship by academically trained African Christian theologians, in both Catholic and Protestant traditions, who consider their work part of the discourse called African theology.[68] Beginning in the 1960s, African theology has developed several strands, among them inculturation theology, liberation theology, reconstruction theology, and women's theology.[69]

Second, in African theology so far, questions of sexuality outside heterosexual frameworks have not received much attention, and there has been little engagement with emerging traditions of lgbt activism and queer thought on the continent. In an overview, Masiiwa Ragies Gunda and I have assessed the ways in which homosexuality is addressed in contemporary African theological writing.[70] We observed that the subject is often avoided, even in the substantial body of work on HIV and AIDS that tends to reflect the assumption that HIV in Africa is a heterosexual epidemic. We further showed that homosexuality has been actively opposed, especially by theologians working in the paradigm of inculturation theology, who tend uncritically to join the choir of those who argue that homosexuality is incompatible with "African values," and who adopt a rather static concept of "African culture," selectively ignoring the historical and anthropological evidence of same-sex sexualities in African cultures and societies. But we also identified another recent trend, in which African theologians are beginning to address questions of homosexuality in more progressive ways. Thus the Kenyan theologian Nyambura Njoroge has argued that the HIV epidemic forces African theologians "to make a U-turn in their teaching and theologizing," as they need to address topics that were hitherto taboo, including homosexuality.[71] This challenge has been taken up by Musa Dube in Botswana, who has developed an African HIV liberation theology in which homophobia and heterosexism are among the structural social injustices that underlie the HIV epidemic on the continent and need to be interrogated. In the face of the devastating impact of HIV and AIDS in the early 2000s, Dube proposes a theology that acknowledges that all life is sacred: "All people, regardless of their color, gender, class, race, nationality, religion, ethnicity, health status, age, or sexual orientation, were created in God's image and are loved by God, who is the source of human dignity."[72] Neither Njoroge nor Dube has developed these arguments further, but other theologians have followed their lead, engaging more substantially with issues of homosexuality. Like Dube, the late Zambian theologian Lilly Phiri stressed the notion of the *imago Dei*, the idea that humankind is created in the image of God, on the basis of which she proposed a theology that recognizes the human dignity and rights of same-sex-loving people.[73] Zimbabwean scholars Lovemore Togarasei and Ezra Chitando, and in particular Gunda, have presented an in-depth and critical interrogation of the popular notion that homosexuality is "un-African," "un-Christian," and "unbiblical," and have suggested alternative readings of both African cultures and biblical texts through a hermeneutics of liberation.[74] Elias Bongmba, from Cameroon, has made a hermeneutical intervention in debates on homosexuality in African Christianity, and has proposed the philosophy of *ubuntu* as a way to interrogate discourses of othering around sexuality in Africa.[75] The South African scholar Gerald West has recently argued for an African queer theology, which he locates firmly in the trajectory of African liberation theologies. Building on the "prophetic" ways in which liberation theology in southern Africa has addressed questions of colonialism, race, and gender, West advocates a queer liberation theology that takes up "the contextual challenge of sexual diversity and the rampant marginalization of different or queer sexualities."[76]

Clearly, a progressive engagement with questions of sexual diversity is a recent and promising trend in African theology. Building on this development, the present book seeks to contribute to a further queering of African theology. I read the case studies of Kenyan lgbt activism vis-à-vis selected African theological writings as much as vis-à-vis queer theoretical, philosophical, sociological, and anthropological, and literary texts. This intertextual reading foregrounds the religious themes in the case studies. Each of the sociocultural texts I discuss presents a critical, creative, and often surprising engagement with Christian beliefs, texts, and practices, rendering these texts grassroots queer theological texts. Bringing them into conversation with relevant writings by African theologians like Edward Antonio, Emmanuel Katongole, and Mercy Oduyoye serves to elaborate on the theological themes raised in the case studies, and to capitalize on the potential for queering African theology. Along the way, this book presents a methodological example of how African queer theology might be developed. Thus, although this book is not a theological project per se, theological voices and themes are a substantial part of the multidisciplinary conversation to which I hope this book will contribute. The engagement with theology, as well as with queer theory and other forms of critically engaged scholarship, gives the book a more constructive edge. I hope this edge will be clear in my discussion of the theme of futurity, to which I return throughout the book, a discussion influenced by my reading of Muñoz's *Cruising Utopia* and by the concern with eschatology in African and queer theological writing.

Accounting for the Ethnographic Self

Between the case studies, this book includes four interludes—short essays, written in an autoethnographical mode, in which I reflect upon some of my experiences during the process of researching and writing the book. Although these personal experiences do not relate directly to the case studies, the idea to include them was inspired by my engagement with the primary material. The function of these interludes is manifold, although there is a risk that they seek to do too much and fail to achieve anything (apart from possibly disturbing the reader, given the rather intimate revelations that some of them contain).

First, they offer me an opportunity to address issues of positionality and to demonstrate reflexivity in a more narrative style. Authors usually address such issues in the introduction of a book, in a paragraph typically starting with a statement like, "As a white, European, middle-class, gay-identifying male, I. . . ." Although each of these categories may apply to me, I feel uncomfortable describing myself in such terms. The meanings of these terms cannot be taken for granted, and simply using them says little about how I understand them, how they affect my identity and subjectivity, and how they affect the ways in which I conduct my research and relate to research participants. Instead of this formal kind of accounting for positionality, I prefer doing so in a more narrative style. Such a style seems to do more justice to the messiness of fieldwork, in which the boundaries between the researcher's private and public selves, the links between the researcher's personal life, academic interests, and political commitment, and the relationships between the researcher and the research participants are all multifaceted, ambiguous, and complicated. Discussing the "transgressive nature of fieldwork" in the study of religion, Rosalind Hackett makes the point that researchers are often drawn into participating in the communities we study in ways that are "not in the 'rule book'—whether religiously, politically, financially, or sexually."[77] My own experiences in the field bear this out.

The messiness of the practice and process of fieldwork is reflected in the interludes themselves, as they are written in a hybrid genre that moves between autoethnographical, reflexive, and confessional writing. As such, they fit into a tradition in anthropology and the qualitative social sciences, where the so-called postmodern turn has given rise to the production of "reflexive, experiential texts which are messy, subjective, open ended, conflictual and feminist influenced," as Amanda Coffey puts it.[78] In addition to being influenced by feminism, my interludes are also influenced by postcolonial and queer perspectives. Each of these critical perspectives is part of the postmodern turn, which has inspired me intellectually and methodologically in the writing of the interludes.

Second, the interludes seek to provide insight into the embodied nature of qualitative research, specifically in the area of religion and sexuality. It is now widely acknowledged that ethnographic research in general is an embodied and relational practice, but the observation that "published ethnographies typically have repressed bodily experience in favor of abstracted theory and analysis" still holds true to a considerable extent, meaning that the person, and indeed the body, of the ethnographer often remains invisible in ethnographic writing.[79] Most ethnographic literature presents a thick description of the research findings, but does not share with the reader the process that led to these findings. But if ethnography and other forms of qualitative research are embodied and subjective forms of inquiry, the messy process of data collection cannot be separated from, and in fact is critical to understanding, the findings.

In anthropology as a discipline, it has become common to acknowledge the bodily nature of ethnographic fieldwork, and some anthropological literature courageously thinks through the broad question of embodiment in relation to the more explicitly erotic and sexual aspects of the embodied process and practice of fieldwork.[80] This acknowledgment has only recently generated new debates in religious studies. Some empirical scholars of religion have emphasized the importance of "taking the body seriously, taking relationalities seriously," and have begun to draw attention to the fact that fieldwork in the study of religion involves "bodywork"—a significant methodological trend toward acknowledging embodiment, relationality, and positionality and demonstrating reflexivity and accountability.[81] What remains underacknowledged, however, is the erotic and sometimes explicitly sexual dimension inherent in the embodied and relational dynamics of fieldwork in general, and (possibly) of fieldwork on issues relating to sexuality in particular. As one colleague, who is involved in the Religion and Sexuality Unit in the American Academy of Religion, responded to my suggestion to convene a panel about this topic, "Of course we all have our experiences, but who would dare to share and discuss them publicly?" In the interludes, I attempt to break this taboo, as some of the experiences narrated here illustrate what it means to say that the fieldwork for this book was indeed bodywork, and I begin by reflecting upon some of the ethical, methodological, and political questions this raises. This opens up further conversations, within and beyond the study of religion, about the embodied nature of fieldwork, including (but not limited to) the question of "sex in the field"—conversations in which those who conduct ethnographic research can openly and honestly discuss and reflect upon our experiences in an atmosphere of respect and integrity.

Third, just as the interludes allow my embodied and sexual self to be written into the pages of this book, they also enable me to account for and reflect upon my religious self—although I find understanding the latter perhaps even more difficult than the former. Robert Orsi has observed that "if sexual relations in the field is the great taboo subject of anthropology, our own religious histories is the great taboo of religious studies."[82] In his book on American Catholicism, Orsi thus reflects upon his own family stories in order to reveal more of his religious history and take a step in the direction of critical self-reflection. Unlike Orsi's book, the present book is about religion *and* sexuality, thus challenging me to face both taboos. In addition, whereas Orsi tends to write autobiographically about religion as a matter of family *history*, for me, religion—in ways I do not always fully understand myself—is part of the ongoing story of my life and influences how I understand myself as part of this world, including in relation to my research field, research topics, and research subjects. As much as the personal struggle of how to combine my sexuality with my conservative Protestant upbringing and with the evangelical Christian faith of my youth belongs to the past, this part of my biography allows me to recognize and sympathize with similar struggles in the lives of the African queer subjects I write about in this book. It also means that there is something at stake for me, personally and politically but also theologically, in writing about these issues. My personal interest and involvement are undoubtedly further influenced by the fact that my initial training was mainly in theology, and that I made my first steps into the field of African studies as a master's student studying African feminist theologians and their work on issues of gender, sexuality, and HIV and AIDS. In my later work, I have broadened my disciplinary position, and nowadays I prefer the more generic identity of a scholar of religion in Africa making use of diverse methodologies. But I cannot deny that certain theological commitments underlie my thinking, and in the process of writing this book I realized that I should make room for that fact rather than hide it behind the mask of a secular academic self. This decision was particularly motivated by the fact that my own body, during the process of writing this book, somehow caught up with some of the theological themes I had worked on previously in relation to HIV and AIDS in African theology. Writing about this in one of the interludes has been a way of making sense of this somewhat ironic turn of events in my personal and academic biography.

Fourth, writing these autoethnographical interludes has been inspired by my critical awareness of the long-standing problem of the othering of Africa in Africanist scholarship, and they are my attempt to address this problem. As Mbembe puts it, "Africa as an idea, a concept, has historically served, and continues to serve, as a polemical argument for the West's desperate desire to assert its difference from the rest of the world. In several respects, Africa still constitutes one of the metaphors through which the West represents the origin of its own norms, develops a self-image, and integrates this image into the set of signifiers asserting what it supposes to be its identity." This problem is particularly apparent in writings about sexuality in Africa, given colonial perceptions of Africa as a backward and dark continent, and of African sexuality as wild and primitive, which continue to influence popular, and at times also academic, representations of issues relating to sexuality—for instance, the "African AIDS crisis" and "African homophobia." Postcolonial Africanist scholarship has taken a reflexive stance in order to overcome colonialist dynamics, but the relationship between the typically white Western scholar of Africa, on the one hand, and Africa and Africans as the subjects of his knowledge, on the other hand, remains problematic. Like African women in the past (but not only in the past), African queer people are typically seen nowadays "under Western eyes," to use the phrase with which Chandra Mohanty famously captured the colonizing gaze of Western feminist scholarship about non-Western women, through which the latter have been systematically "othered." I hope that the inclusion of my self-reflexive interludes addresses, and helps prevent, this othering of the Kenyan queer subjects I write about. In particular, by writing about my own bodily and sexual self, I seek to complicate otherness and draw attention to a shared and embodied human existence. As Mbembe reminds us, "the theoretical and practical recognition of the body and flesh of 'the stranger' as flesh and body just like mine, the idea of a common human nature, a humanity shared with others, long posed, and still poses, a problem for Western consciousness."[83] In writing this book, I have begun to realize the extent to which my own flesh and body, and my identity, are indeed enmeshed with the bodies and identities of those I came to know during the research process: as informants, as interviewees, as friends, and, I hesitantly admit, incidentally as lovers—categories that, in my experience, are not always easy to separate (precisely because of the embodied and relational nature of fieldwork). This has been a rather existential insight. My inclusion of autobiographical and reflexive writings is therefore not just a matter of following the latest trend in ethnographic scholarship, where it has become "increasingly fashionable for individual researchers to 'personalise' their accounts of fieldwork,"[84] but is intended to be a deeply ethical exercise. It is a way of accounting for, and reflecting upon, the fact that "each of us is constituted politically in part by virtue of the social vulnerability of our bodies," as Judith Butler poignantly puts it in a passage to which I return in the interlude titled "Positive."[85]

All of this raises the question of what has been called "queer solidarity," in particular solidarity between the West and Africa. Gayatri Chakravorty Spivak has famously described colonial feminism as a case of "white men saving brown women from brown men," and Rahul Rao has noted that something similar can be observed nowadays in the concern about homophobia in Africa and elsewhere—what he calls "the contemporary eagerness of white gays to save brown gays from brown homophobes."[86] In my own work I have interrogated the latter dynamic, among others, by complicating and nuancing the monolithic narrative of "African homophobia" and, in this book, foregrounding African queer agency. But this is not necessarily enough to prevent the risk that my work will amount to another example of this colonial dynamic. The relationship between Western researcher and African research subjects, and the representation of the latter, especially in a project as political as this one, remains problematic and requires ongoing reflection.

Thus the interludes interspersed between the main chapters in this book are intended to address these four methodological, political, and ethical considerations and concerns. In the interlude titled "Prophetess," between chapters 1 and 2, I reflect upon an incident that occurred when I visited one of Nairobi's Pentecostal churches, which I contrast to my fieldwork experience in Cosmopolitan Affirming Church. In "Bodywork," which falls between chapters 2 and 3, I reflect upon two incidents during my research in Kenya, which illustrate the relational, embodied, erotic, and indeed sexual nature of fieldwork. Between chapters 3 and 4, in "Positive," I disclose my HIV status and use this as an opportunity to reflect upon the ways in which my body has become enmeshed with African queer bodies, becoming part of the history of the pandemic on the continent. Finally, chapter 4 is followed by "Ambassador," in which I reflect upon my political involvement in the subject, and with the subjects, of this book, and upon the complex negotiation of the roles of researcher and advocate.

THE CONTEXT OF KENYA

The case studies presented in this book originate in Kenya, and a brief contextualization is thus required, one that provides insight into the complex dynamics of lgbt activism in that country.

In his 2009 book on Christianity in Kenya, Paul Gifford comments that for most Kenyans, homosexuality "hardly seems a burning issue." This observation might have been correct at the time, but things appear to have changed considerably in the decade since then. In recent years, Kenya has witnessed intensifying public and political debates about homosexuality and lgbt rights, in line with the broader politicization of homosexuality in Africa. To a considerable extent, this is thanks to the growing influence of Pentecostal forms of Christianity in the Kenyan public sphere. Pentecostalism has grown rapidly in recent decades in Kenya, as it has throughout sub-Saharan Africa. The new churches are said to attract the urban middle class in particular, allowing its members consciously to opt into modernity.[87] Yet as much as Kenya's Pentecostal churches may be associated with modernity, they fervently oppose some modern developments, and the recognition of same-sex relationships and lgbt rights is one of them. The influence of these churches and their leaders "has invaded all aspects of Kenyan civic life and their presence is now being felt in the realm of politics, economics, cultural and socio-religious fields," according to Damaris Parsitau and Philomena Njeri Mwaura.[88] The strong Pentecostal involvement in public debates and politics is apparent in the 2010 constitutional referendum, where Pentecostals campaigned (unsuccessfully) against the draft constitution, emphasizing the evils of abortion, Islamic legal courts, and homosexuality.[89] Generally, Pentecostalism has contributed to the politicization of homosexuality in Kenya in much the same way that it has in other African countries, that is, by presenting a form of Pentecostal nationalism according to which Kenya is a "born-again nation" in which Western secular powers assist the devil in imposing homosexuality and lgbt rights on Africa.[90]

But Pentecostal actors are not the only ones to blame for politicizing homosexuality in Kenya. For instance, in response to a 2012 report from the Kenya National Commission on Human Rights that advocated the recognition of sexual minorities' human rights, the Anglican priest Peter Karanja, in his capacity as general secretary of the National Council of Churches of Kenya, said publicly that homosexuality is "against African beliefs and more so our Christian principles."[91] The Catholic Justice and Peace Commission, an official body of the Kenya Conference of Catholic Bishops, is actively involved in mobilizing the antigay caucus in the Kenyan Parliament and in organizing social protests against lgbt rights, such as on the occasion of President Obama's 2015 official state visit to Kenya.[92] Kenya, in addition, has a substantial Muslim minority, especially in the coastal region, among which homosexuality has become deeply politicized in a public discourse that resembles Christian rhetoric, framing homosexuality as "unnatural," "un-African," and "un-Islamic."[93]

The increasing politicization of homosexuality and lgbt rights in Kenya has emerged in parallel to the growing visibility of lgbt activists and communities in the country.[94] In a 2000 essay, the Kenyan writer and activist John Mburu wrote about the "dreams and delusions of an incipient lesbian and gay movement in Kenya." In his account, the Kenyan movement began in the early 1990s, particularly in response to the HIV epidemic and in an attempt to challenge the heteronormative assumptions with which many Kenyans approached issues of HIV and AIDS. Another major challenge, according to Mburu, has been "the pervasive ideology that still portrays homosexuality as un-African and Western [and that] can only be neutralized by an ideal that embraced Africa's various traditions and customs as well as the Western influences that are now an indelible part of Africa's traditions."[95] The ideology referred to here is deeply entrenched in the Kenyan public mind. The first Kenyan president, Jomo Kenyatta—often considered the father of the nation—in his influential book *Facing Mount Kenya* had already asserted that "the practice of homosexuality is unknown among the Gikuyu" (the largest ethnic group in Kenya).[96] His successor, Daniel arap Moi, controversially stated in 1999 that "homosexuality is against African norms and traditions, even in religion it is considered a great sin."[97] These beliefs have been given new salience in contemporary public debates, as seen in statements by Kenya's deputy president, William Ruto, for example, that "homosexuality is against the plan of God" and that "we will defend our country Kenya, we will stand for our faith and our country."[98] Yet this kind of opposition has failed to stop gradual social, legal, and political change.

While Ruto represents a dominant voice in the Kenyan public sphere—exemplifying the phallocracy that characterizes Kenyan political culture—in fact there is a significant level of diversity of opinion on the issue in Kenya.[99] Referring to an antigay comment in 2010 by then prime minister Raila Odinga, Keguro Macharia points out that "five years earlier, such a statement would have elicited mainstream silence or approval[;] this time, however, mainstream newspapers published articles challenging Raila's statement."[100] Beyond the expression of different opinions in the media, lgbt individuals and communities in Kenya enjoy relatively high visibility, compared to their counterparts in surrounding countries, and lgbt activists are correspondingly active in the public domain. This may be the result, in part, of the progressive bill of rights that was incorporated in the 2010 constitution, which, according to Godwin

Murunga, "contributes greatly to the possibility of making Kenya a democratic state by recognizing the human rights and fundamental freedoms of all Kenyans. More importantly, it confers and defends the rights of a diversity of Kenyans in a way that was not possible in the previous constitutions."[101] The new constitution appears to have emboldened lgbt activists and other progressive forces in Kenya. As the prominent activist and lawyer Eric Gitari points out, although the 2010 constitution did not explicitly mention matters of sexual orientation or gender identity, "it nonetheless possessed golden threads of equality, dignity and freedom, better still whose defense had been entrusted to an independent judiciary."[102] Indeed, various legal successes have been achieved in Kenyan courts in recent years. In 2014, for instance, the High Court of Kenya ruled that the Non-Governmental Organizations Coordination Board (NGOCB) should allow a transgender organization, Transgender Education and Advocacy, to register as an NGO, and in 2015 a similar ruling was made for the National Gay and Lesbian Human Rights Commission (NGLHRC). Thus the constitutional right to freedom of association was effectively applied to lgbt groups, and the constitutional right to protection against discrimination was applied to sexual orientation and gender identity. Emboldened by these steps, the NGLHRC in 2016 filed a petition to the High Court calling for the decriminalization of same-sex practices, arguing that the relevant section of the penal code violated the constitutional right to equality, dignity, and privacy. This petition was being heard by the High Court in 2018, and during my final fieldwork visit, in July 2018, activists were optimistic about the outcome. At the highest political level, President Kenyatta has not followed other politicians in Kenya and fellow statesmen in Africa in using virulent homophobic rhetoric. He has repeatedly observed that "for Kenyans today the issue of gay rights is really a non-issue," while at the same time leaving open the possibility of future social and political change on the subject.[103] In the meantime, the Kenyan government is said to have "consistently consulted with LGBT groups and included them in national public health initiatives," especially in programs for HIV prevention and treatment. Referring to these developments, Gitari is optimistic about the future and concludes that, already today, "Kenya stands out as a leader on LGBTIQ equality within sub-Saharan Africa."[104] Macharia is less sanguine, concluding that although the Kenyan government has not followed the example of neighboring Uganda in proposing explicit anti-gay legislation, it nevertheless has actively sought to protect the institutions of family and marriage.[105] There are undoubtedly reasons for both optimism and pessimism regarding lgbt rights in Kenya, yet, as this book demonstrates, there appears to be considerable momentum for lgbt activism in the country at present.

In addition to these forms of legal, social, and political advocacy by the NGLHRC and other lgbt organizations, Kenyan lgbt communities have employed alternative methods to bring about social and political change. Evan Mwangi, for instance, has demonstrated how in recent years community members have actively used digital media as a site of "queer agency" where they combat "homophobic representations of their experiences and desires."[106] The case studies featured in this book represent other sociocultural forms of lgbt activism and queer politics, which fit into a longer tradition of cultural production as a key to social change in Kenya.[107] My research took place primarily in Nairobi, Kenya's capital and largest city, where most of the national lgbt organizations are based. Interestingly, among the officials of these organizations, I encountered relatively little enthusiasm for the question I was studying: how lgbt activism and queer politics might make use of religion as a resource. In other Kenyan cities, such as Mombasa on the coast and Kisumu in the western part of the country, I encountered local organizations that did actively address faith issues and engage religious leaders. As one activist working with the Mombasa-based organization PEMA Kenya explained, "in Mombasa, everything is driven by religion . . . and religious leaders have a voice among the people, so it's important to engage them."[108] Yet in Nairobi, established lgbt organizations seemed largely to avoid religion and faith; when learning about my research interests, activists involved in these organizations would typically respond by sharing their negative experiences with "the church." This observation was confirmed by one faith-based activist (a minister at Cosmopolitan Affirming Church), who told me of the difficulties in collaborating with lgbt organizations in the city, which, in his experience, were wary of religion and pursued a secular lgbt rights agenda.[109] However, in Nairobi as elsewhere in Kenya, religion and faith do matter to many members of the grassroots lgbt community—both in their personal lives and also, therefore, politically.

CHAPTER 1

Kenyan Queer Critique of Christianity and Homophobia

Writing on popular myths about homosexuality in Africa—such as that it is "un-African" and a "Western invention"—Thabo Msibi has underlined the need for "creative and more African-centered" ways of interrogating such narratives.[1] This chapter presents the first of four Kenyan case studies of such creative and African-centered interventions, focusing on the literary writer Binyavanga Wainaina. In line with more general discussions about the African literary writer as a social thinker and about African literature as a vehicle of social and political transformation,[2] scholars have drawn attention to the role of African creative writers and writings in addressing homophobia and the politics of homosexuality in Africa.[3] Although this chapter draws on that scholarship, the case of Wainaina is unique because of the strong autobiographical element in his work: here we have a writer who used a literary story reimagining his mother's deathbed as a vehicle for coming out as gay, and who since then has used his position as an openly gay writer to actively contribute to public debates on matters of sexuality. As Gabeba Baderoon states, "to select the genre of self-writing in which to convey a political position on sexual diversity [is] original and resonant," and it exemplifies "the power of autobiography to shape public debates."[4]

Wainaina is an acclaimed figure on the African literary scene. Among other achievements, he was the winner of the Caine Prize for African Writing in 2002, was the founding editor of literary magazine *Kwani?* in 2003, was nominated by the World Economic Forum as a Young Global Leader in 2007, and until 2013 served as director of the Chinua Achebe Center for African Literature and Languages at Bard College in New York. Considered "Kenya's best-known writer of his generation,"[5] and "one of Africa's most powerful writers,"[6] Wainaina received much attention, both within and outside Kenya, when he came out in 2014. His story was republished on the website Africa Is a Country and by the British newspaper the *Guardian*, while many international media outlets, among them the *New York Times* and the *Huffington Post*, published feature articles about it. In Kenya, Wainaina's confession was a "gay bombshell," in the words of the newspaper *Daily Nation*, as it "shocked the nation and sent the social media abuzz."[7]

The Nigerian-British activist and writer Sokari Ekine has somewhat sarcastically suggested that Wainaina, after coming out, was soon embraced as "the authentic African Queer Spokesperson" by the Western media.[8] Although Ekine's tone is understandable given the enthusiasm with which prominent Western media outlets reported his coming out, there was also excitement in Kenyan and wider African queer circles that a well-known public figure had joined their ranks. Thus the Gay and Lesbian Coalition of Kenya welcomed Wainaina's move, expecting that the courage of such a prominent person would make it easier for other same-sex-loving Kenyans to follow.[9] Wainaina's name is mentioned, and his image is featured, in the Kenyan gay music video "Same Love" (see chapter 2), and an interview portrait of him, written by Kenyan gay activist and writer Kevin Mwachiro, is included in the volume *Boldly Queer: African Perspectives on Same-Sex Sexuality and Gender Diversity*.[10] Several storytellers in the Kenyan queer anthology *Stories of Our Lives* refer to the significance of Wainaina's coming out (see chapter 3). Wainaina himself said that he received "thousands of messages from Africans all over the continent [and] from diaspora Africans," expressing support.[11]

The focus of this chapter on Wainaina, then, is not to follow the pattern of idolization of Wainaina that Ekine observes in the Western media, but to acknowledge the symbolic significance of Wainaina's step, and to examine his contribution to African queer politics. It also allows us to explore how, since his coming out, Wainaina has intervened in the Pentecostal Christian mobilization against homosexuality and lgbt rights in the Kenyan public sphere.

COMING OUT AS INTERVENTION

"I am a homosexual, mum." Under this title, on January 18, 2014, Wainaina published what he called "a lost chapter" from his 2011 memoir, on the pan-African online platform Chimurenga Chronic.[12] As the title indicates, the chapter includes an intimate revelation: Binyavanga, on the occasion of his forty-third birthday, comes out as gay. He does so in a literary style, reimagining the last days of his mother's life and telling her, on her deathbed, the truth about his sexuality. For those confused about whether his announcement was a piece of fiction, he tweeted the next day, "I am, for anybody confused or in doubt, a homsexual [*sic*]. Gay, and quite happy."[13]

One of the reasons that Wainaina gave for his coming out was the death of a friend the preceding year.[14] The friend died at age twenty-three of AIDS-related causes, "because he was too ashamed to ask for a HIV test."[15] This sad death confronted Wainaina with "a certain kind of hypocrisy" because of his status as a closeted gay man, and he felt that he needed to come out in order to clear his mind and overcome the writer's block he was facing.[16] Wainaina also had a political motive: he came out shortly after the passage of controversial antihomosexuality legislation in the Ugandan and Nigerian parliaments. Uganda is the country of his mother's birth, and he is a frequent visitor to Nigeria, the birthplace of his partner (to whom, he announced in May 2018, he is engaged to be married).[17] Explaining his timing, Wainaina said in almost messianic language, "I see my coming out as an intervention, in a moment in time."[18] This statement alludes to the explicitly political significance of his coming out, illustrating David Halperin's point that "*coming out is an act of freedom, then, not in the sense of liberation but in the sense of resistance*" (emphasis in original).[19] On January 21, a few days after his coming-out story appeared, Wainaina released on YouTube a six-part video documentary titled *We Must Free Our Imaginations* in which he describes social, political, and religious homophobia in Africa as "the bankruptcy of a certain kind of imagination" and urges Africans to engage in creative and imaginary thinking. This call to action is in line with the broader postcolonial and pan-Africanist agenda that characterizes Wainaina's work, which seeks to develop "a new way of conceptualizing an Africa free of images of subjection and subjugation," as Rachel Knighton describes it.[20] Thus, for Wainaina, overcoming homophobia is a matter of decolonization.

Three years after coming out, Wainaina made another intimate revelation on Twitter. On December 1, 2016, on the occasion of World AIDS Day, he tweeted that he was HIV-positive "and happy." Interestingly, while Kenyan media reported on his tweet, the Western media outlets that had written extensively about his coming out paid no attention to this second revelation. Perhaps these media did not want their "authentic African Queer Spokesperson" to be tainted by the stigma of HIV. Or perhaps they did not want to reinforce the association of homosexuality with HIV or (possibly with Wainaina's own sarcastic essay "How to Write About Africa" in mind)[21] did not want to reinforce the stereotypical narrative linking Africans to disease. Yet Wainaina himself, by explicitly stating that he was happy regardless of his HIV status, challenged the typical linkage of HIV with disease, physical and mental suffering, and death. Wainaina was clearly and strategically denying that being gay, and even being HIV-positive, in Africa necessarily makes one a victim. He acknowledged that his privileged status as a middle-class Kenyan with an international reputation made it easier for him to reject victim status than it would be for many less well off and less well known gay and lesbian Africans to do so. Indeed, it was this awareness that encouraged him to speak out.[22]

Wainaina's coming out—first as gay and then as HIV-positive—demonstrates his awareness that the personal is indeed political, and that his body is a site of struggle. Knighton, in her review of Wainaina's published memoir, writes that Wainaina's literary politics "centre on the importance of the personal and the artistic, recalibrating theoretical notions of the politicization of African autobiography."[23] With his public confession of these intimate personal truths, Wainaina has put these theoretical notions into radical practice, developing an innovative form of what Achille Mbembe calls "African modes of self-writing," in which the embodied and sexual self is explicitly written into being. This kind of "self-writing" is innovative and significant because it transcends "the pathos of victimization" that, according to Mbembe, has long dominated such modes.[24] In Wainaina's case, this pathos applies not only to the historical experience of colonial and racial subjugation but also to the contemporary experience of both homophobia and HIV stigma, which he seeks to resist and transcend by reclaiming his black, African, gay, HIV-positive body through writing.

Since coming out as gay, Wainaina has become one of the most prominent and vocal African critics not only of homophobia in Africa but also of the religious forces that incite and fuel it. In interviews and on social media he has publicly delivered a strong critique of popular forms of Christianity in Kenya and other African countries. He has been particularly forceful in criticizing Pentecostal Christianity, which he sees as a major factor in the spread of homophobia and in the politicization of homosexuality in Kenya and elsewhere on the continent. As he put it on the popular Kenyan TV talk show *Jeff Koinange Live* shortly after coming out, "What I don't like, and this is where my anger comes from, what I don't like is how public space has been squashed by Pentecostal demon hunters."[25]

As explained in the introduction to this book, in Kenya and other African contexts in which religion is used to reinforce and legitimize homophobia and antihomosexual politics, it is particularly important to draw attention to counterdiscourses and counterpractices emerging in these contexts. Binyavanga Wainaina is a prominent example of Kenyan agency, courage, creativity, and authority in the struggle for sexual diversity and gay rights in contemporary Africa. In fact, given the form and content of his contribution to that struggle, I submit that Wainaina can be thought of as a queer prophet. Referring to a publicly out and proud gay man, a man who is not ashamed of performing gender ambiguity and challenging the conventions of public morality, as a prophet—generally thought of as a pious, zealous, holy man of God—may strike some readers as discordant or even inappropriate. Wainaina himself, when I suggested that he could be thought of as a prophet, responded jokingly that he had "always thought that prophets were very boring people with beards"—not a group with whom he wants to be associated.[26] Yet I propose that we appropriate the figure of the prophet for queer politics, by queering the prophet as a sociopolitical critic. Following the queer methodology outlined in the introduction, my concept of the prophet is neither strictly sociological nor theological. Instead, I invoke prophecy as a creative category in which to think about Wainaina's contribution to queer politics in Kenya and in Africa in language that is contextually meaningful.

One caveat is in order. As much as Wainaina's coming out has been welcomed, and his contribution to queer politics in Kenya and Africa acknowledged, he is also a somewhat controversial figure. His long-term commitment to the well-being of ordinary gay and lesbian Kenyans has been questioned, especially since he moved to Johannesburg, South Africa, in 2017. The Kenyan newspaper *Daily Nation* quotes an anonymous critic who, in response to Wainaina's second coming out (about being HIV-positive), commented: "If he has the energy, he can sustain the struggle for gay men to have access to information and proper medical care. I doubt though, that [Binyavanga] has the energy for any long-haul campaign. Not physical energy: emotional energy and intellectual strength."[27] One may object that this commentator expects Wainaina to play a particular activist role in the area of sexual health that Wainaina never intended to take on. A more fundamental criticism has been voiced by the Kenyan poet Shailja Patel, who has accused Wainaina of publicly defending the man whom she and two other women reported to police for sexual assault. A year after this incident, Patel made her criticism public in a series of tweets, in which she accused Wainaina of misogyny and of "toxic lesbophobia," and in which she called him egocentric and primarily concerned with cultivating his self-image as "The Only Gay Man in Kenya."[28] I am not in a position to verify these accusations, to which Wainaina has not publicly responded. These controversies remind us of the error of idolizing Wainaina, or any other activist, which Ekine observes in Western media. Thus when I conceptualize Wainaina's contribution in terms of queer prophecy, the reader may want to keep in mind that a prophet is not necessarily a saint, and that this chapter is not intended as hagiography.

A QUEER AMONG THE PROPHETS

Kenya has a long tradition of prophets. Many figures in both Kenyan history and contemporary Kenya have been called, or have called themselves, prophet. As a category, whether of self-identification or of identification by others, the term is rather imprecise. A variety of figures in indigenous religions and traditional cultures in eastern Africa, such as diviners, oracles, spirit mediums, and witch doctors, have been described in anthropological and historical literature with the ancient, originally biblical term *prophet*. Reviewing this literature, Douglas Johnson and David Anderson conclude that "the variety of 'prophets' thus found in eastern Africa is indeed bewildering and defies easy amalgamation within a single analytical category."[29] This variety becomes even greater when one takes into account the many self-declared prophets in Kenyan Christian circles, both in twentieth-century independent churches, such as the Arathi or Roho churches, and in twenty-first-century Pentecostal-charismatic churches and movements.[30]

In their attempt to come up with a more precise use of the term *prophet* in East Africa, Johnson and Anderson define the prophet as an "inspired figure" who "must be concerned with the wider moral community at a social or political level" and whose moral authority is believed by the community "to be inspired by a divinity or other source of spiritual or moral knowledge that influences the destiny of the community."[31] I do not to claim that Wainaina necessarily perceives himself, or is perceived by others, as a divinely inspired figure. Baptized as Catholic and later, after his mother's born-again conversion, raised as Pentecostal, Wainaina has confessed that he does not know whether he is "an atheist or a lapsed believer."[32] Interrogating the "ecstasy of madness" that he observes in Pentecostalism, he has also pronounced himself "dedicated to a rational, secular life."[33] More recently, he has suggested that he is reclaiming indigenous spirituality, especially the practice of honoring the ancestors, under the guidance of a South African *sangoma* (diviner and healer) and a Kenyan "spiritual guide." In an open letter addressed to all Kenyans on the occasion of the contested 2017 presidential elections, he spoke out about Kenyan political affairs and suggested that his ancestors had encouraged him to do so. "I would like to say here and now with my ancestors witnessing this that what I am about to say is the truth," the letter stated. He went on to quote the Bible: "believe in the biblical verse that says, 'the truth will set you free'" (John 8:32, in which the word "truth" refers to Jesus's teaching).[34] Wainaina himself thus appeals to both the indigenous motif of ancestral inspiration and the biblical motif of divine, liberating truth to legitimate the source of his moral knowledge and his motivation for making this knowledge public. Given these statements and the ambiguity they create, we can neither assert nor exclude the possibility that there is an element of spiritual inspiration and motivation in Wainaina's prophetic contribution. Thus, rather than suggesting that compared to Pentecostal and other religious prophets, Wainaina is a secular prophet, I suggest that he can be thought of as a nontheistic prophet. I borrow this notion from the political theorist George Shulman, who uses it in relation to African American writer James Baldwin. As Shulman explains, "I call him [Baldwin] nontheistic because he does not announce God's words or point of view as a messenger, but prophetic because, on the avowed basis of experience, social position, and artistic vision, he announces what is disavowed and unsayable and testifies to what he sees and stands against it. I call him nontheistic but prophetic because he announces the vicissitudes of human finitude not by way of God's righteousness in a providentially ordered universe but by way of the exemplary meaning or 'truth' of his experience as a human being and as a 'sexually dubious' black man."[35] Like Baldwin's, Wainaina's prophetic voice is born of his personal experience as a "sexually dubious" black man. That similarity is one of the reasons why Wainaina has frequently referred to Baldwin as a source of inspiration, recognizing him as "black, African, ours"[36] and as a "gay icon of freedom,"[37] and canonizing him as a writer of "new scriptures."[38]

Regardless of the question of divine or otherwise spiritual inspiration that, theologically speaking, is inherent in prophecy, when using the term *prophet* in relation to Wainaina I foreground the historical, anthropological, and literary notion of the prophet as being concerned with the wider community at a sociopolitical level. As the Jewish philosopher Abraham Joshua Heschel famously put it, with reference to the biblical prophetic tradition, "the prophet is an iconoclast, challenging the apparently holy, revered, and awesome. Beliefs cherished as certainties, institutions endowed with supreme sanctity, he exposes as scandalous pretensions."[39] As a sociopolitical critic inspired by an alternative vision of society and human life, the prophet thus stands up and speaks out against the powers that be. In this sense, prophets can generally be thought of as inherently queer, if we keep in mind Halperin's famous description of the term *queer* as demarcating "not a positivity, but a positionality vis-à-vis the normative."[40] As will become clear, Wainaina certainly is such a queer prophetic figure, in the sense that he presents a radical social, political, and religious critique of certain social norms and power structures, and opens up an alternative, transgressive space of sociopolitical imagination.

But Wainaina is also queer in a more specific way, as his prophetic contribution is rooted, in the words of Sokari Ekine and Hakima Abbas, in "a perspective that embraces gender and sexual plurality and seeks to transform, overhaul, and revolutionise African order rather than seek to assimilate into oppressive hetero-patriarchal-capitalist frameworks."[41] This political perspective was his major reason for coming out as gay unapologetically. As he explained in an interview, "I had to come out to be useful. In the closet I could not be useful. I could not think of myself as a writer in the closet while harbouring queer concerns."[42] These words have an almost messianic undertone, as they reflect a sense of calling. To be a prophet is a vocation, and to be a *queer* prophet requires the vocation of intervening in the politics of sexuality. Wainaina is an *African* queer prophet, for that matter, for he does not only intervene in the popular politics of sexuality in Africa but also opens up alternative ways of imagining African queer futures, not least in his YouTube video series *We Must Free Our Imaginations*.

As with prophets in the biblical tradition, Wainaina's name can be read as an indication of his prophetic vocation. The name Binyavanga—which he, as second-born son, following the Kikuyu tradition of his father, inherited from his Ugandan maternal grandfather—is a queer one.[43] As he writes in his memoir, this name "has something to do with mixing things up," and he notes that among the Kikuyu, "your name is a kind of fate." "Being Binyavanga," he continues, "is to me also exotic—an imaginary Ugandan of some kind resides in me, one who lets me withhold from claiming, or being admitted into, without hesitation, an unquestioning Gikuyu belonging."[44] Though for a while he preferred his English name, Kenneth, he now proudly uses Binyavanga and indeed likes mixing things up, as has become clear from his coming out. Having an "imaginary Ugandan" residing in him, and lacking an indisputable claim to Kikuyu identity, Wainaina seems to position himself at the margins of his community—a relative outsider position that is typical of the prophet who critiques the sociopolitical culture and structures of society. His open letter to all Kenyans is a recent example of this kind of critique. Published the day before the rerun of the 2017 presidential election, the letter gave an account of Wainaina's voting patterns in previous elections, and made public that he, a Kikuyu, was now supporting opposition candidate Raila Odinga, a Luo.

Another aspect of queerness, which may apply to prophets more generally, relates to their appearance and performance. In their alternative dress, language, and actions, prophets often stand out from the community. Wainaina is doubly queer in this respect, as his prophetic performance is not simply different from the mainstream but also distinctly queer in the sense of challenging heteronormative conventions of style. One example is his 2014 TEDxEuston talk in London, for which he dressed in a red skirt while talking about traditions of tolerance and sexual diversity in Africa.[45] More generally, Wainaina is widely known for wearing colorful African-print jackets and for the ever-changing colors of his spiky hair, through which he cultivates an Afropolitan gay-male style with an effeminate twist.[46] Furthermore, like many a contemporary Pentecostal prophet, Wainaina actively uses social media like YouTube, Facebook, and especially Twitter to spread his message and reach an international audience.

Two further aspects of Johnson and Anderson's definition of prophets are useful in thinking about Wainaina as a queer prophet. First is the notion that the authority of a prophet depends on "a community who is willing to listen and prepared to respond." In other words, a prophet must be granted legitimacy and authority by his or her community. It is clear that Wainaina has that legitimacy and authority, not only internationally, as we might expect, but also in Kenya, where newspapers and other media reported on his coming out and invited him to appear on TV and other media to talk openly about his experiences and views. Inasmuch as he was given a platform, he also generated public debate and received much response, both positive and negative. Second, prophets always risk being opposed; their message can be rejected by "dissenters or disbelievers within the wider community" or challenged by emerging rival prophets—in an age-old contest between "false" and "true" prophets.[47] Of course, Wainaina's message received a mixed response; many Kenyans rejected it. In this chapter, however, I am interested in how Wainaina himself, as a queer prophet, is contesting the established authority of other Kenyan prophets, specifically Pentecostal Christians.

PENTECOSTALS PROPHESYING AGAINST HOMOSEXUALITY

In order to understand Wainaina's role as a queer prophet, we must compare and contrast him to Pentecostal prophets in Kenya and their recent mobilization against homosexuality. Two cases in particular stand out.

Prophet Dr. David E. Owuor, the leader of the Ministry of Repentance and Holiness (MRH), is a self-declared religious prophet. Owuor, whose long beard reminds one of the typical image of the biblical prophet, has become an enormously popular, though controversial, figure in Kenya's religious scene. Wainaina describes his rise in his memoir, in a chapter dated 2006. "Pentecostals are announcing and denouncing a new Kenyan prophet," he writes. "His name is Pastor Owuor. He says he has a PhD in molecular biology, from Israel. But now God speaks to him. . . . Next December, the prophet says in giant rallies all over Kenya, an earthquake will destroy Nairobi. Bridges, towers will crumble like dust; blood will flow and the river will burst its banks."[48] Owuor, who emerged on the Kenyan religious scene in 2004, became particularly popular after the outburst of postelection violence in 2007–8. He claimed to have predicted this tragic and traumatic episode in Kenya's political history, and said that it could have been prevented if only people had taken to heart his message of repentance and holiness. Thus Owuor successfully used the national trauma of political violence to position himself as a messenger sent by God to bring political reconciliation and healing, along with moral and religious regeneration, to a divided nation.

Interestingly, in an MRH compilation video claiming the "stunning fulfilment" of Owuor's prophecy of "horrific bloodshed," reference is made to "sexual sin" as one major category of sin for which Kenya must repent.[49] Indeed, Owuor appears to be especially concerned, even morbidly preoccupied, with this category of sin in his prophecies. He has frequently addressed what he calls the compromising stand of "the church" on issues of sexuality, has referred to ministers who sexually exploit church members, and has condemned churches that accept or tolerate premarital cohabitation and homosexuality.[50] Owuor may have been capitalizing on the crisis over homosexuality in the global Anglican Communion in order to suggest that the Anglican Church and other mainline churches tolerate, or even promote, same-sex relationships. But he has equally targeted other Pentecostal churches in Kenya, not only for preaching the "deceptive gospel of prosperity" but also for allowing "sexual immorality." One of his sermons reads in part, "Defilement entered the worship teams and the congregation in the forms of homosexuality, prostitution, tight trousers that show their [women's] anatomy, miniskirts, tight skirts with long slits, masturbations, open gay lesbianism [*sic*], deception, slutty dressing, and fleshy immoral dancing during worship services."[51] Owuor consistently presents himself as a prophet bringing moral and spiritual regeneration to the Kenyan nation and the church, and he calls upon people to repent from national and personal sin in order not to incur God's wrath.[52] As a prominent charismatic religious figure, he also has profound political influence. When invited by President Uhuru Kenyatta to pray for the country, he reportedly reminded the president that "righteousness must thrive in order to clear out evil, corruption, homosexuality, immorality and terrorism in the mighty name of Jesus."[53] The clear suggestion is that homosexuality is a major national threat, comparable even to terrorism. In the same way that Owuor and his ministry, in the words of Damaris Parsitau, use women's bodies and female sexuality as "sites of contestation, scrutiny, public debate and discourse, even being the focus of policy debates about social and moral decay in Africa generally and Kenya in particular," Owuor makes homosexuality the site of a moral campaign, not just at the individual level but also at the national.[54] It is his strong belief that the moral fabric of Kenya as both an African and a Christian nation is under threat.

This message is even clearer in the discourse presented by the Evangelical Alliance of Kenya (EAK), an umbrella body of Kenyan Pentecostal and evangelical churches and organizations. In 2014, EAK published a booklet titled *Kenya Let's Pray!* that contained a hundred-day prayer schedule. As Richard Burgess has noted, "prophetic politics is often linked to prayer in Pentecostal practice."[55] This is illustrated in the booklet's foreword, written by EAK chair Bishop Mark Kariuki, whom Wainaina has called "the most visible anti-homosexuality campaigner in Kenya for years."[56] In his foreword, Kariuki uses prophetic language, expressing the hope that the prayer campaign will "serve as a turning point" because Kenya is at a "crisis point," and calls upon all Christians in the country to mobilize and join in prayer against "the spirits of the age antagonizing against the calling of God in this land." The booklet identifies the major threats: they are as varied as terrorism, tribalism, corruption, economic challenges, and, of course, homosexuality. The prayer theme for day 46 is "homosexuality, sexual perversion, drug and alcohol abuse in our children's schools," and it begins with these instructions: "Pray for exposure to public scrutiny those who are covertly working to advance the homosexual indoctrination of our children through the educational system. Pray that God would raise up righteous leaders to successfully contend against the encroachments of the homosexual activists upon our nation's educational system. Pray that defenders of family and protectors of our children's welfare remain strong and courageous and true to their calling. . . . Pray for protection of our children's minds and hearts as they sit in school, college and university classrooms." Elaborating on this theme, the prayer for day 61 reads: "The family unit is under attack from the spirit of the age as men sink further into depravity. Pray that against the so called gay rights (sad wrongs); that these will never be entrenched into our laws." On day 84, Kenyans are instructed "to decree and declare . . . that the financial funding supporting the pro-abortion, anti-family-marriage and homosexual agenda would be cut off. The Lord exposes and thwarts the plans of these evil men."[57] As in Ugandan Christian discourses about homosexuality, children—as the future of the nation—are represented in the EAK material as "a particular locus of social vulnerability."[58] The language of "family values"—probably inspired by the American Christian Right—further demonstrates how this Christian rhetoric serves the construction of a strictly heterosexual national identity, reflecting a broader pattern of the nationalization of sexuality in African Pentecostal settings.[59] Clearly, if the *Kenya Let's Pray!* campaign successfully inspired Kenyan Pentecostal Christians to engage in intercessory prayer against "the threat of homosexuality," such prayer is a form of "political-prophetic praxis,"[60] and it reflects an enormous concern with the moral purity of the nation.

The work of Prophet Owuor and the Evangelical Alliance of Kenya demonstrates that in recent years homosexuality has become a major concern in Kenyan Pentecostal circles and subsequently also in the public sphere. The emerging prophetic Pentecostal discourse reflects the belief that homosexuality is a threat to the moral purity of the nation. It also demonstrates the mobilization of political energies to resist this threat—energies that, in a typical Pentecostal worldview, are believed to come from the power of God and Christ, which enables believers to fight against the tricks and strategies of the devil. Kenya is a Christian country that will prosper if it adheres to "biblical principles"—thus the fervor against the allegedly "unbiblical" practice of homosexuality.

Wainaina's Critique of Christianity in Africa

As a queer prophet, Wainaina has actively and publicly criticized the role of Christianity in the recent politicization of homosexuality in Kenya and, more broadly, in Africa. In particular, he has critically examined popular rhetoric attacking homosexuality as "un-African" and "un-Christian."

Responding to a question by the Nigerian writer Okey Ndibe about the claim that homosexuality is not part of Africa's cultural heritage, Wainaina observes that "it's kind of difficult to talk about an exceptional Africanness when the phenomenon is widely documented in every human society, Africa included." In other words, he challenges the strategic representation of homosexuality as "un-African" by referring to the history or, better, histories of same-sex sexualities on the African continent—a continent that Wainaina described in his TED talk "Conversations with Baba" as "the moral reservoir of human diversity, human aid, human dignity." In the interview with Ndibe, he adds, "And the argument itself has always been made under the banner of the church. They start the conversation with 'it's not African culture because it says XYZ in Leviticus.' But nobody has sought to document any arguments [besides what they read in the Bible]. I think it's a church conversation; it's a conversation that has come into the African space via the church."[61] Blaming the church for politicizing homosexuality, and for making homophobia endemic, Wainaina is particularly critical of arguments that conflate "African culture" with Christianity. Thus, in an interview in the newspaper the *Nairobian*, he states, "People always talk about homosexuality and the African culture but when you ask them to quote they quote the Bible. Is the bible/Christianity part of our African culture? . . . People who say that Africans must be governed according to Leviticus, as far as I am concerned, should not be in any serious podium discussing any serious thing."[62] The fundamental question here concerns the place of Christianity and the Bible in a postcolonial African society like Kenya's. Several African theologians have argued that Christianity is, principally, a non-Western and indeed an African religion—after all, it has had a presence on the African continent since early Christian history, has a strong demographic presence in many parts of the continent, and demonstrates enormous vitality in Africa through contextually meaningful expressions.[63] To the extent that Christianity in Africa has been shaped by the experience of European colonialism and missionaries, many African theologians believe that it can be redeemed from this problematic heritage through a process of inculturation as "a discursive postcolonial African response,"[64] and through African appropriation of the Bible.[65] Even Pentecostal Christianity, which has opposed the strategy of inculturation adopted by Catholic and mainline Protestant churches, has been interpreted by scholars as a local appropriation of Christian faith, successful because it relates to the quest for modernity and globalization while at the same time adequately addressing the spiritual, economic, and political insecurities of the African postcolonial present.[66] In spite of these nuanced and critical interpretations of contemporary Christianity in postcolonial Africa, Wainaina seems to suggest that because Christianity and the Bible were introduced to Africa by the West, they cannot function as sources of moral authority in postcolonial Africa. Wainaina applies the argument of the famous Kenyan writer Ngũgĩ wa Thiong'o in *Decolonising the Mind* to the sphere of religion: where Ngũgĩ suggests that colonial languages are an ongoing force of cultural imperialism, Wainaina suggests that Christianity as a colonial religion and the Bible as a colonial text are more or less inherently imperialistic. It is true that in a tweet on February 4, 2014, he stated: "Show me one decolnised [*sic*] African christian church, and I shall join it." This can be read as suggesting that the existence of a decolonized form of Christianity in Africa is perhaps not completely unthinkable to Wainaina, but that he considers it extremely unlikely.

Wainaina does not elaborate on what exactly a decolonized Christian church in Africa might look like. Yet the point he makes is clear: given that Christianity is an imperialist and "foreign" religion, it cannot be meaningfully used to reinvent a strictly heterosexual "African culture." If Christianity were to be decolonized, it would have to embrace the diversity and tolerance that, Wainaina believes, are typical of Africa's cultural heritage. Such a Christianity would become part of what Ngũgĩ calls a "resistance tradition," and it would oppose "African reactionary forces," including those that nowadays defend the invented idea that homosexuality is "un-African."[67]

In addition to his postcolonial critique of African Christianity, Wainaina also targets the hypocrisy that undermines the moral authority of the church, in particular the Pentecostal church. Referring to the fervor with which their pastors have spoken out against same-sex relationships and gay rights, Wainaina remarks, "I documented, just in the African media since January, 335 cases of gross misbehaviour by Pentecostal pastors. 335. You have documented cases where, in London, there's research showing that the spike in HIV transmission among African women is due to pastors. It's crazy! So I don't understand why we are having a religious, moral conversation around people who harm nobody when, as a continent, [we] are in a grip of something so insanely self-serving, a sin against everybody's moral platform and against everybody's code of goodness."[68] That "something," Wainaina makes clear, is Pentecostalism. One of his criticisms is that Pentecostal ministries are a profit-making industry. In response to one interviewer's suggestion that Wainaina came out as gay in order to receive funding from international donors for gay rights advocacy, he retorted with a smile, "Oh! There is a lot of money in gay business. But if I wanted real money I would start a church."[69]

Wainaina suggests that Pentecostal pastors are not only hypocritical but miss the essence of what the Christian faith is about. Interestingly, he calls on religious concepts in order to criticize the church in Africa for singling out homosexuality as the major moral concern, and gay people as the major category of sinners:

> We are all sinners. That's the contract I know from every church I have ever heard of. We are all sinners, and we all seek sanctuary in the eyes of the Lord. And the sanctuary is a right given to all human beings. And that sanctuary is the sanctuary that the church gives. Its job is not to judge, condemn, influence law or such—it's to give that sanctuary. There is zero noise from any of those churches, even on the back of that law, to just stand up in the media and say, if you are homosexual and you are going through stress, love is in my parish. Come and speak. Not one. I haven't heard one. I think it's extraordinary. So the question becomes: where did the crazy rightwing-ness come from?[70]

Wainaina's suggestion that the church, instead of focusing on the "sin" of homosexuality, should provide a "sanctuary" is in line with recent arguments by several progressive African theologians and church leaders. As the outspoken Ugandan Anglican bishop Christopher Senyonjo (barred from ministry by his own church) puts it: "Jesus' call to his disciples was to preach the good news of salvation to all without discrimination," which presents the model for the church today.[71] The Kenyan theologian Esther Mombo refers to the inclusive love of Christ, and holds that "the church must provide a safe space, free of condemnation, where we will listen to those who are of the gay and lesbian communities."[72]

In a 2015 Facebook post, Wainaina himself invoked the tradition of radical black religious thought, explicitly referring to "the Jesus of James Baldwin and Martin Luther King"—the one who "overturned the political party of the Pharisees who were determined to keep the most marginalized of the people of Judea poor and broken down."[73] This Jesus, Wainaina observed, is "a dead man in Africa"; instead, the Jesus preached to Africans by the church today is a tool and symbol of neocolonial and capitalist domination and exploitation, political oppression, homophobia, and religious intolerance. Denouncing the religious and political orientation of contemporary African Christianity, Wainaina continued, "If Jesus was the Jamaican maroon of his times, hiding from government like Mandela, speaking truth where it was needed, we have abandoned him. Our Jesus wants a gated community, wants diversity deleted, our Jesus wants us to condemn ourselves, tear our hearts apart, beat up our lesbian sister, attack our Muslim neighbor." If the "real Jesus," the Jesus of the Gospels as understood in the tradition of black religious-political thought, were to appear in Africa today, Wainaina went on, the elite African religious and political leaders would incite the masses to make him "bleed in the streets"; his disciples King and Baldwin would be "beaten with stones." A year earlier, he had tweeted that the pastor of former U.S. president George W. Bush "has had more influence on the imagination of Africans than Martin Luther King and James Baldwin."[74] The implicit suggestion here is that white conservative American Christianity has had a greater influence on contemporary Christian thought and practice in Africa than the legacy of progressive black American Christianity has had. Thus Wainaina does in fact point out how African Christianity could be decolonized: through a transatlantic and pan-African reengagement with the radical, prophetic traditions of African American Christian thought, embodied by legendary figures such as Martin Luther King and James Baldwin.[75] A recent historical example of such engagement is the movement of black theology, which in the 1970s and '80s was prominent in both southern Africa and the United States, but which lost its momentum after apartheid ended in 1994 and has since become marginalized in the African Christian theological landscape.[76] Could the current struggle against homophobia and for lgbt rights in Africa provide momentum for renewed engagement? Let us set this question aside for now, but we shall return to it in chapter 4.

A QUEER SATIRE OF PENTECOSTAL DEMONOLOGY

Wainaina asks where the "crazy rightwing-ness" of homophobia and antigay politics in Africa came from. His answer is clear: it came from Christianity, in particular Pentecostalism. His critique of Christianity echoes the concern expressed by another African literary figure, the Nigerian writer Wole Soyinka, who, in reference to the recent popularity and influence of both Christianity and Islam in Africa, has argued that "religion—or, more accurately, fanaticism—has once again, and in such rabid form, bared its fangs in parts of the continent, turning Africa into a warring ground. . . . It threatens the very fabric of a continent that, only a decade or so ago, considered herself immune from the lunacy of faiths."[77] In Wainaina's assessment, it is specifically the Pentecostal belief in, even obsession with, demons that poses the most serious threat, and this belief is the focus of his prophetic critique.

In the African Pentecostal imagination, demons play a central role. A wide range of social, economic, relational, psychological, and medical problems tend to be framed in spiritual terms, and to be explained with reference to demonic spirits, including the devil himself; they are dealt with through deliverance and spiritual warfare.[78] Take, for example, the belief in the "spirit of poverty," which David Maxwell observed among Pentecostals in Zimbabwe. This belief entails the idea that "a believer remained poor because of their spiritual condition" and that "misfortune is passed from generation to generation via demonic ancestral spirits." Through deliverance—"a drama acted out on the body," in which pastors invoke the name and/or the blood of Jesus while praying over and touching or shaking the bodies of those kneeling before them—Christians can be delivered from these evil spirits and regain access to God's blessings and to prosperity.[79] This demonological strain of African Pentecostal Christianity, as Rosalind Hackett points out, "is sustained both by local understandings of human misfortune and spiritual agency as well as the teachings of foreign evangelists."[80] In recent years, demonology has also shaped how Pentecostals in Africa have responded to issues of homosexuality. In public debates, international and local figures promoting gay rights have been "discerned" as agents of the devil participating in a satanic conspiracy to impose homosexuality on Africa.[81] Individuals believed to be gay or lesbian themselves are increasingly targeted by so-called healing and deliverance ministries, or prayer camps, to deliver them from the "spirit of homosexuality" that allegedly possesses them.

Wainaina has made the Pentecostal concern with demons a focal point of his critique. In his 2011 memoir, *One Day I Will Write About This Place,* he writes drily about the outbreak of Pentecostal fever in Kenya in the 1980s, which directly affected his family. His mother left their "polite middle-class Catholic church" for a new congregation, Deliverance Church, headed by Pastor Mark Kariuki (the chair of the Evangelical Alliance of Kenya, mentioned above). Deliverance Church, in Wainaina's memory, was "three hours of guttural noise in Nakuru Town Hall. Screams and tongues, bad microphones and bad American accents. Hell or sweaty ecstasy. Bible study three times a week. Conventions and crusades, bad English, parallel translations of every shouted sweaty sentence, from English to Kiswahili, sometimes from Kiswahili to Gikuyu too."[82] Kariuki made Wainaina's mother believe that her diabetes had been healed, and when she later died of the disease, Wainaina held Kariuki responsible, referring to him as "Pastor Mark 'Demon Remove' Kariuki."[83] Clearly, Wainaina's critique of Pentecostal demonology is motivated partly by this deeply personal experience of his mother's illness and death.

In part 2 of his *We Must Free Our Imaginations* video performance, Wainaina discusses in more depth the growth of Pentecostalism and the widespread concern with demons in Kenya in the 1980s, under the telling title "This Ecstasy of Madness." He explains the outbreak of "panic fever" with reference to the social, economic, and political context in Kenya at the time: the dictatorial one-party state under Daniel arap Moi, the collapsing economy, and the manifestation of a new disease, AIDS, that was killing many young people. Against this background, Wainaina suggests, it is not surprising that people "start getting the feeling that there are these forces" and seek refuge in "these brokers of the forces"—pastors: "The brokers basically are pastors. Their job was to say, 'Listen—me, I control these forces, and I've been given power because I went to Nigeria for Bible study, and inside Nigeria there are demons who run it like a kingdom, which is ruling the whole of Africa. And so I came back and I've been taught how to handle these forces.' . . . So people go demon-hunting. People bring their children to remove the demons. Your heart needs solace—fine. Guys needed the solace. It was a terrible, terrible time."[84] Although he understands people's fear and vulnerability, Wainaina has little sympathy for the Pentecostal pastors who exploited and profited from that fear and anxiety. His response was to dedicate himself to "a rational, secular life" and to use satire to ridicule Pentecostal demonology.

Of particular interest here is a series of messages that Wainaina tweeted on January 6, 2014, shortly before he came out publicly as gay. These tweets were compiled by Aaron Bady under the title "'African Homosexual Deamon'—Binyavanga's Brief Treatise on Demonology," and published on the blog *Brittle Paper: An African Literary Experience*. This series of twenty-one tweets—part of a longer series that day in which Wainaina railed against Pentecostals—opens with the question: "So the deamon for homosexuality, is it French? Coz many Pentecostals say it is not African." Obviously, Wainaina was seeking here to satirically challenge the popular perception in Kenya and other African countries that homosexuality is an un-African Western invention. "Bible Scientists who know the field very well," the tweet story continues, "have deeply researched ALL African knowledge and are sure Gay deamon DID indeed come from the West. Scientists and experts on Bible Africa are sure Homo deamon was imported. I'm not sure though whether by plane or ship. Container number? Homosexuality deamon could very well have arrived, not in a container (carrying Friesian bulls maybe?), it could have come with passengers." A queer satirical blend of irony, exaggeration, and ridicule, this passage makes the popular idea that homosexuality came from the West look absurd. Elsewhere, Wainaina explicitly makes the point that the widespread view of homosexuality as un-African is not based on any historical or anthropological research. But here he continues in the mode of satire: "Homosexuality deamon must have sat around bored for a long long time occupying one or two people, until the internet arrived. When the internet arrived, the homosexuality deamon went digital, and was able to climb into optic fibers. Homosexuality deamon learns fast. Full of trickery. Read a lot and decided to convert from simple analogue deamonhood, to an actual ideology. . . . They called it Gayism and Lesbianism." This humorous account of how "homosexuality deamon" became homosexuality "ideology" ridicules the popular perception of homosexuality as an *-ism*, specifically a political ideology that presents a major threat to the world. Wainaina's tweet series becomes fantastic when he narrates his homosexuality demon possessing the son of a pastor who goes to the Netherlands on a scholarship. Returning together to Africa with the newfound homosexual ideology, their plane is attacked over Sudan by "a chariot of male African homosexuality deamons," specifically Wolof- and Azande-speaking demons, along with two kings, Zulu king Shaka and Buganda king Kabaka Mwanga. This reference is significant; in anthropological and historical literature, the Wolof and Azande ethnic groups (in West Africa and North-Central Africa, respectively) and these two kings (from the Zulus in southern Africa, and the Buganda in East Africa) have been associated with precolonial traditions of same-sex sexualities.[85] Wainaina is invoking the memory of these indigenous African traditions to counter the idea of homosexuality as something imported and "un-African." This passage exemplifies Ngũgĩ wa Thiong'o's point that "creative imagination is one of the greatest remembering practices," because "without a reconnection with African memory, there is no wholeness."[86]

In Wainaina's rich fantasy narrative, the imported European homosexuality demon and the pastor's son, together with the African homosexuality demons and the two kings, spend two weeks in Entebbe, where "they used social media to spread Afro-homosexualism everywhere with a few dutch techniques."[87] Wainaina adds that Yoweri Museveni and Martin Ssempa—Ugandan president and prominent Ugandan antigay pastor, respectively, who both played prominent roles in the drama of the Ugandan Anti-Homosexuality Act—"wanted to make some contacts with some crazy Bush type southern baptist ex-slave owning types." The insinuation here is that antihomosexual politics and legislation in Uganda were at least partly inspired by American right-wing evangelical Christians, whose antigay crusade in Africa is in keeping with the Western enslavement of Africans, representing yet another attempt to control and subjugate black African bodies. African political and religious leaders, Wainaina suggests, are willing to collaborate with and actively seek the support of these white neocolonialist forces, both sides engaging in a marriage of convenience.[88]

The tweet-story is humorous and bizarre—it is not a coherent piece of fiction but a satirical rant full of ridicule and fantasy. It is not clear whether Wainaina deliberately intended to mimic and parody the wild, speculative speech of many Pentecostal preachers—but it is obvious that this satire is his ironic response to the Pentecostal depiction of homosexuality as the devil's work, a sign of the end times, and a national threat as serious as terrorism. As *Brittle Paper*'s editor, Ainehi Edoro, puts it, the text is the result of "storytelling [tipping] over the edge of prophecy."[89] Its prophetic aspect is seen in the exposure and interrogation of popular arguments while creatively opening up a space for new ideas, such as "Afro-homosexualism." It is a queer prophecy, for that matter, because of its creative and absurd style and the way it subverts Pentecostal demonology and shifts the focus from the "demon of homosexuality" to the "demon of Pentecostalism."

CRUISING UTOPIA

In an interesting remark on Pentecostalism and the emerging gay movement in contemporary Africa, Kevin Ward has observed that "like Pentecostalism, gay identities are shaped by participation in a global culture and are almost unimaginable without that participation. Yet both Pentecostal and gay identities struggle to assert their 'Africanness,' and to receive public recognition as 'authentic' African modes of being."[90] The relationship between Pentecostalism and "Africanness" is complex, but one way in which African Pentecostals have dealt with the problem Ward identifies is by reinventing an "African culture" compatible with their own understanding of Christianity and thus strictly heterosexual. Publicly presenting themselves as guardians of "African tradition" and "Christian values," pastors and prophets seek to reaffirm their own "Africanness" by labeling homosexuality and gay people "un-African." This rhetoric has become widespread and has shaped public opinion and political debate in various African countries, as we have seen. Where lgbt groups for a long time were virtually invisible in these countries, their voices rarely heard, Wainaina has become an outspoken public figure who is openly and proudly gay and unafraid of condemning religiously inspired homophobia. In singling out Pentecostalism, he deals with the problem identified by Ward in a way that counters Pentecostal strategy by mirroring it. He accuses Pentecostalism of an imperialist "hindsightisation of [African] culture" and argues that it should decolonize itself and rethink its adherence to Victorian and Puritan values.[91] Referring to himself as a pan-Africanist and Afropolitan,[92] he invokes the history of homosexuality on the African continent to legitimate his own African gay identity and claim a space for African gay people. Whether this will lead to public recognition of gay identities is yet to be seen, but at least Wainaina has created a public platform from which he has moved the debate over homosexuality in Kenya and Africa in new directions. Wainaina prophetically challenges the powers that be, interrogates popular norms, and contests the moral authority of his opponents, the Pentecostal pastors and prophets preoccupied with the "demon of homosexuality." By criticizing Pentecostalism, and contemporary African Christianity more generally, for promoting a conservative and neocolonialist cultural, religious, and sociopolitical agenda, and by reclaiming African traditions of diversity and sexual plurality and engaging with progressive African American traditions of religious thought, Wainaina uses the power of language and imagination, emerging as a prophet, proudly black, African, and queer. Calling upon fellow Africans to free their imaginations from colonialist and homophobic modes of thought, Wainaina the queer prophet also exemplifies José Esteban Muñoz's point that "utopian and willfully idealistic practices of thought are in order if we are to resist the perils of heteronormative pragmatism and Anglo-normative pessimism. . . . Queerness should and could be about a desire for another way of being in both the world and time, a desire that resists mandates to accept that which is not enough."[93] Wainaina, as a gay Kenyan writer and queer social critic, is "cruising utopia" in a way that is reminiscent of the tradition of indigenous prophets in East Africa as well as of the biblical prophetic tradition: through creative performance and inspired speech, he reminds the public that another world—a queer African world—is possible.

INTERLUDE 1

Prophetess

The Nigerian literary writer Tope Folarin won the Caine Prize for African Writing in 2013 with a short story titled "Miracle." The story is set in a Pentecostal church somewhere in Texas, maybe a branch of Winners Chapel International, the Redeemed Christian Church of God, or another church born out of the Pentecostal revolution in Nigeria that now has branches all over the world.

The main character in the story is a young man who, along with many other Nigerians living in the American South, has come to church to experience revival, in particular to witness the healing powers of a visiting prophet from Nigeria—a man who is famous for his performance of "miracles that were previously only possible in the pages of our Bible." When the prophet calls upon people in the congregation to come up and receive their miracle, the young man finds himself walking to the front, with hands pushing him while he tries to tuck away his unbelief. The prophet addresses him, saying, "Young man, you have great things ahead of you, but I can sense that something is ailing you. There is some disease, some disorder that has colonized your body, and it is threatening to colonize your soul." The prophet asks him about his glasses, how bad his vision is, and whether he is ready for his miracle. While the young man feels the mounting sense of expectation from the congregation, he becomes uncomfortable and frightened, his heart beating itself nearly to death. The prophet's hand presses his temples over and over, making him stumble, but each time he is able to regain his balance. The congregation becomes restless and the prophet yells, "The spirit of bad sight is very strong in him, and it won't let go." Finally, the prophet pushes him hard enough, and the prophet's attendants ease him to the floor. Moments later, when he is back on his feet again, the prophet tells him to open his eyes: "My lids slap open, and I see the same fog as before. The disembodied heads are swelling with unreleased joy. I know what I have to do. 'I can see,' I cry, and the loud cheers and sobbing are like new clothing."[1]

I read Folarin's prizewinning story on the plane to Nairobi, where I was headed for my first research trip to Kenya in July 2015. I loved the story because of its realistic and humorous account of a typical Pentecostal experience. Having just arrived, on my first Saturday night I was taken out by some guys to whom I had been introduced by a UK-based Kenyan friend. They took it as their mission to introduce me to the Nairobi gay scene. I thoroughly enjoyed myself, first in a crowded club downtown and later in a more upmarket club in Westlands. Dancing till the early morning hours, I slept for only a few hours when I got home. Realizing that I had come to Kenya not for clubbing but for research purposes, I had set my alarm so that I could attend the 11:00 A.M. service at the Pentecostal Jesus Is Alive Ministries (JIAM), to finally witness the famous bishop Margaret Wanjiru. A little hungover, I went to church only to discover that the 11:00 A.M. service had been cancelled. Yet I was in my fieldwork mood now, and pretty determined. I had seen the sign of another Pentecostal church on the next block, so I decided to go there. This church was much smaller than JIAM, and there was no way I could enter unnoticed. The ushers led me to the front, where I was given a seat in the second row, directly behind the pastors and church elders. It appeared that the service had just started—I had not missed much yet. After some time of praise and worship, prayers and notices, the senior pastor announced with excitement that "the prophetess" was back in church today, after traveling through the country for a while.

The prophetess was invited to the stage, where she began to speak in tongues and then declared that she had received messages from God for some people in particular. She pointed at two or three individuals and started to prophesy over them. Surprisingly, she also had received a message for me, the only *mzungu* (white person) in the church. Pointing at me with her finger, her fiery eyes boring into mine, she spoke of an evil spirit she could discern in my life, a demonic barrier hindering me from realizing my full, God-given potential. Of all the people for whom she had messages, I was the only one who was called to the stage. Asking, or ordering, me to kneel down, she laid her hands on me and started to pray over me. While on my knees, I was reminded of Folarin's story—how ironic to find myself in a similar situation so soon after reading it! Having noticed that the service was being recorded, I decided to try and get hold of the video recording afterward. It would be excellent material for use in my classes—especially for the preparation I do in my class on Pentecostalism in Africa, before taking the students to a service at a mostly Nigerian Pentecostal church in Leeds. As part of this preparation, I warn them that this type of church does not usually allow one to be an observer; they make you participate, whether you like it or not. That Sunday morning in Nairobi, I found out how true this is!

As I thought about all this, the voice of the prophetess became louder and louder, her hands pushing me harder and harder. It was as if she were mobilizing all her spiritual energy to force this evil spirit to leave me. Thinking of Folarin's story, I contemplated the different ways in which I could respond to the performance of spiritual power she was subjecting me to. Should I let my body collapse and fall on the floor? Should I start crying? How to create the impression that I was indeed being delivered? Could I fake deliverance? As I considered these options, I made no outward movement, keeping my eyes closed while feeling the hands of the prophetess pushing me and hearing her voice shouting over me. It crossed my mind that maybe she truly was a woman of God, gifted with a divine spirit of discernment, and that she was able to see or otherwise sense how I had spent the previous night—dancing in gay clubs with handsome Kenyan men, in ways that might have slightly transgressed conventions of public decency (I don't remember exactly). Nathanael Homewood has suggested that Pentecostal prophets (at least in Zimbabwe) are unable to "smell" and thus prophesy about homosexuality.[2] But kneeling on the stage with this prophetess trying to cast out an evil spirit from me, I wondered whether he was wrong.

Like the prophet in Folarin's story, my prophetess became impatient, or maybe she noticed the growing impatience of the congregation that was anxiously waiting to see this *mzungu* delivered. There were no attendants to ease me to the floor, so she decided to give up, for now. Concluding that a very stubborn spirit possessed me, she said she would attend to me after the service. I was allowed to return to my seat. Two hours later, as the service drew to a close, I tried to sneak out of the church. But the ushers prevented me and brought me to the prophetess again. Instead of performing another spectacle of spiritual power, she now took a much kinder and more personal approach, asking me where I was from, what brought me to Kenya, and how the Lord had taken me to church that morning. She also told me that she had woken up that morning with a vision that there would be someone in church today whom God entrusted to her spiritual authority, and as soon as she saw me, she knew I was the one. When she asked for my number so she could contact me later in the week, I lied and told her that I did not have a local SIM card yet. She gave me her number and made me promise to call her. I promised, but I never called.

In the following week I went back to the church three times, trying to get hold of the video recording. I was afraid to see her again, but to my relief we did not cross paths. When I finally got the DVD, I was excited about the prospect of using it in my classes and gave the guy from the media department a tip that was clearly more generous than he'd expected. Once home, I put the DVD in my laptop and started watching expectantly, only to find out that it included the whole service except the performance by the prophetess. Until today I wonder: Had it been cut out because the moment when the Holy Spirit is believed to work most directly cannot be recorded, or because the scene in which I was an unwilling subject of deliverance was such a clear demonstration of what can be described as ritual failure?[3]

Participant observation, as a key ethnographic method, involves the body and changes fieldwork into bodywork in many different and sometimes unexpected ways. An emerging insight in the study of lived religion is that taking seriously the embodiment of the researcher, and recognizing the messy embodied situations into which fieldwork often puts us, helps to "complicate and move beyond the insider/outsider binary," and also to "problematize . . . notions such as detachment and non-involvement."[4] This applies to my visit to this Pentecostal church as much as to the many services I attended at Cosmopolitan Affirming Church, the lgbt church in Nairobi where I conducted one of the case studies presented in this book (chapter 4). There, too, I was made to participate. Although at the beginning of my fieldwork I kindly declined the suggestion that I should preach one Sunday, when I was invited to pray during a church service a few weeks later, I did not hesitate. I was surprised by how easily I could access the register of spontaneous public prayer that I had cultivated in the years of my evangelical Christian youth. True, at CAC I was never subjected to a deliverance ritual or a similar performance of spiritual power. But I was once invited for an interview, during a church service, where I had to spontaneously answer questions about my faith, my sexuality, and my relational life. Again, I was surprised by how easily I could access the evangelical archive within me, this time the register of testimonial language. It must be a sign of my Dutch Protestant–shaped body that apparently I find it easier to *talk* about matters of faith than to participate and engage in an ecstatic performance of spiritual gifts. It is also a sign that in CAC I felt at home socially, emotionally, and spiritually, as the gay spirit residing in me did not have to fear exorcism. In this fieldwork context, my sexual and religious selves were not separated but could both be part of my embodied ethnographic presence.

CHAPTER 2

Kenyan Claim to Queer and Christian Love

Among the inventive and creative expressions that make up the "political bricolage that draws from new forms of technological productions and artifacts" to which African lgbt activists have recently resorted is a Kenyan gay music video.[1] It was released on YouTube on February 15, 2016, by a group of Nairobi-based artists under the name Art Attack. Called "Same Love (Remix)," the song on the video is a remix of the song "Same Love" by the American hip-hop duo Macklemore & Ryan Lewis, who released it in 2012 in response to a Washington State referendum on same-sex marriage. The duo released an explicitly political statement at the same time, reading, "We support civil rights, and hope WA State voters will APPROVE REF 74 and legalize marriage equality."[2] The text accompanying Art Attack's remix reflects a much broader agenda in which same-sex marriage is not the primary concern. Art Attack presented its song to the world as "a Kenyan song about same sex rights, gay rights, LGBT struggles, gender equalities, gay struggles and civil liberties for all sexual orientations."[3] As the title indicates, the song is primarily about love between people of the same gender—and about the struggle for this form of love to be recognized.

Although Art Attack described "Same Love" as a Kenyan song, both the lyrics and the images in the video speak to broader African realities and to the experiences of African same-sex-loving people more generally. Indeed, one member of Art Attack stated that the song was actually intended to be pan-African, and that its production had been inspired by developments in several African countries where homosexuality has become highly politicized. "We wanted it to be a pan-African song," he said, "not just a Kenyan song, a song about Africa, a song about Nigeria, Uganda, our neighbouring country that actually has very strict laws on homosexuality and that views gay people in a very, very bad light, that is Uganda."[4] The "Same Love" music video can thus be considered a cultural expression of African queer politics originating on Kenyan soil, and as an important Kenyan contribution to what Keguro Macharia has called "queer African archives," as discussed in the introduction. Moreover, the song is an African contribution to the growing number of gay music videos, mostly originating in the United States.[5]

In this chapter I discuss the "Same Love" video as a creative sociocultural text that provides insight into the intersections of Kenyan, Christian, and queer identities and politics. After introducing the video, its producers, and some of the controversy around it, I explain how I read the video as a political and theological text. I then offer a detailed reading of the images and lyrics in the video, before presenting a more thematic discussion of the video's representation and imagination of Christianity, Africa, and queerness, respectively. The chapter concludes with an intertextual reading of "Same Love" in conjunction with the essay "'Eros,' AIDS, and African Bodies" by the Zimbabwean theologian Edward Antonio, which allows us to flesh out the video's contribution to an African queer theology of love.

ART ATTACK, "SAME LOVE," AND ITS RECEPTION

Art Attack is the name of a collective of six artists who joined together to produce the "Same Love" video, at the instigation of musician and activist George Barasa. The names of five cast members—Natalie Florence, Soila Cole, Joji Baro, Dayon Monson, and Lorenzo Cruz—are listed at the end of the video. Florence is a popular Kenyan actress and singer who goes by the name Noti Flow. She has been public about her bisexuality,[6] and in March 2016 she released a rather explicit sexual music video with some bisexual scenes.[7] Cole is another Kenyan socialite working in the entertainment industry, and an online source at the time referred to her as Noti Flow's "lesbian lover." The same source introduced Monson as a Kenyan-based actor and model from Tanzania, and Cruz as his "Tanzanian gay lover."[8] Indeed, in the video itself, these four actors appear as lovers, staged as a female couple and a male couple, respectively. The fifth cast member is Joji Baro, a.k.a. George Barasa, who also produced the video and appears in some scenes. The sixth member of Art Attack is an anonymous male rapper. Barasa is associated most publicly with the "Same Love" video. On

February 15, 2016, the day of its release, he wrote on Facebook that the video is "Jojibaro life summarised into one song," suggesting that the song's lyrics are based on his life story. Therefore, he requires a more detailed introduction.

When Kenyan online media write about Barasa, they typically highlight three things: his HIV status (positive), his sexuality (gay), and his profession (usually described as gospel musician).[9] Barasa himself appears to be ambivalent about such descriptions. On the one hand, he uses them himself, such as in this interview: "My name is George Barasa. Or Joji Baro. I am 22 years old. I was born in Nairobi and brought up in Bungoma. I am a Gospel artist. I am Gay. I am HIV/AIDS positive. I am an activist. And I am a drag queen."[10] On the other hand, expressing his discomfort with this public image, he has stated that he feels tired of living in a world "where one has to always introduce themselves as 'Hi am gay and am HIV+!'"[11]

Barasa was outed as gay by the Kenyan newspaper the *Star* in 2011, which wrote about him as "a 21-year-old gay Bungoma school drop out" who has "revealed [that] his present partner is a Kisumu priest."[12] Barasa recounts the repercussions of this outing as follows: "After reading it, my parents were outraged. My family was revolted. And my whole clan was in pure shock. And because of that, I was rejected by my family, my parents and my people. It crashed my soul. Again, I quit St. Paul's Miluki School and came to Nairobi where I engaged in several gay relationships with abandon. I was depressed, naive and young. And I was a hot cake for lusty gay men. Most of whom were married. After my tribulations became too much, I attempted suicide."[13] In addition to his depression, within a year of being outed, Barasa learned that he was HIV-positive. He managed to get his life back on the rails by starting a career in modeling and music, completing school, and engaging in gay rights activism. He established an organization, Out in Kenya, which he led for a few years. In 2013, he was one of the founding members of Cosmopolitan Affirming Church (see chapter 4). Until his relocation to South Africa in 2017, he also ran a shelter for homeless lgbt people in Nairobi and served as the Kenya reporter for the Uganda-based news website Kuchu Times, which claims to be "a voice for Africa's Lesbian, Gay, Bisexual, Transgender and Intersex (LGBTI) community." The American online newspaper the *Huffington Post* featured Barasa in 2016 as one of the key people "fighting homophobia and transphobia in Africa." He was also included in a photograph exhibition, *Love Is Not a Crime: Our Fight in Africa*, organized by Amnesty International as part of the Bilbao International Festival of LGBT Film and Performing Arts.[14] In 2017, he was a finalist for the David Kato Voice and Vision Award, an international award recognizing the leadership of individuals who strive to uphold the rights of lesbian, gay, bisexual, transgender, and intersex people.

As noted above, Barasa is often described as a gospel musician, and it is true that he started his career as a singer in the church he attended in his youth. In 2006 he released his first song, "The Gospel of Unity," and since then he has published a number of other songs with explicitly religious themes. But he has also commented on the "great resistance and backlash" he's received from "the Gospel Industry Heavyweights,"[15] hindering his ability to build a career in gospel music. In a Facebook post marking the first decade of his "ministerial work as a gospel musician," Barasa wrote of his "journey of struggle with my gay secularism."[16] Although this statement seems to separate his religious gospel career from his secular lgbt activist work, elsewhere he has expressed a more integrated understanding of both as a form of "service" to God and humankind. Feeling that the gospel scene was too limited for his professional and activist ambitions, he also produced a number of songs about same-sex-related themes, including "Kuchu Kuchu" (reclaiming the word *kuchu*—originally Ugandan slang for gay) and "Out in the Light" (about coming out). Together with another song, "A Million of Pills" (about living with HIV), these make up what Barasa calls his "Rainbow mini-album." Barasa is a well-known figure in Kenyan popular culture. Often referred to as a "socialite," he receives considerable attention, especially from some of Kenya's online media. He is known for causing controversy for, among other things, his appearance: he likes cross-dressing and prides himself on having fifteen wigs, more than thirty pairs of "sexy high-heels," and an "endless collection of thongs and G-strings and bras."[17] All in all, this makes him a queer popular cultural figure in Kenya.

Combining his interest and expertise in music and advocacy, Barasa has come to define himself as an "artivist," using art for the sake of activism.[18] The anonymous rapper in Art Attack also referred to the band's work as a form of "artivism" because it is "geared towards social change" and "is actually motivated by what we see around in social circles in Kenya."[19] Making use of the "liberatory potential" of digital media[20] and of the "possibilities offered by the Internet to challenge homophobia in Kenya,"[21] Art Attack deliberately made "Same Love" freely available on YouTube. This enabled the group to reach an audience as large as possible, within Kenya and beyond.[22] In the words of the rapper, "Anyone can access it on YouTube; a lot of people are going to see the song, are going to be able to be inspired by the message of the song. We don't tell people 'Be gay,' but we're telling people, 'Let them be!'"[23] According to Barasa, publication via YouTube was also a way of avoiding control by the Kenya Film Classification Board (KFCB).[24] The group did not ask for the board's permission to record the video, as they expected to be denied. Given their limited budget, neither did they seek the legal rights to produce a remix version of Macklemore & Ryan Lewis's original song, or to include scenes from other American visual productions, such as the movie *The Skinny* and the Fox TV drama series *Empire*.

Reception and Ban

Soon after its release, "Same Love" was picked up by some Kenyan media—for example, the online radio station Kiss 100 played it several times in the week directly after the release. On February 23, 2016, however, the KFCB announced that it was imposing restrictions on the video, meaning that its possession, distribution, exhibition, and broadcasting were prohibited. In its official press statement, the KFCB gave two main reasons for its decision: first, the video "advocate[d] for gay rights," depicted "graphic sexual scenes between people of the same gender" and "promote[d] irresponsible behavior," which, according to the board, was "a frontal violation" of its classification guidelines. Second, the KFCB had not given Barasa or Art Attack a license to shoot those sections of the video produced in Kenya, which meant that "the creation of the same video is therefore illegal."[25] The statement further announced that Google had been asked to block access to the video in Kenya on the basis of the "foregoing moral and legal considerations"—a request that Google has to date refused.

In the final paragraph of the statement, the KFCB offered a broader context for its censorship of the video: "The Board's preliminary investigations have shown that incidents of sodomy and other kinds of bestiality are on the rise in Kenya. The Board will work closely with other government agencies to establish the nexus between these cases and exposures to film and broadcast content that promotes such behavior. We believe that this sort of behaviour should be eradicated because it is against the moral values of the country." Peculiar here is the conflation of homosexuality and bestiality, although this is certainly not unique, and it frames same-sex relations as part of a broader culture of moral perversion.[26] The KFCB offered no evidence for its claim that "incidents of sodomy" are on the rise, but it hinted that music videos like "Same Love" are a contributing factor—excuse enough for the board to curb the constitutionally protected right of freedom of expression. The KFCB has also restricted the screening of the American film *Fifty Shades of Grey* (2015), the Kenyan film

Stories of Our Lives (2014), and the Kenyan lesbian-themed film *Rafiki* (2018), all on the grounds that they violate norms of sexual morality.

As so often happens when self-proclaimed moral watchdogs censor books, films, and other forms of art, the KFCB's ban of "Same Love" only piqued the interest of the Kenyan media, which started writing about it, thus generating more attention. The international media picked up the story, thus raising the profile of the gay rights campaign in Kenya.[27] Three months after its release, the video had been watched on YouTube more than 260,000 times, and had received almost twenty-five hundred likes, about eight hundred dislikes, and nearly fifteen hundred comments.[28] Furthermore, especially in the aftermath of the KFCB announcement, it had sparked debate on Twitter and Facebook under the hashtag #Kenyangayvideo. Yet the KFCB's decision and ensuing controversy also had unwanted side effects. One of the video's cast members reportedly had to leave the country because he "started receiving threats and hostility from his Kenyan neighbors after they saw the video," while other members claimed to be "living in fear . . . [of being] arrested and charged."[29] As one member explained, this response was not unexpected: "We are not surprised at all. . . . The controversy that we have received from this song is beautiful! It is really what we like to see."[30] Art Attack deliberately produced a controversial song in order to provoke public debate. As a result of the backlash and his public profile as a gay activist, Barasa himself decided to give up his activism—at least temporarily—and in 2017 he moved to and applied for asylum in South Africa, as he felt that it was "difficult to stay safe" in Kenya.[31]

Transgender Criticism

The ban on "Same Love" received warm support from a seemingly unexpected source—Kenyan transgender activist Audrey Mbugua, the founder and program manager of an organization called Transgender Education and Advocacy (TEA). When the KFCB's chief executive officer, Ezekiel Mutua, tweeted that his board had put restrictions on the video, Mbugua responded quickly, "Well done. Am transgender and am OFFENDED by the song & artists: THEY stereotype transgender people as homosexuals."[32] This was the first in a series of eleven tweets explaining her concerns with the video. Mbugua, who identifies as a transgender woman, felt offended because, in her opinion, the song annexes transgender people into gay activism. It is not exactly clear what incited Mbugua's anger; neither the lyrics nor the images in "Same Love" address transgender issues. Maybe it was the description of the video on YouTube as "a Kenyan song about . . . LGBT struggles"; the use of the acronym might be why Mbugua felt that the video exemplifies "the practice of homosexualizing transgender people" and therefore, in her view, presents a form of "irresponsible activism."[33] It is irresponsible, she clarified, because the song's "propaganda" is harmful to transgender people and has "resulted to death [*sic*]."[34] Previously, she had made a similar claim in a blog post on the TEA website, stating that in the Kenyan gay community, a transgender person in the "nascent stages of her gender transition (male to female)" tends to be associated with gay cross-dressing, and is often perceived as a gay man in the bottom role. According to Mbugua, such a person is easily subjected to "sexual exploitation" because "people misconstrue her gender problems with the desire to be used by men."[35] This, in turn, makes her vulnerable to HIV infection and other sexually transmitted diseases, and thus is potentially life-threatening.

This was not the first time that Mbugua had distinguished the transgender community and its struggles as fundamentally different from other groups under the lgbt acronym. Previously, she had supported the Non-Governmental Organizations Coordination Board (NGOCB, a state body regulating the NGO sector in Kenya) in its decision not to register the National Gay and Lesbian Human Rights Commission (NGLHRC) as an NGO. This happened in a case that was internationally acclaimed as a landmark victory for lgbt activism in Kenya: the 2015 High Court ruling in favor of a petition submitted by NGLHRC director Eric Gitari after the NGOCB had rejected the application for registration several times. In his petition, Gitari pointed out that the objectives of the NGLHRC are to address and advocate for human rights issues "relevant to Lesbian, Gay, Bisexual, Trans, Intersex and Queer (LGBTIQ) individuals, groups and communities in Kenya."[36] As one of the "interested parties" admitted by the High Court, Mbugua, as the representative of TEA, took issue with this. Arguing that the NGLHRC should not be allowed to register as an NGO, she stated that "the transgender community can articulate its own issues" and "did not request this gay and lesbian commission to be our mouth piece."[37] Obviously, Gitari did not appreciate Mbugua's role; he called it "a very unfortunate and ill-advised move" and claimed that his organization offers legal assistance to transgender people as well as to gay men and lesbians.[38] The High Court, in its final judgment, found that Mbugua's arguments against the registration of NLGHRC were "unsustainable" and even "paternalistic in essence."[39]

By actively supporting the rejection of the NGLHRC's application for registration, as well as the ban on "Same Love," Mbugua made public a divide within the Kenyan lgbt community (which, she would argue, is not a single community but one that includes various groups with different, and conflicting, interests).[40] Many Kenyan lgbt activists saw her stance as a betrayal. One of them responded to her welcoming the KFCB's decision with a tweet that said, "Am surprised how after years of struggle world over you think you can go with it alone."[41] George Barasa, in a Facebook post, wrote: "Okay Audrey Mbugua, I think you should join KFCB. And join them alone. Don't drag transgender along because sometime I happen to be one of them."[42] Ironically, this response can be seen as an illustration of one of the issues Mbugua agitates against: the conflation of cross-dressing practices with transgender identity. As much as these responses demonstrate disrespect and misunderstanding, they also express frustration with Mbugua's failure to acknowledge that both transgender people and gay and lesbian people are affected by, and struggle against, heteronormativity. Obviously, the question of the relationship between transgender and broader lgbt activism is a pertinent one for queer politics, and not only in Kenya,[43] but it is beyond the scope of this chapter.

READING "SAME LOVE" AS A POLITICAL AND THEOLOGICAL TEXT

As mentioned earlier, Art Attack refers to its work as a form of artivism. Molefi Asante observes a rich history of artivism in African American culture, specifically in rap music and hip-hop culture, which he relates to the West African tradition of *djelis* or griots, that is, the "traveling poets and artists who not only included, but focused on the politics of the day and the condition of the people as a primary function in their work."[44] Interestingly, through African rap this tradition has returned to the continent in a new, modern form. This artistic journey constitutes a case of "cultural reversioning twice over," with contemporary African artists as "modern griots" reclaiming African-centered concepts that were once the domain of African diasporic traditions.[45]

Regardless of whether Art Attack is familiar with this broader use, or the historical and cultural background of the term *artivism*, the group clearly considers its work along the same lines, as a fusion of art and activism in the struggle for social transformation. Producing "Same Love" as a rap song, and featuring hip-hop artists as actors in the video, Art Attack strategically inscribes itself in the culture of hip-hop music that is so popular in Kenya and throughout East Africa, especially among the youth, and that, just like American hip-hop, is associated with social and political critique. As Mwenda Ntarangwi says of the political significance of East African hip-hop: "Through this music, the youth critique the existing political, cultural, and economic realities and, consequently, join other social and political critics such as the clergy and members of civil society who have dared to challenge and critique oppressive regimes. Hip hop artistes then become important truth-tellers."[46] As will be shown below, the critique expressed in the "Same Love" video targets not only the state and its actors but also the clergy and those sections of civil society that have joined the bandwagon of sociopolitical homophobia. Thus, as much as the song exemplifies a broader tradition of hip-hop as a form of sociopolitical critique, its particular message makes the song stand out from other music in the same genre. As I argue below, "Same Love" presents a creative and courageous queer critique of Kenyan society, and of recent social and political dynamics in Africa more generally.

More than merely a critique, hip-hop music also represents an alternative imagination of sociopolitical realities. Again, in the words of Ntarangwi, "hip hop as performed and composed in East Africa embodies key discourses about African identity, about postcolonial experiences of modernity, and about sociocultural changes that result from multiple factors that interact with the lived experiences of many of the youth performing it. Through the lyrics and choice of specific metaphors of representation, East African hip hop brings together artistes' own historical past within current global realities and then creatively weaves them into a critique of the prevailing sociocultural reality."[47] "Same Love" exemplifies the points made here, not only because the song is based on Barasa's personal experiences, which are taken as reflecting the experiences of gay and lesbian people in Kenya and elsewhere in Africa, but also because the lyrics and images in the video create an aesthetic sense of queer African identity that is negotiated between the local and the global. In this chapter, then, I am interested in how the particular assemblage of images, words, and texts in the video constitutes what Birgit Meyer calls an "imaginary" as a "world-making device"—something that is both "grounded in the material world and takes part in reproducing it as a phenomenological lifeworld that is experienced and vested with meaning."[48] In other words, how does "Same Love" construct and affect a particular Kenyan and African queer imaginary?

Music videos in general have been defined, "simply and perhaps too broadly, as a relation of sound and image that we recognize as such."[49] Added to this interplay of sound and image is the textual aspect, especially in the case of hip-hop, given the political significance of the lyrics. In "Same Love," the importance of the lyrics is emphasized by the fact that the rapper remains invisible in the video—thus deemphasizing features generally considered essential to hip-hop, such as dance moves, outfits, and jewelry. Whereas Art Attack carefully selected and edited the images in the video, and also substantially revised and expanded Macklemore & Ryan Lewis's lyrics, the music itself is copied from the American "Same Love" song. Yet in the Kenyan version, the music has been edited so that it is subservient to the spoken and sung text. My reading of the video thus focuses on image and text, and the interplay between them.

While I hope to elucidate the political significance of the "Same Love" video, I also propose to read the video as a theological text—for the song's lyrics touch on religious themes and even include a quotation from the Bible and a statement about God. One might argue, for that reason, that "Same Love" is a gospel song—a genre that, together with hip-hop, dominates the Kenyan popular music scene and has been described as "the fastest growing musical expression in many parts of Africa today."[50] But "Same Love" does not share most of the characteristics usually associated with gospel music; the song as a whole is not "laden with Christian themes," nor do the performers present themselves as "Christians with a mission to preach the word of God through music."[51] Though it is not a gospel song per se, I suggest that the religious, in fact the biblical, motif in "Same Love" demonstrates the fluid boundary between gospel and hip-hop, and that religion pervades Kenya's popular culture as a whole.[52] Regardless of the question of genre, the function and meaning of the references to religion and of the biblical quotation deserve closer scrutiny, as they obviously shape the song's message and its "imaginary." Reading the song as a theological text provides us with insight into the particular Christian ethos in which "Same Love" conveys its key message about the recognition of same-sex relationships.

There is another reason to read the song theologically, and it stems from the field of African theology, in which there is a strong tradition of engaging with culture—also known as inculturation theology, which is one of the major strands of African theological thought. But culture tends to be perceived in this context as "traditional culture," and the project of inculturating Christianity is typically seen as driven by a postcolonial quest for an "authentically African" expression of the Christian faith.[53] Thus inculturation theology tends to be based on a rather static, and sometimes a reified, idealized, and romanticized notion of "African culture." African women theologians have critiqued the inculturation paradigm for its uncritical attempt to reclaim African cultural beliefs and practices, overlooking their negative effects on women.[54] In a similar way, inculturation theology can be critiqued for being insensitive to the ways in which "African culture" has been invoked to mobilize against same-sex-loving people; indeed, several African theologians have actively used the motif of inculturation to depict homosexuality as "un-African" and "un-Christian."[55] One way to challenge these conservative tendencies is by engaging with the broad category of contemporary popular African culture that shapes modern African identities in a globalized world. To date, however, there has been very little, if any, engagement in African theology with popular culture, including music and music videos. I would suggest that just as traditional African cultural beliefs and practices have been reclaimed by inculturation theologians in order to critique and transform missionary Christianity, popular African cultural expressions can be used to challenge contemporary forms of Christianity on the continent. Specifically, the "Same Love" music video is a popular cultural text that can be used to confront and critique the homophobic tendencies that dominate much of African Christianity today.

THE INTERPLAY OF IMAGE AND TEXT

The video opens with white letters on a black screen spelling out the widely circulated quotation from the late American psychiatrist and media personality David Viscott: "To love and to be loved is to feel the sun from both sides."[56] Next we see footage from a Paris Gay Pride March, with a prominent rainbow flag. Since its first appearance in San Francisco in 1978, this flag "has gradually been adopted by the gay and lesbian community throughout the world as their international symbol" and is now instantly recognized as a "symbol of gay and lesbian pride and solidarity."[57] By including an image of the rainbow flag, "Same Love" inscribes itself into the modern narrative of sexual liberation and diversity. In the following frame, another six-colored flag fills the screen: the flag of postapartheid South Africa, often referred to as a "rainbow nation" and considered by many an African queer person to be a promised land, given its "wonderful constitution that has given access and rights to all lgbt people," as Zethu Matebeni puts it somewhat sarcastically.[58] Matebeni's skepticism about the widespread representation of South Africa as a queer rainbow nation is informed by the critical awareness of the deep divisions—along lines of race, social location, and economic status—within the South African lgbt community. A similar criticism can be made of the rainbow flag itself as a symbol of global queer pride, because it is in fact often used to reinforce a homonationalist and gay-capitalist narrative of Europe and North America as safe havens in a homophobic world.[59] While such critiques are important, the inclusion of the two flags in the video makes clear how strong these symbols are in Kenya and other places that lack basic legal protections of lgbt rights, and it reminds us of the different temporalities of global queer politics. That the producer of "Same Love," George Barasa, himself relocated to South Africa out of concern for his safety in Kenya further illustrates this point. In the video, both flags are used as symbols of liberation and diversity—the first representing the global movement for lgbt rights and queer pride, and the second representing a specifically African narrative of freedom from racial oppression as well as of sexual equality. By putting these images prominently at the beginning of the video, "Same Love" frames its political message as part of both trajectories.

As the South African flag appears, Art Attack's rapper recites the opening lyrics: "This song goes out to the new slaves, the new blacks, the new Jews, the new minorities for whom we need a civil rights movement, maybe a sex rights movement. Especially in Africa. Everywhere. This goes out to you. I feel you." Several images accompany this opening statement. After the South African flag, we see a series of images from peri-urban life somewhere in black Africa: an asphalt street surrounded by small, detached brick houses with corrugated tin roofs; a female figure—or is it a cross-dressing male?—emerging from one of these houses; a group of young men playing football (a.k.a. soccer) on open wasteland; a woman walking on a sidewalk; a child frolicking on a dusty road; a young man cycling through the wasteland. These images, depicting neither the poorest slums nor the modern, upper-middle-class neighborhoods but an environment with which many urban, lower-middle-class Kenyans and other Africans can identify, create a peaceful, almost idyllic, peri-urban lifescape.

This sequence stands in clear contrast to the next series of images, featuring three photos of newspapers with sensationalist, antihomosexual headings. The first photo shows front pages from the Ghanaian state-owned newspaper *Daily Graphic*, with headlines reading "Homos Are Filthy," "Gays Can Be Tried," "8,000 Homos in Two Regions." The next two photos depict the Ugandan tabloids *Red Pepper* and *Rolling Stone*, respectively, the cover of the latter in the hands of its editor, Giles Muhame. Both tabloids were deeply involved in what Kenyan activist Kenne Mwikya has called "the Uganda homophobia spectacle."[60] They actively supported the campaign for the Anti-Homosexuality Bill, introduced by MP David Bahati in 2009, and they competed with each other in their quest to expose the country's "top homos." In October 2010, for instance, *Rolling Stone* published the names and photographs of a hundred people and urged that they be hanged for their homosexuality. Among them was the activist David Kato, who worked for Sexual Minorities Uganda and who was murdered in January 2011. Keeping all of this in mind, it becomes clear why Art Attack's rapper credited the developments in neighboring Uganda with inspiring the group to produce "Same Love."[61]

The three front-page newspaper photos represent the waves of sociopolitical homophobia recently witnessed in different parts of Africa. They remind the spectator that in most of Africa, life is far from peaceful or idyllic for sexual minorities, who fear exposure by the media, prosecution by new antihomosexuality laws, and the general discrimination and marginalization to which they are subjected. They are "the new slaves, the new blacks, the new Jews, the new minorities" that the lyrics refer to, who are in need of the liberation symbolized by the two flags at the beginning of the video. The phrase "I feel you" is addressed to them in particular. The three newspaper photos are followed by two images from Gay Pride marches, one apparently in Istanbul, illustrating that although lgbt liberation may be particularly needed in Africa, it is a global movement. At the bottom of the screen, a line of text appears: "Don't be silent, be heard, gays exist." For a split second, the screen turns black and the sound pauses, before the next segment of the video begins.

My Story

We next see the main actor, Dayon Monson, standing in front of a mirror. The images are accompanied by a keyboard playing a short and simple tune that is repeated ten times. Monson is obviously not doing well. He may be drunk or suffering from a hangover—one image shows a bottle of some spirit—but perhaps his condition is more serious; the same image includes a bottle of hydrogen peroxide, which is used to arrest bleeding and disinfect wounds. In the meantime, the rapper starts singing, faster than before but still articulating clearly: "This is my story yo, my sorry story yo, this is me, this is you, this is us, this is the world, world war, wild war, cold war, love war." The narrative at the heart of the song is introduced here as the protagonist's personal story, which at the same time could be everyone's story—one played out on a global scale, the subject of a global war, a war about love. As mentioned earlier, the story narrated here is based on the life of George Barasa, with Monson reenacting scenes from it. In the song, his story becomes exemplary of the many stories that, in Macharia's words, "collectively populate and haunt Queer African archives."[62]

The next shot is a paradisiacal image of a waterfall—shot at Fourteen Falls in Thika, just forty miles outside Nairobi—surrounded by lush green vegetation against a blue sky; the music becomes more melodic. An aerial view of the landscape—forested hills, the river in the valley hidden by trees—brings to mind the opening of Kenyan writer Ngũgĩ wa Thiong'o's famous novel, *The River Between*. Ngũgĩ describes the river Honia—meaning cure, or bring back to life—as flowing invisibly through the "valley of life" between the forested ridges of Kameno and Makuyu, deep in Kikuyu land.[63] In the novel, the river dividing the two ridges "signifies two contesting ideological positions . . . [or ways] of responding to colonial subjugation"—one that of a traditionalist village and the other of a village converting to Christianity.[64] Could it be that the river in the video similarly signifies the ideological clash in contemporary Kenya over homosexuality, some seeing it as a new symbol of imperialism, others as a symbol of modernity? Or perhaps the landscape and river can be read as staking a claim to the land, a claim of belonging to Kenyan soil. After all, "land is one of the most important foci of identity in Kenya," as Ernest Monte reminds us.[65] The message of the song might be that lesbian and gay Kenyans are children of this land, too, a message further accentuated by the image of a rainbow that appears in the waterfall. A young male couple (acted by Monson and Cruz) are having a playful and romantic time in the river above the waterfall, as the rapper starts singing:

> Years back I fell in love with a male kid in school / He was cool he was funny, always true always shining / My heart told me I was right I could go ahead and love him, I could go ahead and hug him / I could go ahead and have him / He was never judgmental, always stood by my side / Always there when I called him, showed support when I am falling / We spent all the days together, every weekend sharing stories / Summer winter every weather, life was full of all glories / In his eyes there was a sparkle / And my heart was spinning circles, and one day I went and told him that I thought I was a psycho 'cause I was in love with a boy like me / And I told him no one ever gave me joy like me / So he came close, stretched arms and hugged me tight / And he told me never leave me, please love me right / It was strange 'cause I was a man just like him / I really couldn't explain it but I just liked him . . . I did . . . Uh . . . Yeah. . . .

It is the universal story of two youths falling in love—universal apart from the fact that in this case the lovers are two young men. Indeed, the rapper puts emphasis on the phrase "'cause I was in love with a boy like me" by preceding it with a short pause.

As this story is sung, the waterfall images alternate with images of the couple, shot in Paradise Lost, a recreational resort and park just north of

Nairobi: they walk hand in hand on a quiet street, smile at each other, laugh together, take selfies, and pose for each other. The setting changes from the waterfall to a suburban street, and their outfits have changed from a recreational to a more casual urban style: they are now dressed in slim-fit trousers—jeans and yellow chinos, respectively—one youth wearing a slim-fit trendy shirt with panther print, the other a simple black-and-white checked shirt with the same eye-catching necklace and wristwatch as in previous scenes. The outfits cultivate a fashion style that perhaps is not exclusively gay but can be described as "gay-vague," a term referring to a trend in which gay aesthetics have come to influence mainstream mass culture. In the United States and Europe, this urban style is associated with an "indifference about whether one is read as gay or not."[66] Whether this is also the case for Kenya's urban middle class is an open question, but "Same Love" clearly inscribes the male couple in this cosmopolitan gay-vague—and, critics may add, consumer-capitalist—culture.

The two men are portrayed as fully in love and happy together, and the images clearly reinforce the lyrics about the protagonist's falling in love with "a boy like me." This harmony is only interrupted for a second by an image of the protagonist sitting on the floor of what appears to be a bathroom, drinking directly from a wine or liquor bottle. This image appears just after the rapper has sung, "I thought I was a psycho," and it stands in contrast to the lyrics accompanying the image: "I was in love with a boy like me / and I told him no one ever gave me joy like me." Perhaps this contrast is created deliberately to warn the spectator that the story will soon take a different turn. The next lines, about bodily intimacy and love, are accompanied by images that again illustrate the lyrics. First we see the couple walking in an embrace, once more atop the waterfall. We then see more erotic images, not acted by the two male cast members (possibly because of potential legal repercussions) but taken from the American gay comedy-drama movie *The Skinny*: a black male couple, initially standing in a hallway, kissing, and then lying on bed in an intimate position, apparently making love. These are undoubtedly among the images for which the KFCB banned the "Same Love" video. Yet although the two men are partially nude, these images can hardly be called pornographic, as the board suggested.

Next comes the song's chorus, which is copied—both audio and video—from the original version of "Same Love," in which it was sung by the American R&B singer Mary Lambert:

And I can't change
Even if I tried, even if I wanted to

And I can't change
Even if I tried, even if I wanted to
My love, my love, my love
She keeps me warm (4x)

Departing from the rapper's style, the chorus is sung in R&B style. The lyrics convey that sexual orientation is not chosen but is a given, as in Lady Gaga's "Born This Way." Lambert's voice is accompanied by images of a young female couple (acted by Noti Flow and Soila Cole) in a lush green park—the Nairobi Arboretum—soft sunlight streaming through the tall trees. We see the two young women walking, laughing, holding hands, sensually licking an ice-cream cone, and sharing a chocolate bar. (When the chorus is repeated later in the video, we see them kissing, and one woman puts a ring on the other's finger.) Like the scenes of the male couple in the previous segment, these scenes are playful and romantic, the two women presenting an idyll of love and happiness. Their outfits contrast in style: Noti Flow appears in the tomboyish style that she has cultivated in recent years and that she has linked to her bisexuality,[67] wearing denim overalls with the bib hanging down, a loose baseball-style shirt over a tight black top, a prominent nose piercing, an eye-catching chain necklace, dark sunglasses, and orange high-top sneakers, while her lover is much more femme, wearing an elegant sleeveless dress and high heels. Both of them have long curly hair, blonde and black, respectively, have extremely long nails, colored pink and orange, and wear matching pink lipstick and heavy eye makeup. These features are remarkable because lesbian characters—especially butch ones—are usually depicted in films with short nails, short hair, and little or no makeup.[68]

The rapper resumes his rapping as the next segment begins, and the fifth cast member—Joji Baro—appears, dressed in jeans and a denim shirt covered with studs at the top, and wearing one of his wigs. We see him walking alone on a forest lane, a solemn expression on his face. The lyrics, inspired by his life experiences, now tell a much sadder story:

> Years later I told Mummy what I was going thru / I told her I loved a boy and he loved me too / Mummy flipped, started cursing me, running to Daddy / And told Daddy our son's gone crazy already / A decision was arrived to, you're not our son / Pack your bags, shameless heathen, and follow the sun / I sank down to my knees tryna call out to Mama / Mummy said I ain't you Mummy you're the son of the devil / And Daddy said go

> fool 'fore I strangle you, devil / And for the last six years my parents have never seen me / Every day I bleed tears hoping that they wish to see me / And I avoid the public 'cause I am scared of the jail / 'Cause if they ever caught me they would throw me in jail / You're a criminal, how dare you, falling in love, it's a crime to follow your heart and follow your love / I'm breaking the constitution, going thru segregation / Africanization, power to the black nation / Church rules, street rules / Court rules, school rules / Hate is the new love, kill, maim, talk tough / Homophobia is the new African culture / Everyone's the police, everyone's a court judge, mob law, street justice / Kill 'em when you see 'em / Blame it on the West, never blame it on love, it's un-African to try and show a brother some love.

Interestingly, the video subscribes to the model of "coming out" that has become so fundamental to lesbian and gay politics in the United States and other Western nations, but it subtly tweaks this model. The main character in the song does not go to his mum to tell her, "I am gay," as the "strangely specific" speech acts of the coming-out narrative typically have it.[69] Instead, he tells her that he loves another boy. Thus his coming out is not about confirming an identity but confessing an activity—the seemingly innocent and very human act of loving and being loved. Yet this approach does not prevent his coming out from exposing him to the danger of homophobic hate speech and other violent language; he is cursed and demonized by his parents.

While this story unfolds in the lyrics, we see images from the American TV series *Empire* in which a young boy in high heels walks into the dining room where his parents are eating; they look at him in astonishment and his father comes after him. One of the narrative threads in *Empire* is indeed the relationship between a gay son and his homophobic father, the latter being a successful hip-hop artist who runs an entertainment company. The next shot of the "Same Love" video shows Joji Baro, looking bewildered, wearing a ragged white undershirt and carrying two bags, stumbling and falling down in the dust somewhere outside in the bush. This scene is followed by images of the main actor swallowing pills while seated on the bathroom floor, an apparent suicide attempt.

A Pan-African Struggle

The video then shows a series of images meant to illustrate that homophobia is indeed "the new African culture." First we see more antihomosexual newspaper headlines, then a picture of MP Irungu Kang'ata, one of Kenya's most outspoken antigay politicians, followed by scenes from the Protect the Family March, held in Nairobi in July 2015, just before Barack Obama's visit. The point of this march was to inform Obama—in the not so diplomatic words of Kang'ata—that "when he comes to Kenya this month and he tries to bring the abortion agenda, the gay agenda, we shall tell him to shut up and go home."[70] These images are interspersed with scenes from another street protest, by Kurdish people in the Turkish city of Diyarbakır in December 2015, which is violently dispersed by police dressed in riot gear. These scenes express a sense of solidarity with movements around the globe protesting oppression and fighting for social and political recognition. A statement from one of the pro-Kurdish protesters—"their mentality is that if there is something different, they will always block it"—can easily be applied to the struggle for recognition of sexual diversity in contemporary Africa.

The chorus is repeated, after which the rapper sings the final lyrics, continuing the political line from the previous segment:

> Shout out to my brothers Binyavanga, Joji Baro / And my lele sisters everywhere in the struggle / Always love from your heart / Never love from society / The hate is too much, all in the name of piety / Uganda stand strong, Nigeria, Africa, it's time for new laws, no time for new wars / We come from the same God, cut from the same cord, share the same pain and share the same skin / The march is still on, Luther's spirit lives on / It's a bedroom struggle and also a street struggle / Judge less and love more / Stand up and stand tall, talk tough or talk not / We gon' love and love more yo.

We see images of Kenyan gay writer Binyavanga Wainaina, "Same Love" producer George Barasa, Ugandan rights activist and Kuchu Times editor Kasha Jacqueline Nabagesera (to whom Barasa refers as his "mentor"),[71] and the legendary South African bisexual anti-apartheid singer Brenda Nokuzola Fassie (1964–2004). These four figures are presented here as the faces of the struggle for same-sex human rights in Africa. The lyrics link this struggle with the earlier struggle for civil rights in the United States, suggesting that the spirit of Martin Luther King lives on in Africans involved in the contemporary struggle for human rights and dignity regardless of sexual orientation.[72] We hear echoes of the line earlier in the song that associates the American civil rights movement with the contemporary African sexual rights movement, thus hinting at a sense of transatlantic black pan-African solidarity. The pictures of

African queer activists are followed by images from lgbt marches and protests in different parts of the world, alternated with shots from the movie *The Skinny* and scenes of the female couple.

The two female lovers are now depicted in a domestic setting, and the video is edited in such a way as to create the impression that they are in a large, upper-class villa (in fact, the images of the villa's exterior are taken from *Empire*). The luxury villa invokes what Meyer calls an "urban imaginary," that is, a partly utopian vision of life in a modern city with beautiful homes and happy citizens. Whereas the Ghanaian movies that Meyer discusses tend to portray this urban imaginary as upper-class mansions inhabited by nuclear families, "Same Love" presents another vision of the modern urban good life by displaying same-sex intimacy in a domestic setting, specifically, in the bedroom, "the heart of the modern house."[73] Because this domestic setting is relatively moderate in "Same Love," the video puts less emphasis on beauty, wealth, and conspicuous consumption but nevertheless cultivates a style characterized by middle-class domestic happiness and—through the dress of the actors—a cosmopolitan urban identity. The video thus reflects and fuels African queer expectations and aspirations to this kind of modern identity. We see the two female lovers chilling together on a sofa, preparing food in the kitchen—together suggestively holding a pestle in a mortar. Grinding is, of course, a metaphor for female love-making, and the Kiswahili word for lesbian, *msagaji*, literally means "a grinder."[74] Subsequently, we see the couple almost naked in bed, touching, caressing, rubbing, and kissing each other. Of all the scenes in the video, these may be the most explicitly erotic and might be seen as "pornographic"—at least by the KFCB.

In the final repetition of the chorus, the original version sung by Mary Lambert is mixed with the voice of the rapper, who repeats the line "I can't change" several times, adding emphasis to the idea of sexual orientation as an inborn trait. He also raps "He keep me warm yo" while the female voice sings "She keeps me warm," enabling both male and female listeners to identify easily.

Love and Death

The video concludes with the line "Love is patient, love is kind," inspired by the original version of the song by Macklemore & Ryan Lewis, repeated several times. This line is, of course, from the New Testament, the famous passage about love in Paul's first letter to the Corinthians (13:4). Yet Art Attack has included a substantially longer paraphrase of this poetic biblical text:

Love is patient
Love is kind
Love is selfless
Love is faithful
Love is full of hope
Love is full of trust
Love is not proud
Love is God and God is Love

The lines are recited in slow motion, like the opening lyrics, in a clear, loud voice. In the background, female voices echo the first two lines—"love is patient, love is kind"—melodically. The quotation not only exemplifies the use of the Bible in contemporary African popular culture, but also demonstrates the fluid boundaries between the genres of hip-hop and gospel music. With its explicit political and pan-African message, "Same Love" is not a typical gospel song, but it fits into the tradition of hip-hop music in East Africa as an expression of sociopolitical critique and as a negotiation of postcolonial African experiences of modernity and globalization. Yet the quotation of a highly symbolic biblical text and the invocation of the Christian notion of God as love show how Christian beliefs and texts have become part of, and are reproduced through, popular culture in Kenya and other parts of the continent.[75] Moreover, it demonstrates not only that the Bible has become "a site of struggle" where "the debate on homosexuality is being fought" by homophobic African religious and political leaders,[76] but that the same site is engaged by African lgbt activists in support of their cause. "Same Love" adds another chapter to the long history of appropriating the Bible in Africa;[77] it is an African queer appropriation of the biblical text read through a hermeneutics of love. The concluding line, "Love is God and God is Love," does not appear in 1 Corinthians 13, but it reflects a strand of texts in the Bible associating God with love.[78] The song ends with the widely circulated quotation from the American actress Loretta Young (1913–2000): "Love is not something you find / Love is something that finds you." The inclusion of quotations about love from both the Bible and Western popular culture demonstrates that the lyrics of "Same Love" are part of a global discourse of love, but one that has particular political significance in the African context. By putting the notion of love at its center, the video offers a correction to several dominant discourses. First, there are the sexual health discourses in Africa, in which same-sex love is often described in terms of "men who have sex with men" and "women who have sex with women," thus reducing intimate relations to the act of having sex and removing any emotional affection.[79] Second, there is a longer tradition of Western scholarship and popular writing that "has reduced African intimacy to sex."[80] This problematic representation is part of a history of colonial discourses about African sexuality as "primitive, uncontrolled and excessive" that dehumanized Africans and subjected them to humiliating policies.[81] Third, both in the West and in Africa, this notion of hypersexuality is often used for gay people, particularly for gay men, who tend to be presented as promiscuous and as "purely defined by sex."[82] Against this background, the message of "Same Love" is that both Africans and gay people share the human capacity to love. Yet, as Lynn Thomas and Jennifer Cole point out, "claims to love are often claims to modernity," and this appears to be the case with the "Same Love" video.[83] Its depiction of romantic, playful love, the middle-class setting and gay-vague cosmopolitan styling of its characters, and the inclusion of fragments from Western popular culture all add to the suggestion that Africa is indeed part of the modern world, and as such should recognize lgbt sexualities, identities, and rights.

The central theme of love in the final segment of the video is contrasted with the image of the main actor, who has swallowed pills in an earlier scene, collapsing on the floor—at the very moment that the rapper sings "Love is God and God is Love." An image of a handwritten suicide note appears on the screen:

> *I'm tired, tired of the pressure, tired of the pain, tired of the stigmatization.*
> *Tired of the insults and the attacks and the hate!*
> *Goodbye world!*
> *Mummy, I love you.*
> *Wish I wasn't born this way.*

The contrast between lyrics about love and images of suicide makes the point that in a world filled with insults, attacks, and hatred, not everyone finds love—on the contrary, many people find suffering and death because of rejection and hatred. The theme of suicide reaches its climax at the end of "Same Love," illustrating Judith Butler's insight that life becomes unlivable for those who are "recognized as less than human" or "not recognized as human at all." The video invites its viewers to reflect critically on the "schemes of recognition" in society, and on the question of who, in the dominant schemes, "qualifies as the recognizably human and who does not."[84]

How should we interpret the video's ending with suicide, which resembles a pattern in queer cultural production more generally in which "queerness and that particular modality of loss known as suicide" are often linked?[85] Does "Same Love" subscribe to Lee Edelman's polemical thesis of giving up on the future, in which queerness is ultimately linked to, and defined by, the death drive? That seems unlikely, given the video's adoption of a Christian and pan-African discourse. Neither in Christianity nor in African philosophies is death the end; rather, it is the beginning of new (after)life. In indigenous African religions, ancestors are seen as "the living dead," while in a Christian context death is linked to the hope of resurrection. Moreover, I agree with José Esteban Muñoz's criticism of Edelman: "to write or conjecture about suicide as a queer act, a performance of radical negativity, utopian in its negation of death as ultimate uncontrollable finitude, and not to think about what it symbolizes for a larger collectivity would be remiss."[86] It seems to me that, against the background of a general anxiety in Kenya and East Africa about a perceived increase in suicides,[87] "Same Love" draws attention to the generally overlooked problem of queer suicide, that is, suicide committed by people, especially youths, who are not recognized as fully human in the first place, because of the norms of recognition relating to sexuality and gender, and whose deaths therefore are considered trivial by society. The act of suicide in the video, then, is a prophetic statement that creates awareness of, and speaks out against, the reality of queer suicide. What Achille Mbembe writes about the colonized subject, that "as for his/her death, it mattered little if this occurred by suicide, resulted from murder, or was inflicted by power,"[88] is the implicit critique in "Same Love" of how African societies today respond, or fail to respond, to the death of queer people who are, after all, "the new slaves, the new blacks, the new Jews, the new minorities." Their death is the collateral damage of the necropolitics of the homophobic postcolonial state. Significantly, although the video ends with suicide and death, the person on whose life the song is based—George Barasa—is still alive, in spite of having gone through suicidal moments. This discrepancy can perhaps be seen as an allusion to the possibility of overcoming social death, that is, the possibility of the resurrection of the African queer body. In that case, the video may touch on a deeply Christian theme, central in black political theology: the belief, as Mbembe puts it, that "the final truth of death is in the resurrection—in the infinite possibility of life."[89] This possibility, from a Christian perspective, is intricately connected to the eternal and abundant love of God. The video's coinciding references to suicide and divine love may then also make the claim that queer folk who see no alternative to suicide will not fall out of the embrace of God's radical love.[90]

The song's equation of gays and lesbians with "the new slaves, the new blacks, the new Jews" inscribes the experience of same-sex-loving people in Africa in a longer history of racial and ethnic oppression and persecution. Whereas Frantz Fanon, among other postcolonial thinkers, has reflected upon the similarities (and differences) between antiblack racism ("negrophobia") and anti-Semitism, "Same Love" suggests that homophobia should be considered as yet another expression of systematic discrimination and oppression. As Barasa explained, the similarity between blacks, Jews, and same-sex-loving people is that members of each of these groups share a history of their humanity's being called into question, if not denied, on the basis of religion, ethnicity, race, sexual orientation, or gender expression.[91] As Butler put it, members of these groups fall outside the schemes of recognition in society. The reference to blacks and slaves is part of a longer tradition, particularly in the United States, of lgbt activists describing the oppression of lgbt people as "similar in nature although not in history to that of African Americans" through the use of "metaphors of chains and enslavement."[92] The reference to Jews, moreover, evokes the memory of the Holocaust, which is significant for two reasons. First, it implicitly suggests that the sociopolitical oppression of African gay and lesbian people in the early twenty-first century is somehow comparable to the Jewish experience of the Shoah or Holocaust in the mid-twentieth century. Within the field of Holocaust studies, it is recognized that "if the Holocaust was the quintessential genocide—defined as the intended destruction, in whole or in part, of a national, ethnic, racial, or religious group—it was neither the first nor the last."[93] Although sexuality is not mentioned here as a basis for genocide, homosexuals were, of course, also persecuted and murdered by the Nazis. Whether one can speak of systematic "intended destruction" of gay and lesbian people in contemporary Africa is questionable, but genocide in contemporary scholarship is not always limited to homicide but can also be cultural in nature. For instance, Jean-Paul Sartre famously referred to colonization as a "cultural genocide."[94] In both its homicidal and its cultural forms, genocide is about social death; it seeks to destroy the identity and social vitality of a group.[95] The transatlantic slave trade and racial oppression under apartheid in South Africa have also been referred to as forms of genocide, and indeed as "black holocausts."[96] The lyrics of "Same Love" implicitly suggest that the persecution of same-sex-loving people in a range of African countries constitutes yet another chapter in this history—a "queer genocide" as a cultural cleansing in which certain Africans seek the social death of fellow Africans because they engage in behavior perceived as "un-African."[97] The antihomosexuality laws introduced in Uganda, Nigeria, and The Gambia are the latest manifestation, in Mbembe's words, of "laws that underpin and organize tragedy and genocide" in the African postcolony.[98]

The implicit allusion to queer genocide in "Same Love" is also significant because it counters a particular narrative about homosexuality in East Africa, specifically Uganda, concerning an incident in the late nineteenth century, the period of the arrival of colonialism and missionary Christianity. This narrative, famously documented by the Catholic priest John F. Faupel, uses the notion of "African holocaust" to refer to the murder of a group of twenty-two young men serving as pages in the royal court of the Buganda kingdom, who, following their conversion to the Christian faith, reportedly refused to have intimate relationships with the king, Kabaka Mwanga.[99] Officially canonized as martyrs and saints in both the Catholic Church and the Anglican Church, their story has become foundational to the history of Christianity in Uganda and plays a critical and complex role in recent debates about homosexuality in that country.[100] "Same Love" can be read as a counternarrative to Faupel's story of African holocaust, not only because of its implicit allusion to queer genocide but also by its reclaiming of Christianity in order to affirm the possibility of same-sex love in Africa.

CRITIQUING AND RECLAIMING CHRISTIANITY

The "Same Love" song makes a few explicit references to religion. When the protagonist comes out to his parents, his mother tells him that he is "the son of the devil," while his father goes further and calls him "you devil." These phrases exemplify the demonization of homosexuality in popular Christian discourses in Africa.[101] Whereas Binyavanga Wainaina critiques these discourses of demonization through the use of satire (see chapter 1), "Same Love" presents a more subtle, but no less fundamental, criticism by making clear the effects of such discourses: mothers and fathers who deny and reject their own children. In other words, the video exposes how demonization leads to interhuman alienation.

The lyrics later make a brief reference to the church: "Church rules, street rules / Court rules, school rules / Hate is the new love." The point here is that different spheres of society, including the religious sphere, and different social institutions, including the church, share an abhorrence of homosexuality and have joined forces to preach hate. The consequence is that gay people are not safe anywhere; there is no room left for them, as homophobia has been generally embraced as "the new African culture." The hatred that gay and lesbian people experience in society is directed at them "in the name of piety." Religion has become a cover for the expression of hate, the violation of other people's dignity, rights, even their lives. The lyric "judge less and love more" seems to be addressed to religious people in particular. As Noti Flow commented in an interview, "The Bible clearly says, 'Only God can judge,' so please, just let them [gays and lesbians] be, don't judge them, don't discriminate them, it's not correct, it's not fair."[102] In addition to these textual references, at least one scene in the video has an implicitly religious connotation: the images of the Protect the Family March, organized by a number of Kenyan Christian organizations, among them the Evangelical Alliance of Kenya, the Catholic Justice and Peace Commission, and the Kenya Christian Professionals Forum. The march exemplifies the role of religious bodies in the political mobilization against homosexuality in Kenya.

Clearly, "Same Love" critiques religion—Christianity in particular—for its key role in the politicization of homosexuality in Kenya and in Africa more widely. In this respect, it is in line with the public critique of religion expressed by Binyavanga Wainaina. However, more than Wainaina, "Same Love" also explicitly appeals to religion in a positive way. The line "Uganda . . . Nigeria, Africa . . . we come from the same God, cut from the same cord, share the same pain and share the same skin" reflects a sense of pan-Africanism based on a notion of the African race as created, or uniquely designed, by God. Such a notion is reflected in the prose poem "Credo" by the twentieth-century African American intellectual W. E. B. Du Bois. This religiously inspired version of pan-Africanist thought is also known as Ethiopianism, after the country that, according to the Bible, has "stretched out her hands to God" (Psalm 68:31). Ethiopia is also a country that was never subjugated by colonial rule. In the early twentieth century, Ethiopia thus became the symbol of a movement for religious and political autonomy, both for Africa as a continent and for its diaspora. This movement was rooted in the belief, promoted by another pan-Africanist thinker, Marcus Garvey, that "God Almighty created us all to be free."[103] "Same Love" also refers to Martin Luther King, who was not only the famous leader of the African American civil rights movement but also a Christian minister. The "spirit" of King mentioned in the lyrics may refer both to his spirit of black resistance and to the tradition of black religious thought that underpins it. At the end of his world-famous "I Have a Dream" speech,

King expressed his hope for "that day when all God's children . . . will be able to join hands and sing in the words of the old Negro spiritual, 'Free at last, Free at last, Great God a-mighty, We are free at last.'"[104] King's was a vision of racial liberation and reconciliation; "Same Love" suggests that the same prophetic spirit underlies the struggle for queer liberation.[105]

The song's most direct and significant appeal to religion, as discussed above, comes at the end, with the paraphrase of 1 Corinthians 13:4. Art Attack explicitly appropriates the Christian concept of love here, broadening it to include love between people of the same gender. This appropriation of Christian love is significant because love has received very little attention in African theological discourses so far, as I discuss in more detail below.

CRITIQUING AND REIMAGINING AFRICA

East African hip-hop has been described as "a genre of music that is both a product of globalization as well as a medium to critique globalization."[106] "Same Love" can clearly be read as a product of globalization: it is a remix of an originally American song, and the lyrics are in English; it does not include a single word in Kiswahili or any of Kenya's local languages. In addition, the actors who play the male and female couples in the video reflect global fashion styles, and the video includes images of Gay Pride marches and protest marches in different parts of the world. The video also includes snippets of American movies and TV, and it presents the African struggle for the recognition of same-sex love as part of both the international lgbt movement and the global struggle against discrimination on the basis of race, ethnicity, or sexuality.

It is harder to see how the video critiques globalization. If anything, "Same Love" is concerned with critiquing African realities. Instead of blaming Western cultural, economic, or political forces—whether colonial governments, missionary Christianity, or American evangelicals—for their historical role in creating these realities, the song blames African societies and institutions that have made homophobia "the new African culture." The suggestion is that postcolonial discourses of Africanization have in fact led to the marginalization of a whole class of people who are treated like "the new slaves, the new blacks, the new Jews." Rather than represent an Africa "that is cosmopolitan, holding onto its traditions while embracing transnationalism and transcultural realities,"[107] the song criticizes Africa for blaming homosexuality on the West, for calling it a Western invention, and for claiming that "it's un-African to try and show a brother some love." Thus "Same Love" critiques Africa for failing to be cosmopolitan and for conservatively sticking to a set of invented "African values" instead. In doing so, the video acknowledges African agency, holding African actors responsible for homophobia in Africa. Its reference to homophobia as "the new African culture" runs the risk of reinforcing the negative perception of Africa as a homophobic continent; but the phrase serves to succinctly capture recent developments in different parts of Africa through which homosexuality has become strongly politicized.

As much as the song critiques Africa, it also alludes to the possibility of an alternative Africa—one that has the capacity to recognize and uphold same-sex love. This is visible in the opening shots of the video, when the South African flag is depicted as the symbol of an African success story in achieving liberation, securing equality, and recognizing diversity, in terms of both race and sexuality. Ngũgĩ's observation that "South Africa [is] an integral part of the black self-imagination" and that the "liberation of South Africa was key to the social liberation of the continent" appears to apply to the African queer imagination and the struggle for queer liberation on the continent, too.[108] Furthermore, the reference to same-sex-loving people as "the new blacks" in the opening lyrics implicitly frames the struggle for gay and lesbian rights as part of an ongoing struggle for African liberation. Such a framing, as Macharia has pointed out, is not unproblematic, because it suggests that "African liberation discourses were [merely] silent about the figure and role of the homosexual," when in fact homophobia can be found "at the heart of African liberation narratives."[109] This may be true, but South Africa's liberation movement, the African National Congress, is an exception, for the ANC has a history (albeit somewhat ambiguous) of engaging with lesbian and gay activism.[110] "Same Love" specifically invokes this South African legacy. Moreover, the phrase "new blacks" suggests a broader pan-Africanist perspective in which the lgbt rights struggle in Africa is related to the civil rights movement in the United States, and in which the legacy of a figure like Martin Luther King Jr. can be invoked in support. It is an example of what Ngũgĩ has called creative imagination as a remembering practice, with African and black memory as a "link between the past and the present, between space and time, and the base of our dreams."[111] For the makers of "Same Love" (as for many pan-Africanist thinkers), Christianity is not an inherent obstacle to the creative imagining of an alternative Africa; instead, the song refers to the concept of God's creation as the source of African unity and solidarity.

The original American version of "Same Love" has been criticized for shaping its characters in a heteronormative way, foregrounding their "desire for relational stability, monogamy, middle-class prosperity, and longevity." Produced to advocate marriage equality, the American video allegedly emphasizes "sameness [so as] to convince a heterosexual audience of the similarities they share with gay men and women."[112] From this perspective, the representation of gay and lesbian identities in the American version is not radically queer but instead adopts a strategy of normalization. Does this critique also apply to Art Attack's Kenyan remix? A detailed comparative analysis of the two videos falls beyond the scope of this chapter, but a few comparative remarks can be made, which may provide a deeper understanding of the representation of queerness.

Unlike Macklemore & Ryan Lewis, Art Attack did not launch its video as part of a campaign promoting same-sex marriage rights. Thus, whereas Macklemore and Lewis had a strategic interest in presenting the video's protagonist as being in a long-term loving relationship—it depicts him falling in love as a young man, introducing his partner to his parents, getting married in a church, and, finally, on his deathbed, his husband by his side—the Kenyan version shows none of this. Although there is a subtle allusion to marriage in the shot of Noti Flow placing a ring on her girlfriend's finger in the park, the Kenyan video lacks the emphasis on longevity, stability, and ostensible monogamy. It neither suggests nor denies that people in same-sex relationships cherish the heteronormative norms and values of an overwhelmingly straight, Christian society. Its emphasis is entirely on romantic love and joyful intimacy, thus stressing the romance and playfulness of same-sex love without necessarily inscribing it in a heteronormative order.

In addition, Macklemore & Ryan Lewis's video features arguably rather "virtuous" and "tame" expressions of same-sex intimacy in domestic settings, hardly posing any threat to the heteronormative order.[113] As Barasa claims, the original version of the video is "predictable," while his remix goes "to the limit" and is more "gross."[114] Indeed, the expressions of intimacy in the Kenyan video have a more suggestive character, display more nudity, and are shown not only in domestic but also in public settings. The public performance of joyful romantic intimacy, by both the male and the female couple, is set in the green outdoors—Fourteen Falls Park, Paradise Lost Park, and the Nairobi Arboretum, all popular leisure places of the Nairobi middle class. Although these recreational areas are public, the video always depicts the couples in quiet surroundings, with no other people to witness their romance. Since the public is absent, the outdoor expressions of intimacy remain private, and at first glance do not seem to disrupt the heteronormative order of public space. Indirectly, however, they can be seen as disruptive, most obviously in the setting of the female couple in the Nairobi Arboretum. The arboretum is located just beyond the city center, near State House, the official residence of the Kenyan president. It is literally in the president's backyard, and as such it is heavily patrolled by the police. Furthermore, as Hervé Maupeu points out, "The Arboretum is constantly taken over by prayer groups, most often by Pentecostals. Several gospel music videos have been made there. . . . Thus, this park takes part in interdenominational religious events that correspond to the vague [Christian] national ideology that cements the country."[115] Thus, although the arboretum does not allow political demonstrations, it is a highly symbolic terrain of cultural and political citizenship in Kenya. By using it as the setting for romantic same-sex intimacy, "Same Love" challenges the hegemonic political and religious narratives with which the park is associated in the public mind. Every kiss in public can be considered a performative act, but whereas a kiss between a man and a woman reaffirms heteronormativity, same-sex kisses disrupt the heterosexual order of public space, and therefore can be seen as *kairotic* and as a strategic move toward queer world-making.[116] From this perspective, the public expressions of intimacy in the "Same Love" video, especially those set in the arboretum, can indeed be read as disruptive of Kenya's dominant heteronormative culture.

Another aspect of heteronormativity not infrequently reflected in same-sex relationships is a distinct pattern of gendered performance. In male same-sex relations, this is manifested in a strict dichotomy of top/bottom roles, while in female same-sex relations it is reflected in the butch/femme binary. Anecdotal evidence during my fieldwork in Kenya confirms that these distinctions are important for people's identification of self and others. (I still remember a conversation with a butch-identifying lesbian I got to know in Nairobi. For some reason she had decided that I was a "total top," while the straight-identifying friend with whom I went to visit her, in her opinion—and to his astonishment—looked "very bottom.") Correcting such popular perceptions, Ishtar MSM, a Nairobi-based organization for men who have sex with men, posted an article by one of its members on Facebook titled "The Power in Being Versatile." The article argued that the strict identification with top and bottom positions is "a sad mirror of heterosexual relationships. When one is always the 'man' and the other is always the 'woman,' it has the potential to bleed into other aspects of your lives."[117] This was confirmed in my conversations with research participants. They would tell me that sexual positions are related to socioeconomic power, with the masculine "top" in a male same-sex relationship typically being the one providing for his feminine "bottom" partner and being the "head of the house" if they live together. (It is worth noting that sexual positions are consequently unstable, for they depend on changing economic circumstances and can change from relationship to relationship. Indeed, hegemonic notions of sexual activity and passivity can be "particularly unstable markers of erotic belonging.")[118]

Interrupting this heteronormative scheme, "Same Love" depicts the male couple as rather equal in their gendered styles of dress and interaction—there is no obvious masculine/top and feminine/bottom partner. Barasa confirmed that this was intentional and was designed to make clear that gay relationships are not all about anal sex, and that male partners, regardless of their sexual position and identification as bottom, top, or versatile, can share intimacy, romance, and love.[119] The female lovers in the video, at first glance, may suggest a more distinct butch/femme pattern. And yet the butch (supposed to be the dominant partner in bed) has acrylic nails far too long to finger her partner, and indeed is shown in a more passive position in the bedroom scene at the end of the video. Moreover, both women, as noted above, have long hair and wear makeup and jewelry, defying a strict butch/femme dichotomy. So, in a more subtle way, they can also be read as subverting a strictly defined heteronormative order.

Queer World-Making

Although the Kenyan remix of "Same Love" may be more queer than the American original, I have been taken aback on several occasions by responses when I screened the video at academic presentations. Viewers sympathetic to radical queer theory in particular often appeared not to like "Same Love." Their responses can be understood in relation to the work of two exponents of radical queer theory, Lauren Berlant and Michael Warner. In their 1998 essay "Sex in Public," they address what they call "sex as it is mediated by publics." The context for their argument is the United States in the 1990s, where they observed a "project of constructing national heterosexuality." This heteronormative project, they argue, is based on a relatively modern notion of sex and intimacy as private. A hegemonic culture of heterosexuality has subsequently emerged, they contend, in which "a complex cluster of sexual practices gets confused . . . with the love plot of intimacy and familialism that signifies belonging to society in a deep and normal way" and in which "community is imagined through scenes of intimacy, coupling, and kinship."[120] The problem with this scenario, according to Berlant and Warner, is that a range of sexual expressions and practices, and the people involved in them, are constructed as abnormal and as outside (or even as a threat to) this cultural script of sexual citizenship. Homosexuality may at best be tolerated, as long as it remains private and invisible to the public.

Berlant and Warner promote what they call the "radical aspirations of queer culture building," which they describe as the creation of "not just a safe zone for queer sex but [of] the changed possibilities of identity, intelligibility, publics, culture, and sex that appear when the heterosexual couple is no longer the referent or the privileged example of sexual culture." An alternative term for this project is queer world-making, and a key instrument in this process is what they call counterintimacies: "Making a queer world has required the development of kinds of intimacy that bear no necessary relation to domestic space, to kinship, to the couple form, to property, or to the nation."[121] Such kinds of intimacy become counterintimacies and contribute to queer world-making only when they do not restrict themselves to the privatized forms typically associated with sexuality but are public, or, as Berlant and Warner put it, counterpublic. In a later essay, Warner has developed this notion of the counterpublic, describing it as a situation "in which a dominated group aspires to re-create itself as a public and, in doing so, finds itself in conflict not only with the dominant social group, but also with the norms that constitute the dominant culture as a public."[122] In the case of counterintimacies, the premise of the dominant heteronormative culture to be contested and transgressed is the privatization of sex and intimacy. Instead of imitating heterosexual culture "by betrothing themselves to the couple form and its language of personal significance, leaving untransformed the material and ideological conditions that divide intimacy from history, politics, and publics," Berlant and Warner emphasize the need for queer folk to actively and publicly perform counterintimacies. "The queer project we imagine," they write, "is not just to destigmatize those average intimacies, not just to give access to the sentimentality of the couple for persons of the same sex, and definitely not to certify as properly private the personal lives of gays and lesbians. Rather, it is to support forms of affective, erotic, and personal living that are public in the sense of accessible, available to memory, and sustained through collective activity." As a prime example of such a nonstandard, transgressive counterintimacy, the authors discuss a performance of "erotic vomiting" that they once encountered in a leather bar in New York. The performance was a scene of "intimacy and display, control and abandon, ferocity and abjection," which contributed to queer world-making because it made "sex the consequence of public mediations and collective self-activity in a way that made for unpredicted pleasures."[123]

Compared to the performance of erotic vomiting, the depiction of romantic intimacy by two same-sex couples in the Kenyan "Same Love" video may seem rather vanilla. One can argue that the video sentimentally upholds what Berlant and Warner call "the couple form" and "the love plot of intimacy," which they suggest is an imitation of heteronormative culture. From that perspective, "Same Love" does not feature counterintimacies and thus does not contribute to queer world-making. Yet without suggesting that "Same Love" is beyond critique, I would present three objections to that view of the video.

First, online publication of a same-sex music video, which became the subject of national controversy and debate, most certainly contributed to the emergence of a queer culture, or counterpublic, in Kenya. Using Berlant and Warner's words, the video does depict "forms of affective, erotic and personal living" that are made "public in the sense of accessible, available to memory, and sustained through collective activity." The video widens the range of sexual possibilities available to the Kenyan public mind by prominently featuring same-sex intimacy and thus disrupting the normative pattern of heterosexuality.

Second, the KFCB considered the video so sexually explicit and transgressive, so graphic, that it banned it. The video's depictions of intimacy were banned precisely because the KFCB perceived them as counterintimacies, as a threat to the project of building and defending a culture of national heterosexuality based on the privatization of sex and intimacy. For the same reason, as noted above, the KFCB banned the queer films *Stories of Our Lives* (2014) and *Rafiki* (2018), and also *Fifty Shades of Grey* (2015), which depicts a heterosexual but not privatized, romantic, or familial expression of sex and intimacy.

Third, as noted earlier, the settings in which same-sex intimacy is performed in "Same Love" are highly significant, given the political and religious meanings associated with the Nairobi Arboretum by the Kenyan public. To use Berlant and Warner's words, the video does not just create "a safe zone for queer sex" in the privacy of the bedroom; by claiming the arboretum as a site where same-sex intimacy can be publicly enjoyed, it changes the "possibilities of identity, intelligibility, publics, culture, and sex." In the Kenyan context, where the domestic or private enjoyment of gay and lesbian sexuality is already criminalized, the public performance of such enjoyment is obviously considered even more offensive. Hence the kiss between the two female partners, exchanged in the symbolic setting of the Nairobi Arboretum, becomes a politically significant act and, indeed, a counterintimacy—perhaps, in fact, more transgressive than the performance of erotic vomiting in the relatively safe zone of a New York leather bar.

I do not mean to defend "Same Love" from any criticism at all, only to acknowledge the many different and context-specific ways in which queer world-making can take place. As Nathanael Homewood observes, "for Berlant and Warner, queer worldmaking must be radical, anti-normative and actively aggressive politically," which in his opinion "unnecessarily discards a number of queer ways of being" and "unnecessarily sets boundaries on queer resistance." Homewood applies this insight to the sphere of religion as well: "Queer intimacies are also found in sanitised, heteronormative publics. In the normative words and acts of religious rhetoric and ritual, queer counterintimacy in a very heteronormative (even explicitly homophobic) space illustrates that there are many alternative ways of publicly enacting intimacy."[124] This observation reminds us of the video's invocation of an explicitly Christian concept of love, its declamation and paraphrase of 1 Corinthians 13:4—a biblical text commonly read at church weddings and thus deeply associated with the institution of (heterosexual) marriage. How should we interpret this claim of love, specifically a biblical and Christian view of love?

TOWARD AN AFRICAN QUEER THEOLOGY OF LOVE

The concept of erotic love has received little attention in African theological discourse to date. The Nigerian Catholic theologian Agbonkhianmeghe Orobator invokes the biblical idea of God as love and interprets this concept as God's being in a "permanent, loving relationship" with humankind.[125] Yet he does not relate this concept to the human capacity for love. Another Catholic theologian, the Kenyan Wilson Muoha Maina, takes the idea of God as love as the fundamental basis of the "call for a Christian to love others," which he considers the "basic principle of religious and social transformation."[126] Yet Maina appears to be referring to nonsexual love, often associated with the Greek concept of *agape*, and not about erotic or sexual love, usually associated with the Greek word *eros*.[127] This orientation echoes a long tradition in Christian thought in which the two kinds of love are opposed to each other, agape being privileged over eros. One of the very few African theological treatises on love as eros was penned by the Zimbabwean Protestant theologian Edward Antonio. As early as 1997, Antonio published an essay, "Homosexuality and African Culture," in which he critically interrogated arguments opposing homosexuality on the basis of an imagined "Africanness." I am more interested here, however, in a more recent essay, which is not concerned with homosexuality in particular but with erotic love and sexuality more generally.

In a 2010 essay titled "'Eros,' AIDS, and African Bodies: A Theological Commentary on Deadly Desires," Antonio offers a reflection or, in the words of the subtitle, a commentary, on issues relating to sex and love in African contexts. He starts with the critical observation that the HIV epidemic in Africa has made eros (which he acknowledges is an originally Western [Greek] term for sexual love and erotic desire, raising questions about intercultural hermeneutical coexistence, simultaneity, and translatability vis-à-vis African contexts) and death two sides of the same coin. Antonio then pursues a twofold agenda: first, he seeks to interrogate the ways in which Western discourses about the HIV pandemic in Africa have seriously misrepresented African modes of sexuality. His concern here is with the public health discourse that explains the prevalence of HIV in Africa "through a largely Western construction of what has been called 'a hypersexualized pan-African culture' in which Africans are stereotypically depicted as marked by an excessive libidinal complex." As a case in point, Antonio discusses a widely circulated essay on the HIV pandemic in Africa by John Caldwell, Pat Caldwell, and Pat Quiggin, which argues that there is a distinctive African sexuality and that it reveals an alternative civilization, different from that of the West. Antonio counters that by "making African sex and sexual behavior one of the fundamental distinguishing features of African civilization, Africans are ontologically conceptualized and represented in terms of their sexuality"—a views, he argues, that reinforces "a long history of stereotypical Western portrayals of Africans as sexually immoral, exotic, aberrant, and totally other." This line of thought has shaped the public health response to the HIV epidemic, Antonio suggests, resulting in a behaviorist approach of promoting "safe sex"—an approach that problematizes both sex and love: "To the extent that sex is hitched to love, sex-as-love becomes existentially threatening. How can love be the medium or agent of threat, danger, and destruction? I want to suggest that given this cluster of issues, there really is no safe—that is, unproblematic—way of talking about sex and love in Africa anymore; there is no straightforward way of connecting 'eros' and love. Any such connection faces the challenge of suffering and death of individuals and communities." Against this background, Antonio presents his second agenda, of drawing attention to the challenges of HIV and AIDS for theology and reflecting upon the theological understanding of eros in this context. "In Africa," he writes, "HIV is most commonly spread through sex where the figure of something like 'eros' is at work. Given the devastating nature of HIV/AIDS, is 'eros,' understood as God-given love, possible? Can we theologically make sense of 'eros' as love in the presence of massive social death, especially where the latter is the effect of the former?" Clearly, Antonio struggles with these questions, writing that in the context of AIDS, eros "is turned into a site of dereliction, lamentation, and mourning, a place where the love of God is itself radically called into question." Only at the end of the essay does he offer some constructive theological thoughts, drawing on the close relationship he perceives between the idea of safe sex and the Christian idea of salvation. He suggests that eros should be thought of as "subject to the dynamics of God's self-giving as salvation," meaning that eros is not just about libido and cannot be reduced to sex as a mere biological act, but is a form of "responsible, mutual self-giving."[128]

Whereas Antonio treats eros as a major social and theological problem, "Same Love," as a piece of popular culture, takes a more straightforward approach. The song's lyrics are about love, and the video's imagery depicts this love in a romantic, affectionate, and erotic way—"Same Love" is about eros broadly defined. The link between eros and disease, so central to Antonio's thinking, is absent from "Same Love," which is particularly remarkable given that the producer himself is HIV-positive—a fact that apparently did not restrain him from presenting love and eros positively in the video. Antonio's essay refers to AIDS as a widespread life-threatening disease, which was the case in the 1990s and early 2000s in several parts of Africa. "Same Love," by contrast, emerged in a context where antiretroviral treatment was widely available. Although access to treatment continues to pose challenges, in principle, HIV in contemporary Africa is no longer a death sentence, thus freeing eros from its close relationship to sickness and death. By featuring two Kenyans who are openly gay and openly HIV-positive—Binyavanga Wainaina and George Barasa—and depicting them as healthy, strong, and successful, "Same Love" aims to break the stereotype of people living with HIV as "thin, weak, and vulnerable."[129]

True, "Same Love" does draw a link between eros and death. But the cause of death, in the video, is not a sexually transmitted virus but a social virus that affects the physical, emotional, and spiritual well-being of same-sex-loving people, marginalizing them, stigmatizing them, discriminating against them, shaming and humiliating them, rejecting them, sometimes unto death by suicide. The song counters this dark reality theologically. The paraphrase of 1 Corinthians 13:4 and the closing statement "Love is God and God is Love" place erotic love and intimacy squarely and unequivocally in the arena of God's all-embracing love. Thus, indirectly but quite radically in the Kenyan and African context, the song claims that God's love is broad enough to encompass and inspire love between people of the same gender. The song can be read as a corrective to African theological discourses that either are silent about love or follow the long tradition in Western Christian thought that separates and privileges agape over eros, seeing eros first and foremost as a problem, both socially and theologically. The message of "Same Love" is that eros is a gift from God to humankind, to be celebrated by all people, regardless of their sexual orientation. One might even argue, in keeping with recent work in queer theology and black (African American) theology, that the song's statement "Love is God and God is Love" implicitly suggests that God is found in the erotic, and that human eroticism is embedded in the relational and embodied nature of God.[130] In a context in which African theology has largely remained silent about homosexuality, and where some progressive theologians have begun to argue for acceptance of homosexuality on the basis of theologies of liberation and justice,[131] "Same Love" calls on African theologians to adopt a much more radical African queer theology that takes eros seriously as a theological category—not only as something that poses a threat to the body, as in Antonio's account, but also as something that brings pleasure to both body and spirit and is rightly to be enjoyed.

INTERLUDE 2

Bodywork

"So are you a top or a bottom?" The person who asked me this question was my host in a town somewhere in Kenya. When I had been in the country the year before, he had sent me a friend request on Facebook—apparently, we had a mutual friend—introducing himself as an lgbt activist. We chatted a bit, but I had too little time left to arrange a meeting. Returning to Kenya a year later, I decided that I should not focus exclusively on the capital city, Nairobi, but should also visit other parts of the country. So I sent this Facebook friend a message, asking if I could come and visit him to learn about the work he and his organization were doing. He responded that I was most welcome, and that he would be happy to arrange some interviews for me with other key figures in the town. He recommended a simple hotel, only to suggest a week later that I was welcome to stay at his place and could use the money I would save on food and transport costs for the two of us during my visit. Accepting such hospitality is, of course, a good ethnographic (and human) practice, and so accept it I did.

When I arrived that evening, he was waiting at the bus station. We did some shopping and went to his place—a tin-roofed three-bedroom house on the outskirts of town. He prepared a meal that we shared over small talk. He then started asking questions, initially about my work and research, which I was happy to talk about. I asked about his involvement in the lgbt organization and about the lgbt community in the town more generally. It soon became clear that he was not really involved in any organization but was working on a private initiative, offering support to some young gay men, providing them with condoms and lubricant and ensuring that they got tested for STDs periodically. In the course of our conversation I became somewhat irritated by his demeanor, and by the rather negative way in which he depicted the lgbt community in the town, in particular by his stereotypical and judgmental depiction of gay youths as promiscuous, that is, sexually amoral and irresponsible.

He soon began asking more personal questions. Was I gay? Was I in a relationship? Who in my relationship was the head of the household? Had I had ever slept with a black guy? Did I think it was true what they say about black men? Was I a top or a bottom? And so on. I answered the first two questions straightforwardly but gave evasive answers to the others, which I considered irrelevant, even inappropriate. I sensed that my host was interested in me in a way I was not at all ready for—a suspicion that was strengthened each time he mentioned that he had never been with a white guy. As I repeatedly refused to respond in kind, he became increasingly irritated. My reply to his question whether I was a top or a bottom—that I don't believe in such a binary scheme of sexual preference—failed to satisfy him. He kept pushing the head-of-the-household question, ignoring my reply that my partner and I share an equal relationship and tend to make decisions together. I was taken aback when he said, "In our culture, there always has to be one who's the head of the house." He explained how these gendered roles in a same-sex relationship are connected to sexual roles. It became clear that the head-of-the-household question was simply another attempt to find out whether I was a top or a bottom. I got tired of the conversation, which was going nowhere, and told him I needed to sleep. He showed me my room and I went to bed.

A few minutes later he came into my room, saying that his bedroom was too warm. He lay down next to me and soon began touching me. My body froze. Yet given the situation—I was a visitor in a house with somebody I hardly knew, in a town where I did not know anyone else, it was late at night—I did not resist his advances. Apparently, this encouraged him, for he asked, "Can you suck me?" The question sounded more like an order. I tried frantically to think of a way out of the situation, but some moments later found myself reluctantly sucking him. When I paused briefly, he asked, again making it sound more like a command than a question, "Can I fuck you?" By then I had gathered enough courage to decline, and told him clearly, "No thanks." After a pause, he left my room. Breakfast the next morning felt awkward, but we did not talk about what had happened. During the day we were busy in the town, where I conducted several interviews with people he had arranged for me to meet. Once back at his place, we had supper; I went to bed soon afterward, using my early departure time the next morning as an excuse for turning in early.

The incident stayed on my mind for some time and made me contemplate a range of questions. Could I have known that something like this might happen, and should I have managed my host's possible expectations more clearly from the outset? Why was it a struggle to set clear boundaries, when it became more and more obvious that he had a sexual interest in me? A close friend and colleague with whom I shared this experience observed that the way I told the story reminded her of how victims of sexual abuse often tell their stories, tending to blame themselves for what happened. Let me emphasize that I am not suggesting that this incident was a case of sexual abuse. But it does illustrate the complex situation of power and vulnerability in which I found myself, which allows sexual contact to become intrusive, if not downright abusive.

I worry that sharing this story may reinforce a pattern in colonial and racist writing of white fear and anxiety about black sexuality. In an attempt to address and balance this risk, I present a counterexample below. First, however, let me explain how the incident with my Kenyan host has made me think, again, through the taboo topic of "sex in the field." In spite of critical work on this topic,[1] when the issue is raised, it is usually in the context of research ethics, with an emphasis on educating the researcher as to his or her relative power vis-à-vis research subjects. "Sex in the field" is usually presented as a simple case of the researcher's sleeping with his or her interlocutor, which research ethics codes and committees tend to consider inappropriate. Yet the reality in the field is not always as simple as university codes and committees would have it be. Fieldwork is an embodied activity, and "the field" is a site of desire and vulnerability, both physically and emotionally. Researchers and research participants develop social relationships like any other, characterized by like and dislike, trust and mistrust, closeness and estrangement, expectation and frustration, and these emotions often unfold in complex ways. Depending on the specific field situation, researcher and interlocutors have changing levels of agency and power.

As much as these dynamics can create difficult situations and lead to negative experiences such as the one described above, they can also give rise to positive—though still potentially problematic—experiences of friendship and intimacy. One of the reasons why the fieldwork underlying this book was so enjoyable for me overall was that I could be open about my sexuality. This undoubtedly added a layer to the fieldwork experience, as it allowed for a certain level of affection, flirtation, and touch in the ways in which I engaged with research participants, and they with me. At the same time, I was very much aware of the risks involved, and was keen to manage expectations from the outset—which is why, when introducing myself to the congregation of Cosmopolitan Affirming Church, I put much greater emphasis on the fact that I am *married* than I usually do, strategically deploying a protective pretension of monogamy. This did not stop some members, however, from approaching me, whether directly or indirectly, and expressing an interest in me. Although managing this interest was relatively easy, the greater difficulty, in my experience, is the management of more subtle manifestations of erotic subjectivity and of the fluid boundaries between embodied relationality, friendship, intimacy, and sex. In the course of my fieldwork for this book, I hung out quite a lot with queer folk in Nairobi—in church, in nightclubs, and at parties. In these settings, I not only observed but participated, naturally, in the culture of dancing, close hugging, and other forms of intimate bodily contact. In this context, it is not enough to say that fieldwork is bodywork,[2] as bodywork turns out to be work of physical intimacy and erotic desire in which it is not always clear what is good or bad, right or wrong, for the question of sex in the field becomes embedded in multiple and messy layers of relationality, embodiment, and erotic subjectivity.[3]

In spite of my initial determination not to have sex in the field, I came to realize that this decision created an artificial boundary based on the questionable assumption that sex, more than other embodied and intimate forms of human interaction, is inherently problematic. Perhaps it was for this reason, or maybe because of my weak flesh after a period of celibacy, but mostly because I was simply attracted to his handsome looks and charming personality, that I did not strongly resist when one of my research participants, whom I had befriended during my research but whose playful advances I had previously avoided, invited me to visit him at his home. Again, accepting such an invitation is, of course, a good ethnographic and human practice, but this time I was less ignorant of the potential consequences. That evening, he made us dinner, we watched a movie, and he insisted that I stay over because it was too late to go home. It made for an intimate and passionate night, which I fully enjoyed. I share this experience not in order to promote sleeping with research participants. In fact, I still wonder whether I transgressed a professional boundary that I should have respected. Yet my point is precisely that such boundaries easily become blurred in the field, when befriending participants and engaging in embodied interactions. I have long hesitated to reveal this experience, especially given the new public sensitivities in the era of the #MeToo movement—but if we need anything in this era, it is open and honest conversation about the complexities of our embodied human interactions in all spheres of life.

Reflecting upon his erotic encounters in the field, the anthropologist Ralph Bolton writes, "The taboo on sexual involvement in the field serves to maintain a basic boundary between ourselves and the Other in a situation in which our goal as ethnographers is to diminish the distance between us. Sex is arguably the ultimate dissolution of boundaries between individuals. Indeed, good sex creates a physical and emotional connection in which it may be difficult to determine where 'I' stop and 'the other' begins."[4] This statement can be (mis) interpreted as advocating the instrumental use of sex in fieldwork in order to overcome the problem of othering. Although I do not think that such a reading does justice to Bolton's intentions, I do acknowledge, more than Bolton does here, that although sex can dissolve boundaries, it can also cause complications and become a hindrance in fieldwork. The encounter with my second host has, overall, been a good one—for both of us, I believe. Soon thereafter, I left Kenya and returned home, but we have stayed in touch since then.

It is important to approach sex in the field with caution and care, because there are valid concerns about power and also because of the need to manage the expectations and emotional attachments of both self and others. Yet I do sympathize with Bolton when he suggests that the taboo on sexual involvement is based on a somewhat problematic distinction between the ethnographic self and the ethnographic other, as well as on a puritan view in which sex is a very distinct area of human interaction governed by different rules from those that apply in other embodied exchanges. A queer approach to ethnography requires that we navigate relationships, intimacy, and sex in the field in ways that are ethically responsible and reflexive, with a critical awareness of the workings of power and mutual vulnerability, but without necessarily strictly complying with written or unwritten research ethics codes based on assumptions about disembodied research.

CHAPTER 3

Kenyan Queer Stories of Sexuality and Faith

A relatively recent trend among African lgbt activists is to document "queer Africa" by building archives of life stories. One example of this trend is the anthology *Stories of Our Lives*, initiated by the Nairobi-based arts collective The Nest. Starting in June 2013, over a period of two years, project members interviewed Kenyans who identified as lesbian, gay, bisexual, transgender, intersex, or otherwise queer about their life experiences. The idea behind the project emerged in 2012, when the Anti-Homosexuality Bill was pending in the Ugandan Parliament, and The Nest—described by one member as a collective "comprising a bunch of queer people"—became concerned about the legal and political consequences of populist rhetoric about homosexuality as exogenous to Africa.[1] The result is an archive of more than 250 life stories from queer Kenyans throughout the country, with interviews in nine cities, towns, and rural areas. Five of these stories were dramatized and turned into the film *Stories of Our Lives*.[2] Soon after its release in 2014, the film was banned by the Kenya Film and Classification Board because it has "explicit scenes of sexual activities" and "promotes homosexuality which is contrary to our national norms and values."[3] A book with the same title came out the following year and presents the greater part of the stories archived under the project. In contrast to the film, the book was never banned, and I found copies on display in bookshops in Nairobi. Structured around seven thematic sections—"Memories," "Childhood and First Times," "Identity," "Society and the Future," "Coming Out," "Love, Sex and Everything in Between," and "Religion and Spirituality"—*Stories of*

Our Lives (*SOOL*) gives a comprehensive account of the diversity of contemporary Kenyan queer lives and experiences.

This chapter offers an analysis of the stories collected in the book, examining what Ken Plummer calls narrative sexualities. If telling sexual stories is a way of bridging "the local micro-sexual culture (of who we are and what we do) with the wider more abstract sexual meta-culture,"[4] then reading Kenyan queer sexual stories provides critical insight into the ways in which lgbt Kenyans narratively construct and negotiate their own experiences and identities in relation to the sociocultural context of Kenya and of Africa more broadly, on the one hand, and to global lgbt and queer discourses, on the other. My reading concentrates on three major themes: first, the narration of sexuality, with a particular interest in the ways in which lgbt and queer categories are narratively appropriated and negotiated; second, the narration of place and belonging, with a particular interest in Kenyan queer geographies; and third, the narration of religion and faith, with a particular interest in Kenyan queer theologies. I begin, however, by discussing the political and theological significance of queer storytelling more generally.

THE SIGNIFICANCE OF QUEER STORYTELLING

The work of The Nest has a political edge, expressed in its aim of "exploring troubling modern identities, reimagining African pasts and inhabiting mythical African futures."[5] The project of documenting the life experiences of Kenyan lgbt people—generally referred to in *SOOL* by the umbrella term *queer*—contributes to that aim and was motivated by the desire to claim space, "to make room for Kenyans and Africans in that space of queerness."[6] As explained in the book's introduction, the collected stories defy the culturally, socially, and politically "enforced silence" on homosexuality and other things queer, and they complicate and add nuance to the stereotypical representations of lgbt people that abound in the media, political discourse, and religious circles in Kenya and elsewhere on the continent. Thus the stories are, in fact, "counterstories" that resist dominant tales of sexuality; with them, *SOOL* presents an example of "narrative politics" in which stories are activated for the purpose of promoting a particular sexual politics.[7]

The Politics of Queer Storytelling

The Nest's project was inspired by the notion, well developed in postcolonial, feminist, and queer scholarship, that narration is a way to "reclaim the agencies of people who have been excluded from cultural and political centers and for whom epistemic and political agency remains a struggle."[8] Michael Jackson points out that "we tell stories as a way of transforming our sense of who we are, recovering a sense of ourselves as actors and agents in the face of experiences that make us feel insignificant, unrecognized or powerless."[9] Somehow, this holds true generally—stories require agents, and in autobiographical storytelling we as human beings tend to construe ourselves as agents, movers and shakers in the stories of our own lives. Yet for people who historically have been marginalized or excluded from society, or whose identity and agency have been denied, this aspect of storytelling is particularly important and explicitly political. "Telling their own stories enables them to claim epistemic authority as well as to counter the objectified, dehumanized representations of them circulated by others," in Shari Stone-Mediatore's words.[10] This point was confirmed by one of my research participants, a young Kenyan gay man in training to become a journalist, who emphasized the importance of telling "our stories in our own perspective and dimension." As he explained, "It's not every day you hear gay related stories in the Kenyan media so it is up to us to tell our own stories."[11]

The political significance of storytelling resides not only in the way it allows people to reclaim agency, but also in how it makes public things that hitherto were private. As Jackson puts it, "the power of storytelling [is] to connect us with others, finding common ground and reclaiming a public world."[12] Again, this is what The Nest had in mind: "Through these stories, the self-representing queer Kenyan grants the reader permission to explore private and intimate worlds—WHERE THE VAGARIES OF QUEER PUBLICNESS, SILENCE, INTIMACY, MILITANCY AND LOVE HAPPEN" (xiii). Both the telling of the stories as such and their publication in a book transform private into public meanings and claim public space. Plummer's words about sexual stories in general certainly apply to *SOOL*: "sexual stories can lift what were once private tales into the public world, transforming and reorganizing the public knowledge and political awareness of sexual worlds."[13]

Capturing the significance of storytelling for academic research, Sarojini Nadar (quoting Brené Brown) describes stories as "data with soul." Stories contain meaning and knowledge in the ways that people narrate their experiences and construe their identities, and in their relations to others and the world. Reflecting upon the role of stories in black and feminist studies, Nadar identifies five ways in which narratives are of key epistemological significance: "Firstly, stories can be used to engender suspicion of master narratives. Secondly, stories are a tool of knowledge gathering as well as knowledge sharing. Thirdly, stories by their very nature object to objectivity by privileging subjectivity. Fourthly, stories make us reflexive as researchers, and finally stories engender a yearning for change that can be translated into a working for social transformation."[14] Nadar writes here about the narratives of women, particularly women of color, but her comment can be applied to the narratives of other marginalized groups, such as queer Kenyans. The significance of these stories is at least threefold. They most certainly engender suspicion of, and in fact present counterevidence to, the popular master narrative of homosexuality as "un-African." They are indeed a source of knowledge and meaning, providing insight into queer self-representation and queer world-making. To acknowledge the political significance of queer storytelling is to acknowledge and attend to the yearning for change and transformation that speaks from the pages of *SOOL*. This, I believe, is a crucial beginning of social transformation toward sexual justice. In other words, queer storytelling is a form of queer world-making.

The Theology of Queer Storytelling

While many of the stories in *SOOL* are about sex, love, intimacy, and relationships, they are also about religion, faith, and God. Indeed, a member of The Nest told me of the collective's surprise at the "evolved theologies" many of the interviewees came up with.[15] This is particularly significant given the tradition of storytelling as a crucial methodology in African theology.

Emmanuel Katongole has argued that African theology should be suspicious of metanarratives about Africa that conceal the realities of actual people. He specifically mentions the metanarrative of the African Renaissance, proclaimed in the 1990s by several political leaders. Raising the question of where his "semi-literate, rural mother" and other "ordinary Africans" stand in this narrative, Katongole suggests that they may experience the renaissance—especially when it comes in the form of economic liberalization—as a catastrophe. Thus he argues that the task of theology is "to challenge the various metanarratives that claim validity simply because they come from the top, but which fail to take people's life histories seriously," and he emphasizes the fundamental need for theology "to remain on the ground—within the realm of small stories, within the narrative context of the African's ordinary struggles and aspirations."[16]

Applying Katongole's argument to another metanarrative in need of deconstruction—that of homosexuality as "un-African"—requires acknowledging that this narrative does not simply come from the top but is fiercely defended by many Africans. Thus Katongole's somewhat simplistic notion of "ordinary Africans" needs to be interrogated, as it appears that many people at the grassroots level are willing to buy into a politically invested narrative that writes their sons and daughters, brothers and sisters, neighbors and friends out of African cultures and societies and denies them their citizenship, human dignity, and rights. As *SOOL* attests, the narrative of "heterosexual Africa" has been catastrophic for many lgbt Kenyans who, while growing up, learned that their experiences and desires do not fit into this socially dominant narrative. Yet the same stories attest that in many respects, these lgbt individuals are "ordinary Kenyans" and "ordinary Africans," too. Thus, extrapolating Katongole's argument (whether he agrees or not),[17] it can be argued that African theology should be written in such a way that African lgbt people can locate themselves within it.

As a model for such a narrative queering of African theology, one might adopt a strategy similar to that through which African women and feminist theologians have debunked patriarchy and male dominance in African theological and Christian circles.[18] As Mercy Oduyoye points out, "African women [theologians] accept story as a source of theology and so tell their stories as well as study the experiences of other women including those outside their continent, but especially those in Africa whose stories remain unwritten."[19] When African women's theology emerged in the late 1980s, storytelling was adopted as an important means of revealing the "hidden histories of women of faith in Africa," and as a key to reclaiming and reimagining *his*tory as *her*-stories. Out of the idea that women's voices have been muted in the dominant narratives of faith and church in Africa, telling women's stories is considered the key to reclaiming these muted voices and asserting women's identities: "The act of story telling—of delving into the past—encourages retrospection and reflection on our experiences. We begin to see our past in a new light and this consequently makes us read the present differently. Story telling shapes and reshapes our identity, recasting the images we have of ourselves as women." The telling and sharing of often painful stories is thus both deeply political and therapeutic: it grants women agency, shifting them "from being observers and victims into participants and actors in history," and it puts them in a process of "narrative therapy" through which "healing and wholeness can come to African women who have [experienced] and who continue to experience the effects of sexism and other forms of discrimination."[20] Storytelling is seen as the beginning of transformation—of the church, of theology, and of society—so that the humanity of all people will be recognized and gender justice can be realized. The therapeutic dimension of storytelling applies not only to those who share their stories but also to those who hear or read those stories and recognize themselves in them. As a friend, to whom I had given a copy of *SOOL*, wrote me later, "Going through the book *Stories of Our Lives* felt like revisiting various experiences I've had as a gay man living in Kenya. From my relationships in high school, to my first time being in a gay bar, to having strong feelings for a close friend who happened to be straight. My experiences will never be heard by the world, but the book gave me hope because other Kenyans who share similar experiences have told it to the world."

For African women theologians, storytelling is not only a historical but also a deeply theological method, a way of reconstructing "her-theologies."[21] This storytelling takes various forms, but one important tradition is the reading of biblical stories in the light of contemporary African women's experiences—for example, the New Testament narrative about Jesus calling Jairus's daughter back to life with the words *Talitha cumi* ("little girl, arise"), which is read as a story about life and hope in the midst of women's experiences of poverty, disease, and oppression. This biblical story has in fact provided the motif for what has been called "Talitha cum hermeneutics of liberation" and subsequent "Talitha cum theologies."[22] Another tradition reconstructs the biblical themes and religious motifs in women's stories into a more or less systematic theology from the grassroots—for instance, the oral Christology reflected in the references to Jesus Christ in women's stories and prayers.[23] A third tradition is the autobiographical narrative, where personal stories—about experiences of struggle, vulnerability, and liberation in the context of the family, culture and society, the church and the academy—are shared and reflected upon as a means of both narrative therapy and narrative theology.[24]

By bringing in women's experiences, African women theologians have broken the silence on issues of gender and sexuality in African communities, and have developed a strong critique of patriarchy as a sexist ideology. Until recently, however, this has largely been done in ways that take heterosexuality for granted. African women theologians have hardly begun to tell, share, and reflect upon the stories of women in same-sex relationships, and of lgbt people more generally, and have not yet developed a systematic critique of heteronormativity.[25] Her-stories and her-theologies are being told and reconstructed in a heterosexual, if not a heteronormative, framework. Consequently, queer voices remain muted in African theology, in much the same way that women's voices were once muted. I would argue that storytelling is a crucial means of breaking this silence, enabling queer-stories and queer-theologies to become part of the African theological conversation.

Many of the stories in *SOOL* open with a line in which the narrators introduce themselves and their sexuality. In the words of Keguro Macharia, these opening lines present an "articulation of being"[26]—more specifically, an articulation of sexual being in the world. Some typical examples read:

> I am a male-to-female transgender. (5)
> I realized I was bisexual when I was ten. (14)
> I identify as a queer Kikuyu woman. (23)
> I'm a lesbian. (29)
> I'm very, very gay. (69)
> I am an intersex person. (81)
> I'm a male sex worker, and I'm gay. (91)

The narrators use English and originally Western terminology to describe their sexuality. *Gay* and *lesbian* are the most commonly used categories, but *bisexual*, *transgender*, and *queer* are used several times, and *intersex* once. In the stories themselves, the Swahili words *shoga* and *kuchu* appear incidentally, but never in the opening lines as categories of self-identification. One might conclude that in order to narrate themselves into being, the storytellers consider the lgbt framework and its underlying modern notion of sexuality and gender as an identity to be particularly helpful. But this would be a mistake.

In many cases, the self-signifiers are not as stable as they at first appear to be. This is why Macharia argues that *identity* is a difficult word to use: "More than one story takes off from the first line to cycle through a series of identifications and negations. . . . Points of departure, first lines don't always make it till the end."[27] Take, for example, the opening paragraph of one story: "I'm twenty-two years old, and I'm bisexual. I've known for two years now. I just found myself getting feelings for my fellow men. In high school, I had such a crush on a certain guy, so I just realized like that. Actually, I'm not really bisexual because I'm not interested in girls that much. I just socialize with them. I've had sex with only two girls but guys . . . I like it. I enjoy it more" (36). The initial identification as bisexual is renounced four sentences later. One might suspect that this man's hesitation about straightforwardly identifying as gay reveals his internalized homophobia. Later in the story, though, he says that when people call him *shoga*, he has learned to respond boldly, "Yes I'm a fag and I'm dating your dad" (37). Thus, having rejected his self-identification as bisexual, the storyteller proudly embraces the derogatory term *shoga* (translated as "fag"). The reader is left wondering why the narrator does not introduce himself as *shoga*, or gay, from the start if, as he claims, he no longer lives in fear but is proud of who he is. One reason may be that the word *shoga* is considered too derogatory to be used as a term of self-identification. For example, the narrator of another story tells how he once went out clubbing with friends in "outrageous drag"; when he walked home the next morning, people shouted at him, "'*Shoga*! *Mamako*!' Fag! Your momma!" (137). *Shoga* is thus popularly used as an insult for men who dress in drag or are otherwise considered effeminate. Apart from the example quoted above, not a single narrator in *SOOL* embraces the term. In this regard, *SOOL* reflects a more general hesitance about the word *shoga* that I observed during my fieldwork. See, for instance, the following conversation in the WhatsApp group of Cosmopolitan Affirming Church on January 21, 2016 (chapter 4):

A: The word *shoga* doesn't sound cute to me. Isn't there another fabulous name to use. Coz we are fabulous and unique, the world just doesn't know it.
B: True [A], people use that to insult us, so it's really not good to use it.
C: I love the name *shoga* . . . ha ha ha.
B: OK [C], bet that should be your new nickname.
C: *Shoga* can mean a good friend nt necessary a gay . . .
A: No baby don't allow to be called "*shoga*." *Shoga* sounds like a dragon name from ancient china
D: Sure *shoga* is mean!! . . .
E. *shoga* is a frnd frm Swahili perspective. if u did riwaya ya utengano then u must av come across that word. bt in current situation its used to refer to gays
F. I think its how the homophobic society uses it that it makes it sound nasty . . . were it to be used to refer to a friend, then it wld be received with a more positive attitude.

Basically, this discussion considers the question whether *shoga* is inherently derogatory or could be redeemed and reclaimed. The latter possibility is apparently located in the broader meaning of the word—"close friend"—without the necessary connotation of gayness. Obviously, there was no unanimity about this, and neither in CAC nor in my wider fieldwork was the word *shoga* widely used. Thus *SOOL* in this regard appears to be representative of the Kenyan queer vernacular, and reflects the tendency to adopt English terminology, which reflects the globalization of the language of sexual identity.[28]

Although this globalization of queer language is rooted in "the global circulation of a gay men's English that originates in the United States,"[29] some of the stories in *SOOL* suggest that the word *gay* is associated with a particular lifestyle with which not all men engaged in same-sex relationships want to be identified. As one storyteller, who begins by stating, "I am gay," puts it, "I don't like the sound of it, it doesn't speak of me, because being gay is tied to a certain lifestyle, a certain way of being and expressing yourself, like having an interest in interior decoration" (200). Thus the conflation of gay with both a sexual preference and a particular, mostly urban and cosmopolitan, cultural style makes the label less than appropriate in some situations.

We can see the instability of self-signifiers in another *SOOL* story, which begins, "Growing up, I never liked playing with boys, I used to play with the girls" (34). Later in the story, the narrator recounts how he started to realize that he was gay and says that "nothing will change that," only to add that he plans to marry a woman because he wants to have children. And he describes the experience of sex with a woman as "awesome." One might assume that this is a familiar story of a gay man trying to fit into a heteronormative paradigm, and that his statement is a deliberate performative speech act in which he attempts to assert his heterosexuality. But if that were the case, then why would his story conclude with the experience of a foursome with three other guys, which he describes as deeply enjoyable, indeed, as his "most memorable moment of being queer" (36)? The reader is left puzzled by the apparent inconsistencies and shifting articulations of sexuality in the story.

The two stories just quoted appear to make firm claims about stable sexual identities, which then prove to be quite unstable. In some of the other stories in *SOOL*, narrators explicitly express reluctance to use clear, black-and-white identity categories in the first place. This may be because they are still discovering who they are, as one narrator suggests: "I identify as confused, in that phase of experimenting. I would say I am bi-curious, I just don't know" (31). The implicit suggestion seems to be that after the phase of experimentation, one will move to the next phase, in which one has worked out and come to terms with the "truth" about oneself: whether one is "truly" hetero-, homo-, or possibly bisexual. But who's to say that experimenting will just be a phase? In this particular story, confusion about sexuality appears to be related to confusion about the gendered self. Could it be that this and other stories reflect a level of confusion because the binary schemes of sexuality as hetero- or homosexual, and of gender as male or female, are indeed too rigid for the often ambiguous and complex experiences, practices, and desires of the Kenyan queer bodies behind the text?

Another form of hesitation to identify with lgbt categories is expressed here: "The question of what I identify as has never been easy for me to answer. I identify as a person. I find myself attracted to men, but I also find myself attracted to women. However, I find myself more attracted to women, especially over the last five years. Over the last couple of years I've been living as a lesbian. Before that I was living as a bisexual" (59). Though she first declines to identify herself sexually in any clear-cut or binary way, this narrator proceeds to reveal that after living as a bisexual for some time, she has more recently been living as a lesbian. The expression she uses is not *being* but *living as*, which moves the understanding of sexuality from an ontological level to one of lived practice. A similar understanding is reflected in the statement of another storyteller, who says, "I used to be gay but I am bisexual at the moment" (200)—a statement that challenges any reification of homo- and bisexuality as stable and coherent categories.

Some narrators express fundamental discomfort with stable signifiers of sexuality and opt instead for the label *queer*. They say, for instance, "I identify as queer. Queer to me is an undefined space" (152). This use of *queer* as a term of self-description follows a trend that emerged in the United States in the early 1990s and since then has spread more widely, including, recently, to Africa. The use of the term *queer* in this way is a product of the poststructuralist critique of lesbian and gay identity politics and of the emerging understanding of identity as provisional, dynamic, and contingent.[30] In this conceptualization, the term *queer* suggests a way of being beyond stable categories of sexual identity, as in this comment from another story: "For me, queer is a wider spectrum, which to me means that I would be comfortable dating anyone of any gender or sexuality. . . . I still have a problem with the word queer because it's a label and I really don't like labels. But I feel that's the word that I've found so far that I'm most comfortable with" (26). This statement seems to allude to pansexuality, foregrounding gender-blind emotional connection, rather than gender-based sexual attraction, as the basis of desire, love, and relationship. The move beyond sexual identity politics is reflected in yet another story, which uses *queer* as an intellectual and political stance: "I identify as queer. It is not only a term which speaks to my sexuality—which is gay—but it also refers to a certain set of political identifications that my gayness means that are ethically and politically affiliated to certain kinds of politics. . . . I discovered that our notions about sexual orientation, and the foundational stability of heterosexuality were actually very false. Over a period of time, I've cultivated what I'd describe as radical queer politics, which orient me to identify myself as queer today" (208, 211). It becomes clear in the remainder of this story that this radical queer politics specifically relates to gender norms, as the narrator tells how he realized that he was gender-nonconforming long before he realized he was gay, but that he has come to embrace his identity as an effeminate gay man.

It appears that "the one size fits all LGBT framework," as one narrator calls it (200), is too limited. For one thing, the meanings of the words covered by this acronym, as well as of the word *queer*, are far from stable; they shift from story to story and context to context. This framework is based on a notion of sexual identity as stable and coherent, while many of the stories describe fluidity, ambiguity, and incoherence. I agree with Judith Butler that the narrative configurations of confusion "operate as sites for intervention, exposure, and displacement" of the reified ways in which sexuality and gender often are conceptualized.[31] One may wonder why many narrators employ the lgbt identities framework in the first place. Although this is not directly clear from the stories, there may be several reasons. For instance, because the media, the internet, and activist discourses have made this framework easily available to the storytellers, and because they associate it with access to a global discourse of identity and rights, with an international community, and with funding, traveling, and (online) dating and networking opportunities, it is not surprising that many people would naturally use lgbt terms and categories in describing their identities and situations, even when they are not a perfect fit.

Coming-Out Stories

The topic of "coming out" comes up frequently in *SOOL*—yet another indication that Kenyan queer experiences are shaped by a discursive model of sexuality that originated in the West. Plummer describes coming out as the "most momentous act in the life of any lesbian or gay person," because through this act "they proclaim their gayness—to self, to other, to community."[32] This may be true in Western societies where homosexuality is more or less accepted, and where coming out is encouraged as an act of sexual emancipation. The underlying assumption is that sexuality is a defining aspect of our identity and being, and that openness about one's sexual identity is therefore a matter of personal authenticity and a political claim to recognition. But how does this work in Kenya?

One narrator explicitly recounts that he prepared himself for coming out to his parents by reading articles on American websites. Surprisingly or not, his parents responded much more negatively than the American parents he had been reading about. The only liberation that coming out actually delivered was relief from the "burden of being their good son" (263). He talks about his coming out, and his parents' rejection, in almost religious language, as an experience of "death and rebirth at the same time," apparently because coming out gave him the freedom to lead his life as he wished, with friends who accept and support him.

Several stories narrate positive experiences of coming out to siblings, friends, and colleagues. One narrator explained this in terms of progress and modernity: "The general public is starting to realize that gay people are here to stay and it's not just a phase. When I came out to my friends in 2009, they took it better then [*sic*] I think they would have before. Being a lesbian is no longer shocking to the educated folk. I think it's going to get easier" (226). The suggestion here is that people nowadays, especially younger, more educated people, are more likely to accept lesbian and gay people than used to be the case. They are open, even if they are "staunch Christian[s]," as one storyteller put it, to learning that "sexuality is not something that a person chooses, it's something you're born with" (42).

Yet coming out to parents, who obviously are from another generation, is usually a different, and much more difficult, experience. Some of the *SOOL* narrators were not just rejected by their parents but were called "devil worshipper[s]" (260), were sent to a Christian therapist or pastor, were kicked out of the house and disinherited. Thus it is no surprise that a number of narrators do not plan to come out to their parents at all. "The moment you come out to your parents, it becomes their burden too, because then they have to worry about how it reflects on them. . . . Also, my sexuality has little to do with them. I love them and I want the best for them, but my sexuality is just that; it's mine" (294); "I am not out to my family, and I wouldn't want to come out to them. They don't ask. Why would they? They don't bother. My parents are conservative, they don't ask such questions" (35). Both of these statements allude to the importance of keeping one's sexuality private. As the second one makes clear, the idea of "don't ask, don't tell" is often linked to the parents' conservatism—it is not necessarily that they are actively opposed to homosexuality but that sexual matters are not talked about in the first place. This may be linked to what Marc Epprecht calls the "culture of discretion" that traditionally surrounds matters of sexuality in general, and of homosexuality in particular, in many

African societies.[33] Such a culture, which allows same-sex intimacy as long as it is kept strictly private and hidden, is obviously at odds with the modern push toward disclosure and openness.

Several stories address the difficulties that result when the modern model of coming out is applied in the contemporary Kenyan context, where homosexuality is traditionally seen not so much as a distinct identity but as a practice that can perhaps be tolerated as long as it is discreet. One narrator questions the suitability of this model in the first place: "I am very close to my mother, but I have never felt the need to tell her. I have never told my siblings, I don't think they need to know. I think that relates to the politics of definition. Why should I feel obligated to tell anyone? Coming out is such a big obligation. It is seen as a big part of being in the movement. You are not seen as part of the movement if you do not come out, if you don't say who you are to your family" (258). This person views the act of coming out—of defining and disclosing one's sexuality according to a set of "strangely specific" speech acts[34]—as a compulsory precondition of membership in "the movement." Why should he be pressured to follow this discursive model, with its inherent "politics of definition," that is, the problem of verbally expressing those intimate aspects of one's life that may already be intuitively known by others who can tolerate it precisely because it remains unspoken? It is interesting that this narrator begins his story, "I am sort of out to my family. I think they know. It comes out in little slips in conversations. They don't have the language for it. I think my brother knows, he has never brought it up though. My mother sort of suspects I'm gay. Most times she ignores my effeminate expressions" (257). Apparently, there are ways of queer living that are "sort of out" without requiring "coming out." Such ways of queer living can exist precisely because of the silence, the hesitation to publicly name and define one's sexuality, and the discretion that this allows.

Writing about sexuality in a completely different context (the classical period), Michel Foucault comments that "there is not one but many silences," and argues that "we must try to determine the different ways of not saying such things."[35] Rather than associate silence necessarily with powerlessness, and coming out with agency, the story of this Kenyan gay man, who resists the pressure to come out and instead dwells in a space of discretion, underlines the need to think about different silences, some of which may be interpreted as agency, power, and resistance. As Sylvia Tamale puts it, "in many African cultures silence can be as powerful and as empowering as speech," and Stella Nyanzi has argued that the deliberate silence of same-sex-loving individuals and communities in The Gambia can be read as both "a protective posture" and a "powerful mode of resistance."[36] Although in Kenya, unlike The Gambia, lgbt organizations tend to follow the strategy of publicness promoted by international lgbt movements, several stories remind us that this strategy is not suitable or desirable for every Kenyan queer. Thus, as Gabeba Baderoon, in line with other queer postcolonial scholars, urges us, we must explore "the potential of protective and nourishing forms of silence," and question "the normativity of the 'coming out' narrative."[37]

What emerges from many of the *SOOL* stories is a strategy of selective coming out—to friends but not to family, to siblings but not to parents, at work but not in church. Such a strategy is informed by considerations of privacy, discretion, safety, and employment, as well as by the aforementioned resistance to the "politics of definition." Obviously, it is easier to follow such a strategy when one lives in an urban area, where life tends to be more anonymous than in smaller towns. While some narrators seem quite happy with being partially out, one storyteller describes that position as making him feel less than "fully fledged" (22); for him, apparently, being fully out is key to self-realization and something to which he aspires. The stories also make clear that the strategy of being selectively out can be difficult to control. There is always the risk of being outed by others. For a number of the storytellers, coming out was not a voluntary act of self-disclosure but was beyond their control, as their sexuality was discovered by friends or relatives who disclosed it to others in the family or community. This experience is often traumatic, for obvious reasons: one may not yet be ready to disclose an intimate part of oneself, cannot control the ways in which such disclosure happens, and cannot prepare for the reaction.

In short, the coming-out experiences narrated in *SOOL* reflect the variety of decisions people make, and the factors they consider, regarding the disclosure of their sexuality. Whereas in Western societies coming-out stories generally follow a recognizable pattern, and are characterized, as Plummer (almost religiously) puts it, by an "epiphany, a crucial turning point marked by a radical consciousness raising," these Kenyan stories do not simply attest to "redemption and transformation" but are equally about ongoing conflict and struggle.[38] This is, of course, because homosexuality is such contested terrain in Kenya, where openly lesbian and gay identities are deeply controversial.

Intimate Citizenship

Although many of the *SOOL* stories do not fit neatly within the coming-out genre, narrowly defined, in a broader sense they can in fact be seen precisely as coming-out stories. Through storytelling, "the self-representing queer Kenyan grants the reader permission to explore private and intimate worlds," say the book's editors (xiii). Precisely because of this aim to make public what hitherto has remained largely private and taboo, *SOOL* engages the field of "intimate citizenship." Plummer coined this term "to hint at worlds in the making, worlds in which a public language of 'intimate troubles' is emerging around issues of intimacy in the private life of individuals."[39] This development is necessitated by the fragmentation and pluralization of traditional notions of gender, sexuality, relationships, and the family in the modern period, and the resulting transformation and contestation of what we mean by intimacy. In Kenya and elsewhere in Africa, homosexuality has become one of the key sites where private intimacy has been politicized, made an issue of public concern and indeed a marker of citizenship. "Intimate citizenship," Plummer writes, "ultimately suggests new communities of stories, new ways of storytelling, and new ways of making dialogue. It suggests new ethical strategies that are moving into the public sphere and that are starting to configure the ethical worlds of the future."[40] *SOOL* can be seen as an example of enacting intimate citizenship, as its stories narratively construe ethical lives while negotiating moral and political dilemmas and conflicts. The emerging picture of Kenyan queer intimate citizenship is far from homogenous, for the narrators present different ethical strategies for dealing with sex, love, relationships, marriage, and family.

Many of the storytellers recount their sexual experiences with seeming enthusiasm. They describe their first experiences of same-sex intimacy, and they talk about their current sex lives, often in detail. A good number of them seem to have moved beyond discussing sex in the moralizing terms common in Kenyan public discourse. For them, sex is something to be consumed and enjoyed. One storyteller begins, "I identify as someone who likes sex. I love pleasure" (217). However, others are more concerned about their sexual lifestyles, partly because of the risk of HIV and other sexually transmitted diseases, and partly because of public perceptions. "When I accepted that I was gay," one man says, "I did have that whole 'sexual awakening' phase, where all I wanted to do was just fuck. I didn't care with who, I didn't care about what or when or where, it was just like thirst. I just wanted to get as much sex as I possibly could. . . . That didn't last really long. I found out early that I'm picky, which is a good thing because there's that stereotype about homosexuals being promiscuous" (218). The adoption of a more restrictive sexual lifestyle is informed not only by the narrator's being "picky," but also by his cognizance of the public perception of gay promiscuity, which he believes hinders social acceptance. In contrast with the transgressive queer politics mentioned earlier, his attitude reflects a strategy of assimilation to normalcy.

The different ways of dealing with casual sex are also linked to different notions of intimacy. While some narrators see sex as just about fun, others take it more seriously. "There's nothing casual about that connection with another human being," says one storyteller. "I think it's deeply spiritual, and so I don't just throw it around" (234). Emotional notions of intimacy are reflected in narratives about romance and love, which are as common in *SOOL* as narratives about sex. These stories are particularly relevant in view of our interest in intimate citizenship, because the language of romantic love demands political recognition.[41] Significantly, this claim is not stated directly but is made narratively. The power of storytelling allows readers to recognize themselves in the stories, and this is certainly the case with the experience of falling in love and feeling heartbroken. "I have never, ever loved anybody the way I loved that guy," says one narrator. "I am completely unable to move on. Some days, I can't even go to work. I'll just sit in the house. I couldn't eat, or I was eating too much, everyone was asking me why I was gaining weight. Even my mother noticed I was falling apart" (14). Regardless of their sexuality, readers will be able to identify with universal experiences like this one; such stories thus disrupt the othering of same-sex-loving people, as they point toward the ubiquitous human desire for and struggle with love.

Even though love is a universal experience, it is not sought or experienced in the same way by all people across time and space but has its own cultural logic. Thus I draw attention to the particular cultural politics underlying the narratives in *SOOL*. As Jennifer Cole and Lynn Thomas state in their book *Love in Africa*, "claims to love are often claims to modernity." This is not to say that love did not exist in Africa traditionally, but that the ways in which love is understood, expressed, and claimed are shaped by particular ideologies and embedded in wider processes of cultural, social, and economic change. Thus many of the *SOOL* accounts reflect a concern with romantic love, as illustrated by the use of phrases such as "the love of my life" (59). Thomas and Cole point out that "the novelty of the Western ideal of romantic love . . . lay in its privileging of individual desire," whereas in precolonial Africa, romantic love was subordinated to the interests of family and community.[42] Obviously, the embrace of this ideal is particularly strategic for people who want to shape their relational and love lives on the basis of same-sex desire, because in the current Kenyan context this usually requires a break with invested familial and community expectations and interests. The modern ideal of (heterosexual) romantic love is deeply ingrained in African popular culture and endlessly reproduced in fiction and film. This is reflected in *SOOL*, in this statement, for instance: "I love commitment. I love being in relationships. . . . It's not just about sex. If you keep shagging everyone you lose a bit of yourself. Sometimes you shag so many people you feel empty. It becomes meaningless and boring. But when you are with someone you love and you spend time together, it's like an investment" (78). This narrator explains his preference for sex linked to romantic love with reference to the risk of STDs, but also with reference to age. His concluding comment—"at my age, I want to be in a serious relationship" (79)—reflects the ideal of long-term partnership defined by singular commitment and stability, or monogamy.

In the global capitalist economy, the ideal of romantic love has been commercialized, most tellingly in the promotion of Valentine's Day. According to Rachel Spronk, this holiday has been embraced by young middle-class professionals in Nairobi as a way of "affirming a cosmopolitan identity."[43] It is no surprise, then, that several *SOOL* storytellers mention their Valentine's Day practices, among them sending cards, flowers, or chocolates to a lover, taking a partner out for dinner, and doing other "mushy, soft things" (122). As much as this may express cosmopolitanism and middle-class status, it also presents another illustration of the modeling of same-sex relationships after the ideal of romantic heterosexual relationships. This ideal is further associated with what Thomas and Cole call "companionate marriage—the ideal that situates emotional closeness as both the foundation and goal of marriage."[44] Although narrators know that marriage as a social institution is not available to them, several accounts do reflect adherence to this notion of romantic companionship as the foundation and goal of relationship. One, for example, says that love is "not about what's in your pants" but about "whose soul your soul connects with" (26).

While for some narrators, same-sex relationships modeled on straight marriage are an ideal to strive for, others plan to enter into a heterosexual marriage—not out of romantic love but because of social and cultural pressures. One says, tellingly, "This is Africa, I have to be realistic. So even though I know getting married will not be easy for me, and being with a woman will not be easy for me, I will still go through it. I have to start a family; it is what is expected of me. My parents are very traditional; I feel obligated" (231). The twofold obligation mentioned here—to marry a woman and start a family—is explained with reference to the African context in which the narrator is trapped, a subject to which we shall return. Suffice it to say here that some configurations of intimate citizenship seek to comply with sociocultural norms rather than to transgress them.

The wish to start a family is not always motivated simply by a sense of obligation or pressure, of course. In several stories, it appears to be a deeply personal desire. "I want to have my own kids," says one storyteller. "Two of them. I want to raise them full of love. After all, what are we doing all this for—all the investing and things—if it's not for our kids? I'll probably hook up with a lesbian and have kids. I want both my children to be related on both sides; me as the father, and her being the mother, and then we can co-parent regardless of being queer, and just be there for our kids" (79). This narrative about the queering of family life hints at a queer world in the making. Others suggest that friendship and support networks within the lgbt community function as an alternative family. As one narrator puts it succinctly, "Blood isn't always thicker than water. I'm seeing gay people forming stronger bonds amongst themselves than they have with their families. Friends are becoming the new family" (233). This is, of course, particularly important for people who have fallen out with their biological family because of their sexuality. It is yet another example of the new ethical worlds configured in these stories, centered around queer solidarity.

Narrators in *SOOL* follow a variety of strategies for navigating sex, love, relationships, and family, and the strategy of the volume as a whole is exactly to make public this diversity of Kenyan queer experiences. The stories add nuance and multiply notions of intimate citizenship in Kenya, and they challenge the hegemonic status of heterosexual citizenship, demonstrating that intimate citizenship, and sexuality more generally, is always contextual, configured in relation to particular geographies of belonging and identification.

NARRATING PLACE AND BELONGING

How do Kenyan queers relate to their country, compare the Kenyan situation with the situation in other African countries, negotiate Kenyan and African identity, and understand themselves as Kenyan, African, and global citizens? A close reading of the references to place in *SOOL* provides insight into the geographies of sexuality.

Kenya

Given that many stories contain negative experiences—of being rejected by family, expelled from school, evicted by landlords, dismissed by employers, harassed by fellow Kenyans, and preached against by pastors—it is no surprise that the overall picture that emerges from *SOOL* is one of an ambivalent relationship with Kenyan society. After being publicly harassed while out with friends, one storyteller realized that "this was the real Kenya, and this is what gay people go through" (238). In the real Kenya, in his experience, queer folk live in constant fear of humiliation, pestering, aggression, and violence from fellow citizens, and cannot count on protection by the law or the police. The awareness of this lack of protection is disempowering, as is evident in a story about sexual harassment. "One thing that made me really sad about that situation," says this narrator, "was that I felt like I couldn't get justice for that. I couldn't walk into the police station and say, 'This man tried to rape me,' because I was too scared. . . . I couldn't go to the law for protection, which is what it should be there for" (246). Experiences like these, and they are common, make queer Kenyans feel insecure and alienated, and cause them to wonder what kind of future they have in the country. As one of them puts it, "Sometimes I think, 'I'm not meant to be here.' When I say here, I mean Kenya. Because why am I in this environment that is so hostile?" (218). The feeling that they are not "meant to be here" raises fundamental questions about the politics of sexual citizenship in Kenya, and the impact that it has on the sense of social belonging and identification. Some dream of leaving the country. Others attest to how sexual citizenship is reclaimed: "I want people to know that it's not shameful to love another man. . . . I am a homosexual, and very proud of that, and I am a Kenyan," says one (227). Claiming a place under the Kenyan sun, this storyteller speaks out against the law "that states that two men are not allowed to express love" and that "excuses the violence we see, the killings we see, the firings, the dismissals, the prejudice, the eviction from rental houses, the exclusion from family" (227). This account, like many others, clearly constitutes an "act of citizenship"—a performative deed anticipating a queer Kenyan citizenship that is "yet to come."[45]

Several narrators criticize what they consider the hypocritical sexual culture in Kenyan society, where keeping up the appearance of respectability is all that matters.

> I don't think we as Kenyans have dealt with our identity as people, and of course that includes our sex. We're still pretending to be Christians, with that fucking statistic of being 70% Christian. There's nothing 70% Christian about all the unsafe sex that is going on in this country. And that's not just the gays—because us gays are always labelled as being promiscuous. But even the straights are having a lot of unsafe sex; with other people's

wives and husbands, relatives, strangers, when drunk, in cars. Even the kids are busy having sex when they're thirteen, fourteen, in school, with house-helps. But when the sun rises, everyone goes back to pretending that they're respectable, and everyone goes back to judging "others." The gays, the single mothers, the perverts. But there's no "other" when it comes to sex. It's the same thing for everyone, that uncontrollable force that makes logic go out of the window. (233–34)

The *SOOL* stories tend to associate Kenyan society as a whole with moral pretense, public intrusiveness, and societal hatred, but the narrators also make some interesting comments about regional differences within the country. Nairobi is generally associated with relative anonymity and freedom; people are allowed to enjoy there what one narrator calls the gay lifestyle: "The gay lifestyle is only tolerated in the Nairobi metropolitan region. It is very urban and peri-urban. It exists only in those urban spaces" (200). Another man describes attending his first gay party in Nairobi. "That day I felt free. It was scary and amazing at the same time. I entered this place and saw only men. Men hitting on each other, men kissing, men in drag. It was so interesting. I thought I was in another world" (115). Queer Kenyans who live outside the capital often imagine it as a place that is much better than the rest of the country. "In Nairobi people know their rights a little better but in the regional level, the stigma is everywhere," one comments (84). The suggestion that the awareness of human rights is higher among lgbt people in Nairobi, and that the stigma attached to lgbt people there is lower than in rural areas, is probably accurate, thanks to the various lgbt organizations and community groups in Nairobi, and also to the relative anonymity that the capital offers. One lesbian-identifying woman says of her town, "I wish this was Nairobi. This town is too small. There are some clubs you can't enter if you're a lesbian or gay, and they tell you they can't serve you. . . . Sometimes I think it's not as hard in Nairobi—maybe people there aren't too shocked to see lesbians. But here?" (132). These accounts reflect and reinforce an urban-rural opposition that is typical of queer geographies more generally, in which rural areas are associated with moral conservatism and oppressiveness, and urbanity with anonymity and liberalism. As in the cities of Europe and North America, where modern homosexuality emerged in the nineteenth century,[46] the formation of gay and other queer identities in Kenya has been enabled by the processes of urbanization and globalization during the late twentieth and early twenty-first centuries. Yet the rural-urban binary also has a highly symbolic value. In the words of Kath Weston, "the gay imaginary is not just a dream of freedom to be 'gay' that requires an urban location, but a symbolic space that configures gayness itself by elaborating an opposition between rural and urban life."[47] Being gay or queer, in this imaginary, is thus by definition conceived of in such a way that it can only, or best, be realized in the modern, cosmopolitan, anonymous city.

SOOL storytellers often mention Mombasa, Kenya's second-largest city, as well. But whereas Nairobi is associated with a modern, urban, cosmopolitan gay lifestyle, this coastal city appears to be associated with a culture of male sex work.[48] Several stories relate experiences of commercial sex in Mombasa. "I worked in Nairobi as a sex worker for six years," says one man. "I left Nairobi because of the environment and in search of greener pastures. I kept hearing Mombasa was the better environment for gays. . . . Mombasa is a nice place for sex work, because of the tourists. There's good money, and it's a lot easier to get a client in Mombasa" (93). Western tourists, as several stories recount, make Mombasa attractive—at least financially—for both dating and sex work. As one narrator puts it bluntly, "with *mzungus* [white people], you don't have to ask for money. They just give it to you. . . . Some even pay you and still send you money via Western Union when they get back home" (93).

Yet the narrator who referred to Mombasa as a "greener pasture" is less positive about the city on second thought and concludes that it "isn't that great either" (93). Tourism is seasonal, so there is a lot of down time. He further narrates negative experiences, including being beaten and raped by Swahili men. His reference to these "Swahili men" (whom he distinguishes from "Indians" and "Africans") echoes historical tensions between the different racial groups in the coastal region that are rooted in a particular history of sexual politics. Another narrator evokes this history in detail. "I have learnt that sodomy was historically used as a way of degrading slaves," he says. "It was a power tactic to finish the pride of the slave. A man penetrated like that was finished as a man, but the one who penetrated him was seen as a true man. That idea remains, and so gay men who are tops are not seen as being really gay. Gay men who are bottoms receive all the insults" (230). Indeed, Mombasa and the East African coast more generally have a well-documented history of same-sex practices and of slave trade. Although it is not clear whether coastal Arabs used male anal intercourse to degrade slaves in the way this narrator suggests, the use of anal penetration to psychologically emasculate male slaves and colonized subjects is certainly not uncommon.[49] Outside the context of slavery, male homosexuality in coastal East Africa has been closely linked to age, status, gender, and power, with the receptive partner—usually referred to with the Swahili word *shoga*—typically being younger and of lower economic status, and thus associated with femininity.[50] The statements from the men quoted above suggest that these histories continue to shape perceptions of and attitudes toward homosexuality in Mombasa, and that these perceptions intersect with attitudes about race.

The names of smaller cities and towns have been removed from *SOOL* in order to safeguard the anonymity of small-town participants. Yet references to small-town life are found in various stories. Towns are associated with conservatism, narrow-mindedness, gossip, and a lack of anonymity. "The rumours that I was gay started to spread in my town," one man recalls. "Every time I'd walk on the streets, I'd hear people saying, '*Shoga yule.*' He's a fag. That used to bother me so much. I didn't feel safe. I run away from that town and came to [name of town blacked out]" (165–66). Many small-town dwellers who had similar experiences express the desire to relocate, typically to Nairobi, where queer life is believed to be safer and more open and free. Yet some stories attest to the strategies of survival that queer folk in small towns develop, and, more than that, of claiming space for themselves, both physically and psychologically. One narrator persuaded the manager of a local club to allow queer people to meet there for parties, and even pressured the manager to expel a "whole bunch of rugby people" who frequented the same venue and were causing problems (87). Such stories disrupt a strict rural-urban opposition, and suggest that queer space-making is possible outside metropolitan areas. While smaller towns tend to be spaces of alienation and rejection for sexual minorities, they can also be made into spaces of belonging, and different queer folk navigate this tension in different ways.

References to village life are few in *SOOL*, indicating not only that stories were collected in predominantly urban and semiurban settings, but also that young urban queers in Kenya may not maintain connections with their rural homes, as other urbanized Kenyans tend to do.[51] One storyteller mentions in passing that she was raised by her grandparents in a village, while another refers briefly to being sent to the ancestral village for circumcision. The most elaborate account of village connections comes from a gay-identifying man from a village in western Kenya. He describes "an elderly guy who used to bathe at the river. . . . If you showed him your ass, he would throw you fifty cents. That was the perspective I had of homosexuals. In the village they would use that guy to scare young children. . . . He was viewed as a mad man" (193). The narrator claims that this experience made a permanent impression on him; he became introverted and even suicidal, and lived in deep fear of being considered a "mad man." Indirectly, his story also confirms that same-sex eroticism, in one form or another, was not unheard of even in parts of Kenya far away from the modern urban centers, thus contesting popular claims that there was no such thing as homosexuality in traditional Kenyan cultures.

Africa

Concern about life for queer people in Kenya prompted some narrators to make positive comparisons with other African countries. Two neighboring countries, Uganda and Tanzania, are each mentioned once in *SOOL*—Tanzania as a place where transgender people are more common and accepted, and Uganda for having a large and vibrant gay community. The latter statement in particular may come as a surprise, given Uganda's international reputation as possibly "the world's worst place to be gay" owing to its infamous Anti-Homosexuality Act.[52] Yet, as one narrator suggests, the Ugandan gay community is not only big and vibrant but also close-knit; its members are "meshed together" and "check on each other," a positive state of affairs he finds missing in Kenya. Less surprising, perhaps, are several positive references to South Africa, the country widely seen as representing the continent's "dream of love to come."[53] Because it was impossible to marry his partner in Kenya, one storyteller thought, "Maybe we could get married in South Africa and then come back here" (82). Whether because of the country's legal provision for same-sex marriage or its constitutional protection against discrimination on the basis of sexual orientation, another narrator states bluntly that "South Africa is easy—they don't have homophobia." Yet he tempers this perception by adding that the so-called rainbow nation does "have issues with xenophobia and with racism" (90). Nevertheless, the fact that the two openly and high-profile Kenyan gay public figures discussed in previous chapters—Binyavanga Wainaina and George Barasa—have both relocated to South Africa reflects the strong association of this country with African queer freedom.

While the identification with Kenya is ambivalent, most of the explicit references in *SOOL* to Africa as a geocultural entity are negative. One narrator, having shared his experiences of abuse and harassment as a gay-identifying male sex worker, concludes by saying that he is "tired of Africa now" and dreams of being taken to Europe by a man willing to marry him (95). Others explain their decision to conceal their gay identity by arranging a heterosexual marriage as the natural result of living in Africa. "I'm in this Africa so I must marry," one says simply (206); another, quoted above, explains, "in the future, I want to get married to a woman. This is Africa, I have to be realistic. . . . I have to start a family; it is what is expected of me" (231). One of *SOOL*'s female narrators explains this expectation with reference to the dominant cultural view, in which women are always attached to men: "African women are raised from childhood to belong to a man and to children. Nothing in between. We can't belong to ourselves, and when we try, we're told we're being selfish. . . . Men are—apparently—the only ones who can give women legitimacy as human beings" (198). These statements reinforce the association of Africa with homophobia, heteronormativity, and patriarchy. The storytellers make little direct effort to reclaim Africa as a sociocultural space that could accommodate their queer lives. Whereas young middle-class and presumably heterosexual urban Kenyans have been described as being "occupied with issues of Africanness" because "they experience modernity as particularly problematic,"[54] this does not appear to be a concern for the queer Kenyans in *SOOL*. This may be because they identify more straightforwardly with a globalized queer culture, and dissociate themselves more explicitly from what they see as the conservatism and oppression of African culture and tradition. Many of their stories are about the complex negotiation of family ties that link them to this culture and tradition. Although not explicitly reclaiming Africanness, *SOOL* provides insight into the manifold ways in which queer people lead their lives on Kenyan soil and under the African sun.

Europe

Western Europe (and not, surprisingly, North America) appears to be at the heart of the global queer imagination reflected in *SOOL*. In addition to the rural-urban binary that dominates queer geography on a national scale, there is an Africa-Europe opposition formulated along similar lines: Africa stands for conservatism, oppressiveness, and homophobia, while Europe stands for liberalism, tolerance, and freedom. The gay sex worker quoted above adds, "I wish a man would come and ask me to marry him, and take me to Europe. . . . I want to go to Holland, I know all the crazy things happen there. I want to go and be a stripper there" (95). Several narrators dream about migrating to Europe. Of all European countries and cities, the Netherlands and its capital, Amsterdam, exercise the most pull; apparently they are symbolic of a place where queer life can be lived to the fullest—because same-sex marriage is legal, because of the vibrant gay scene, and because of the liberal culture and the anonymity in which sex can be enjoyed. Several narrators tell about their experiences of, or fantasies about, attending gay clubs and saunas in European cities like Amsterdam and London. The risk of such narratives is that they reinforce, on the one hand, a sense of queer Afro-pessimism, and, on the other hand, a sense of European homonationalism. Yet the idea of Europe as a site of queer aspiration and fascination appears to be deeply rooted, as I observed throughout my fieldwork: many research participants asked, more or less directly, whether I could arrange boyfriends for them back home. These requests were often couched in racial language, with the suggestion that "whites" would make more trustworthy and reliable partners than "blacks" (financially and otherwise).

School, Home, Work, Club, and Church

In addition to matters of geographical location and identification—within Kenya, the African continent, and globally—five categories of spatial location appear to be crucial in the stories: school, home, work, club, and church space.

Many narrators recount their first experimentation with homosexuality at school in their teenage years, though the initial awareness of being gay or lesbian dates in several accounts to primary school, as early as standard 2, 3, or 4.[55] The first sexual experiences, of kissing and touching, usually occurred in the higher grades of primary school, standard 6, 7, and 8. Most stories recount the years in high school (forms 1–4), where students are typically between fourteen and eighteen years old, as a period of active sexual experimentation, often facilitated by the fact that many high schools are single-sex and/or boarding schools. The memories of this period, however, vary greatly. One narrator enthusiastically refers to boarding school as "a free world" with "a lot of playing around happening," and with sexual encounters taking place in the showers and dormitories during the evenings and nights (97). Other accounts are more negative, featuring bullying by schoolmates and being reprimanded publicly or suspended from school after being caught in compromising situations. One narrator was expelled from high school three times because of "lesbianism" (14); another shares his experiences of harassment and concludes that "our high schools are very homophobic" (21). Storytellers who went to university often point to the higher level of freedom they experienced there, compared to high school. "You're not going to suspend me in university because of my sexuality," says one. "I'm not staying on campus. I have my own house. Whatever I do in my house is my business" (45). Yet university experiences also vary; a student at a Christian university describes its "crazy rules," as a result of which his "gay life in university was dead" (116).

The home can offer a level of privacy rarely possible in a school setting. "Being a lesbian is hard," says one woman, "but there are times when it's good. I love being a lesbian when I'm in the privacy of my place" (52). Finding and keeping housing, however, can be difficult; some of the stories describe constant struggles with landlords and threats of being evicted. Although home is often associated with safety and freedom, several stories refer to a lack of privacy, especially when people live with family, or when nosy neighbors are keeping a close eye on others. Some of the stories describe sharing a place with a partner, often under the pretense of being cousins or friends. This pretense can be hard to maintain in the long term, of course. As one narrator puts it, "After staying with another woman for ten years, you can't keep telling people that she is your room-mate, or your sister" (215). Clearly, as much as the home is associated with privacy, it cannot be taken for granted.

The workplace is another category frequently mentioned, demonstrating that employment and career are as important to queer folk as to other Kenyans. *SOOL* is full of stories about jobs in business, law, tourism, farming, medical care, NGOs, and the informal sector. As in other areas of life, experiences of being queer at work differ greatly. One narrator, who deliberately took a job at a Christian law firm, had to quit when they found out he was gay and "the work environment became very hostile" (2). Recounting a similar experience of having worked "in places that were really homophobic," another storyteller learned her lesson: "It taught me not to mix work and my personal life. So I stopped mentioning that I was queer" (28). There are exceptions to the rule, however. One man says that he is "out at work, and everyone seems to be OK with it" (256). Initially, he had to deal with many "stupid questions" and "misconceptions," but gradually his colleagues came to accept him as they realized he was "just like them" in his struggles and ambitions at work.

Nightclubs and parties are a fourth spatial category. When narrators speak of clubs, they are usually referring to (semi)public music and dancing venues that cater to a general audience. The risk in such spaces is that when you behave in too queer a manner, or demonstrate same-sex intimacy too visibly, other people may start bothering you, waiters may refuse to serve you, or security may chase you out. Describing a night out with queer friends, one narrator recounts how the five of them were "dancing and kissing, and looking for opportunities to be intimate," and someone else "took photos in the club that night and circulated them to the whole town" (85). In spite of such risks, *SOOL* contains numerous stories of flirtation, romance, and intimacy at clubs, and suggest that there is a certain level of discretion and tolerance in at least some clubs, even those that are not strictly queer. However, a number of stories also relate negative experiences, and many of the storytellers prefer private parties, which provide much more safety and freedom. "This is why I stopped going out," says a transgender-identifying person who was chased out of a club. "The only parties I feel comfortable going to are queer parties" (8).

A fifth spatial category in Kenyan queer lives is places of worship. Most of the references by far are to Christian churches, but a few stories refer to mosques and one to a Hindu temple. Many of these stories are about childhood and youth experiences with religion, though several people continued to attend places of worship after they discovered their sexuality and developed queer identities, and they often actively participate. "I go to church," says one woman. "I'm even the choir mistress! I sing, and I take those people to heaven. Let them listen to me, and stay with their questions" (303). Statements like this illustrate that many queer Kenyans find ways to combine their sexuality and faith, as discussed below in more detail. As much as people go to church or mosque for religious reasons, places of worship are also an important part of people's social life and can even provide opportunities for dating. As one narrator puts it, "in our church we have guys in the praise and worship team who are gay—even some of the ushers are gay" (305). Others, however, have stopped going to church, and some of those who do attend church frequently feel ambivalent there. "I know that being gay is against the Bible," one man confides. "So whenever I'm in church I remember, 'Oh my God, I'm gay.' When I start praying and doing church stuff, it's like I'm mocking God" (305). Being in church reminds this person that he is a sinner, even making him think that his worship is an insult to God. Similar experiences of alienation, of queers feeling out of place in church, are shared in several other stories, explaining why people often withdraw from church more or less gradually. "Whenever I think about going to church, I rethink my decision and decide it's better if I stay home and pray," says one. "There is no difference between someone who goes to church and someone who stays at home praying, as long as you believe" (306). Others use the same strategy of privatizing faith to keep going to church, but while ignoring pastors and fellow Christians who condemn gay people: "If anyone wants to gossip about me on the side, that's their problem. I don't know what they have come to do in church, I know I've come to see my God" (317).

A few *SOOL* accounts distinguish between Catholic and Protestant churches, the latter generally being described in more negative terms. One narrator observes that, "mostly in Protestant churches, you get pastors who condemn homosexuals" (306). Talking about a traumatic experience at boarding school, another narrator recounts that she had gone to Catholic Mass one day, only to find out afterward that her girlfriend had at the same time made a public confession at a Protestant church service: "She talked about how she was living in sin, and she was having a relationship with a girl, and she named me" (43). This narrator links Protestantism to the practice of public revelations, and prefers Catholicism precisely because of the relative anonymity it offers. "At least Catholics don't ask newcomers to stand up and be seen," she says. "So I don't have to suffer through those awkward moments. Where I go, you get in, you pray, worship and leave. That's it" (68).

The complex geographies of Kenyan queer lives are all ambivalent and entail multiple risks. At the same time, these stories demonstrate the considerable skill required to navigate in the wider world, and they provide insight into the multilayered process of queer world-making.

NARRATING RELIGION AND FAITH

The almost universal truth that there are "religious stories we live by" appears to apply to Kenyan queers as much as to other human beings.[56] That religion is a theme in many of the *SOOL* stories may come as no surprise, given the prominent role of religion in Kenyan society. What may surprise some readers is that many of the stories not only refer to a religious upbringing but attest to an ongoing religious commitment, active participation in faith communities, or relentless faith in God. In their religious stories, narrators interweave and interact with the narratives, symbols, and moral codes of various religious traditions.

Analyzing the ways in which people from religious backgrounds manage the tension between their faith and their homosexuality, scholars have distinguished four different modes or strategies of negotiation, each of which can be found in *SOOL*.[57] The first, *privileging faith over sexuality*, is underrepresented in the volume, which is understandable given that people were invited to participate precisely because of their sexual orientation. At least one story does exemplify this strategy, however; it involves a young man who attempted to give up on being gay after a frustrating dating experience.

> It was such a hard time for me. I even locked myself in the house for almost a whole week. One of my friends told me I needed to start thinking about moving on. After some time I thought, "Maybe I'm not gay." So I decided to get born-again. I tried these godly things. I had talked to this guy who I considered my mentor. I told him what I was going through and he told

me I should give being a born-again Christian a try. I really tried, but it just didn't work. I think I wanted to get deep into the church to help me get over losing both my best friend and my potential boyfriend. (122)

Being both gay and a born-again Christian is presented here as impossible, the two things being mutually exclusive. The narrator of this story had earlier described himself as bisexual, and so giving up on being gay may have seemed an option for him. But it did not turn out to be a viable option, especially after he "bumped into a very cute boy" whom he had been dating ever since.

The second strategy, *privileging sexuality over faith*, is reflected in various stories. Several narrators say that they are attending church less frequently or have stopped attending altogether. Participating in "organized religion" leaves a bad taste in one narrator's mouth "because there are so many bad things that come about from the church" (316). These bad things include both condemnation of homosexuality but also the moral hypocrisy of religious leaders and straight churchgoers. One narrator considers himself a deist: "I believe there is a God but I don't believe in religion," he says (42), which captures the attitude of several others—although the significance of this belief in God seems to vary, from a merely rational awareness of the existence of a supreme being to a strong personal belief in and relationship with God (discussed in more detail below). Several others cite intellectual reservations about faith, and one person explicitly describes himself as an atheist. This man had begun to question the rationality of belief in God in high school, had come to identify as a "secular Christian" and then had pursued "a mish-mash of Christianity and Buddhism," before finally deciding he was an atheist. "I try not to see myself as cynically rebelling against religion and God on account of my sexual orientation," he says. "But sometimes it seems to me that that is what happened" (313). This person gave up on faith in God in order to make room for his sexuality; other accounts reflect a privileging of sexuality over faith in more gradual steps. Some chose to live out their sexuality while believing that this might be a sin. We can see this in the account quoted above from the person who felt that he was mocking God by praying in church, having internalized the view that "being gay is against the Bible" (305). In cases like this, although sexuality is privileged, a certain level of religious involvement continues.

The third strategy is one of *compartmentalization*, with people commuting between the spheres of religion and sexuality without necessarily trying to reconcile the two. As one lesbian narrator put it simply, "I am a homosexual, and above all I am a Christian. My sexuality and spirituality don't have to balance out on a scale—they are different" (160). A gay Muslim man made a similar statement: "I feel that there is no problem with the Islam religion and my sexuality" (308). The general feeling among those who compartmentalize appears to be that it's not necessary to attempt to explain how their sexuality and faith relate to each other. "The relationship between my sexuality and my spirituality doesn't bother me," says another narrator. "I go to church every Sunday and Wednesday. When a car runs down, you take it to the garage. God made me, and He knows all the parts that I'm made of. When I go to church, I'm going to see my God so He can fix me and any problems I'm having" (317). Whereas other narrators suggest that God is everywhere, or can be encountered at home, this storyteller believes that God is to be met in church. He apparently does not see his sexual orientation as a problem that needs fixing—for him, the relationship between sexuality and faith is simply not an issue.

Several accounts do present some reflections, however rudimentary, upon the relationship between sexuality and faith, and thus approach the fourth strategy, of *integrating and reconciling* the two spheres. The *SOOL* stories do not necessarily offer deep or detailed thoughts on how queer sexuality can be justified from a biblical or theological perspective. But they do reflect an effort to reconcile homosexuality and religious faith. "I go to church," says one woman, "and I ask myself many questions. Even the other day when Binyavanga came out, people were forwarding us many messages telling us to read the Bible, read Romans chapter this or that verse. I know all of those verses, but I don't think I am wrong. It's not my fault that I'm not attracted to men. . . . I don't think being gay is bad. I'm happy with my life" (131). This narrator does not try to come up with an alternative interpretation of the biblical texts that people use to tell her that homosexuality is wrong. In stating simply that her lesbianism is not her fault, she implicitly suggests that it should not be thought of as a fault at all. Her self-acceptance, with its implicit proposition that God has nothing against queer people, presents an ethic of happiness in its simplest form. In other accounts, this suggestion is more explicit. "I believe God is interested in the state of your heart and nothing else," says one such account. "I won't even argue with people about homosexuality. I believe God is for all" (303). The attempt to integrate sexuality and spirituality kept some people going to church despite the homophobic rhetoric and attitudes they might encounter there. "I think I'm a good Christian," averred one such person. "I don't think being gay affects my religion. I go to church, and I don't have a problem with the church, though sometimes you hear the pastor condemning gays. . . . I'm used to it though, I know in the end it's just me and my God" (305).

Grassroots Theologies

Just as queer people negotiate the relationship between their sexuality and their faith in various ways, so do their stories incorporate narrative theologies, especially Christian theologies centered on God and Jesus Christ. I am primarily interested here in which theological pathways hinder, and which ones promote, the integration of faith and homosexuality. By identifying which pathways or strategies move queer people closer to that kind of integration, we may find resources for a grassroots African queer theology.

Through their religious socialization in church and family, many lgbt people have learned to *associate God with punishment*. As one *SOOL* narrator observes, they are told in church that homosexuality is an "abomination" in the eyes of the Lord (27). This term comes from Leviticus 20:13, which says that a man who lies with another man has committed an abominable act and that both men should be put to death. The biblical story of Sodom and Gomorrah likewise recounts God's destruction of whole cities because—according to popular readings—their inhabitants were guilty of "sodomy." A *SOOL* narrative by a young woman about her mother finding out about her sexuality reflects this connection between punishment and homosexuality. "I got an email from my mother asking, 'What is going on?' It was a 2–3 page email talking about how she will not have any homosexual children in the family, and how I have turned away from God and how I need to repent my sins before His wrath is unleashed upon me" (25). Interestingly, the speaker's mother does not cite Leviticus, which refers only to male homosexuality, but invokes Romans 1, which speaks of the "wrath of God" toward both women and men who "exchanged natural sexual relations for unnatural ones."

As much as this idea that homosexuality angers God and incurs God's wrath may be instilled by pastors and parents, it can be deeply internalized and cause emotional anxiety and existential conflict. One woman who at first seemed to have accepted her sexuality nevertheless says, "Sometimes when something goes wrong in my business, I wonder, 'Is God punishing me? Should I just stop being a lesbian?'" (51). This simple thought reflects a "theology of retribution," which has its roots in both the Bible and indigenous religious epistemologies, and is widespread in African Christian circles.[58] Sexual sin in particular is believed to provoke God's wrath and punishment.

Ironically, the same theology can actually affirm people of faith in their sexual orientation. A narrator who grew up in a "very poor family" sees the contours of his life as an indication that God has blessed him. "If it were not for God," he begins, "I would not be where I am, in spite of everything. . . . I haven't even gone to any college, it's just the hustle. I started out washing toilets in a hotel! But you come into my house and it is comfortable, nice chairs, all of that. I believe God is a caring God. He doesn't choose only men that love women" (303). This man believes that God is only interested in "the state of your heart"—not in people's sexuality. This view is the other side of the coin of a theology of retribution: health, wealth, and well-being can be interpreted as signs of God's blessing and of God's positive inclination toward people with the right state of heart, even as a sign of divine approval of their sexuality. But such a theology is an unstable basis for an affirmative theology of sexuality, precisely because people's fortune tends to be unstable.

Neither the negative image of a punishing God nor the affirmative idea of God blessing people regardless (or even because) of their sexual orientation is dominant in *SOOL*. A much more prevalent notion is the association of God with love, as exemplified in these two comments: "I believe that God loves everyone, so I don't think it's a big deal to be gay and serve God at the same time. I think I love God, nothing will change that. I'm gay, nothing will change that" (35); "I know God loves me. I know he loves me the way I am. Don't let anyone tell you as a gay person that God doesn't love you. It's religion that has something against homosexuality, not God" (304). The first statement emphasizes the universality of God's love: divine love includes and embraces everyone, regardless of sexual orientation or gender identity. The second puts it more intimately, emphasizing the narrator's personal spiritual knowledge of being loved by God. Autobiographical storytelling here becomes testimony and source of truth. It illustrates what Dawne Moon calls "the truth of emotions in everyday theologies": feelings, in this case the feeling of being loved by God, "come to represent truth—not only the truth about sex but, as there is no truth without its guarantee in the divine realm, the truth about God." The advantage, of course, is that claims of personal experience and emotion as a source of intimate knowledge are difficult to contest. This applies as much to the American context Moon writes about, where, thanks to the cultures of psychotherapy and self-help, feelings have become an "almost sacred form of knowledge," as to the Kenyan context, where, thanks to Pentecostalism, a religious culture has emerged that centers around a "politics of affect."[59] Significantly, the category of experience is also crucial to a queer theological understanding of divine revelation. As Patrick Cheng points out, the doctrine of revelation "is more than just a matter of scripture or reason. It is also a matter of experience. Specifically, the doctrine of revelation can be understood as *God's coming out as radical love*."[60]

The *SOOL* narrator seems aware of the pastoral and political significance of sharing his story, for in his personal testimony of divine love he is calling upon queer folk to know that they are accepted and loved by God regardless of what people tell them. His distinction between institutional religion and God is significant, as it demonstrates how queer people sometimes use particular images of God to criticize the church and distance themselves from it. This distinction is echoed in other testimonies. "I felt that God loved me no matter what, no matter who I was," says one, "but I didn't feel the same from the church" (27).

The association of God with love is often related in the stories to the concept of God as the creator. Sometimes this is expressed in general terms: "I believe in God because He's the creator. He's the provider. If you get something, you thank God, if you don't get anything, you still thank God. God is everything. He doesn't care if you're Muslim, Hindu or Christian. Even if you're a sex worker, you just know God is looking at you and providing for you. My mother was Muslim and my father was Christian, I [have] never been to a church or a mosque, but I believe in God" (95). The religious worldview reflected here is deeply rooted in African thought, in which human existence has its origin in God, who created and maintains the world. Earlier in this story, the narrator introduced himself as an HIV-positive gay male sex worker who ran away from home at age fourteen and has led a tough life on the streets ever since. Despite his lack of religious upbringing or involvement in any faith community, and even in spite of a life that few would envy, this man believes that God watches over and provides for him, and for everyone, regardless of religious affiliation or sexual orientation.

The same basic idea of God as creator and provider is reflected in other stories, sometimes in more personal ways directly related to sexuality. "God knows why He created me," says one. "God knows why I feel the way I feel, because this is not something induced. . . . So I don't think God made a mistake making me. It's humans who make a mistake in judging me" (313–14). Another narrator explicitly suggests that sexual diversity is part of God's design. Other people tried to make this man believe that God does not like queer people, "but I looked around me," he says, "and I realized God is a diverse God, and people were trying to standardize Him and His creations" (304). This grassroots theology, which puts difference at the heart of the understanding of God, challenges what Marcella Althaus-Reid has called T-theology, totalitarian theology that tends to homogenize God and also creation.[61]

The ideas of God as love and God as creator merge in the account of one storyteller whose faith was strengthened by his sexuality.

> Before I really accepted who I was, I used to feel like I was really sinning. . . . I fasted and prayed about it, and I told God if He wanted me to be straight then He should take the feelings away from me, and that I didn't want to meet anyone who was queer. Then I'd bump into nice men, bond, fall in love. . . . If He didn't want me to be gay, then I wouldn't be this way. You are born this way, you cannot be made into anything else. You can't help who you are attracted to. I guess it's God's will. . . . So I reconciled with it and I am happy. I pray to God, and I love Him very much. I think He loves us just as we are. (77)

This account, like some of the others, conveys a sense of what has been called "gay Christian essentialism,"[62] the belief not only that lgbt people were "born this way" but that God deliberately created them this way—that their sexual orientation is part of God's plan and that God loves them just the way they are. This deeply affirmative belief enables lgbt people to accept their sexuality and to reconcile it with their religious faith.

Grassroots Theologies of Christ

Only three accounts in *SOOL* refer to Jesus Christ, but they provide valuable insight into what can be called queer Christology. One narrator explicitly claims that he is struggling to find an alternative understanding of Christian faith, beyond the traditional theologies preached in churches.

> Maybe there is a different way of looking at Christianity, Jesus and religion, but as at now that is very distant to me. It is so frustrating to me because I think Jesus would be an awesome person being God. I would like to know him better but I don't know how to begin to know him. . . . The significance of this is just amazing; that someone can be nailed on a cross and die for someone else. I think that person is the perfect guy. I want him in my life. I would like to know Jesus in a different way. (302)

The desire to know Jesus "in a different way," a way that affirms queer identity and sexuality, reflects the need for a theology that makes sense of Kenyan lgbt experiences and allows imagining a queer world. The suggestion that a theology based on the sacrificial and atoning death of Christ—the belief that Jesus died "for us," which is at the heart of Kenyan and other African forms of the

Christian faith—is particularly significant in light of Cheng's claim that atonement is a queer doctrine because it "erases the boundaries between 'insiders' and 'outsiders' . . . [and] dissolves the boundaries of sexuality and gender."[63] Intuitively, this *SOOL* story lays down a potential stepping stone toward a grassroots queer theology.

Another stepping stone is also concerned with Jesus Christ, but more with his life than with his death. Recalling the New Testament Gospels, this narrator creates her own version of "Talitha cum theologies," mentioned above.

> My favourite story in the Bible is the one where Jesus drank from the water pot of a woman accused of being a prostitute. Jesus did not care whether she was a prostitute or whether she was HIV positive. God sees us for who we are. He sees what is good in me. He is up there telling his angels that there are things that I am doing that are better than what the Christians who are pointing fingers are doing. There is no big sin or small sin before the eyes of God. Being a homosexual is irrelevant to him. (164)

This woman appears to be referring to John 4:7–26, the story of Jesus and the Samaritan woman at the well. The Gospel does not describe the woman as a prostitute, but it does mention that she has had five husbands and is currently living with a man who is not her husband, thus depicting her as a sexual outlaw. That she is a Samaritan adds to her marginalization, as in biblical times Jews tended to consider Samaritans foreigners and treat them with hostility. The narrator may be conflating the story of the Samaritan woman with elements from other Bible stories, among them John 8:1–11, about the woman caught in adultery and brought before Jesus by the Pharisees, and Luke 7:36–50, about the "sinful woman" (popularly known as a prostitute) who pours perfume on Jesus's feet.

These and other New Testament narratives have frequently figured in the writings of African women theologians to illustrate Jesus's countercultural relations with women, through which he, in the words of Mercy Oduyoye and Elizabeth Amoah, "has become for us [African women] the Christ, the anointed one who liberates, the companion, the friend."[64] The reading of such narratives by these theologians is often characterized by a hermeneutics of identification, with women in contemporary Africa being written into the biblical stories about Jesus's interactions with women. A telling example of this is the poem "I Am the Woman," by the Ghanaian theologian Rose Teteki Abbey, in which the poet identifies with several marginalized or stigmatized New Testament female characters. Such identificatory and in fact emancipatory readings can be found at the grassroots level as well. The comment of the Kenyan narrator—who describes herself as "a lesbian, a sex worker activist and mother of three children" (162)—that Jesus did not care whether the Samaritan woman was a prostitute or HIV-positive exemplifies the creative way in which many African Christians engage with biblical stories, relating their own context to the text and reading the text in the context of their own experience. That HIV was unknown in the time of Jesus is irrelevant. What matters is the narrator's direct identification with the woman in the biblical story, whom Jesus treated with respect and compassion, defying the narrow-minded bigotry of those who found his contact with her scandalous in the context of the prevailing culture of the time.

The Bible may once have been a tool of imperialism in Africa, but it has now been widely and popularly adopted, in the words of Gerald West, as an "African icon" and through complex processes of appropriation has become a "people's Bible."[65] Not only have black Africans appropriated and reclaimed the Bible from white Western missionaries, and not only have African Christian women appropriated and reclaimed it from a male-dominated church and academy; as we can see in several of the *SOOL* stories, sexual "outcasts" have now begun to appropriate and reclaim the Bible as well. Like Abbey's poem, the passage quoted above reflects an empowering reading of scripture: Jesus's accepting attitude toward a stigmatized woman is taken as proof that "God sees us for who we are" and that one's sexual orientation, HIV status, or involvement in sex work is irrelevant.

The direct equation of Jesus and God is typical of African grassroots theology, in which "Christology is not a discourse" but a personal relationship through which believers "discover for themselves that Jesus reveals God."[66] The *SOOL* narrator quoted above clearly presents Jesus as revealing the image of an accepting God whose love liberates queer people from the prejudice and discrimination of a homophobic society. Although this Kenyan lesbian's appropriation of Jesus may seem highly transgressive, it follows a model that is common in feminist and other traditions of liberation theology in Africa and in African Christianity more generally. As Paul Gifford summarizes African Pentecostal beliefs, the Bible "is not just a record of covenants and commitments to others in the past. It is not a historical document at all—it is a contemporary document; it tells of God's promises to me. It tells my story; it explains who I am."[67] Although she follows a common pattern, the lesbian's statement is innovative in two ways—vis-à-vis African theology, it adds sexuality to the more established concerns with gender, race, and socioeconomic status in African liberation theological discourse, and vis-à-vis Pentecostalism, it enables a queer reclaiming of the Bible and challenges homophobic Christian rhetoric.

Another *SOOL* account takes Jesus's embrace of queer people to a more radical level, calling Jesus himself "fucking queer." "Christ was a very odd man," says this narrator. "He was odd, because He was a thirty year old man, wasn't married, didn't have kids, was celibate—as far as the reports go—and He was uprooting married men from their homes to walk around the country with him, leading rallies . . . , sitting with prostitutes, having His feet washed by them. He was a strange, strange man. . . . He was fucking queer. Not in the sexual way, but in that way that He was so outside the boundaries that usually surround a man of His age" (312). Not only did Jesus himself transgress the expectations of marriage, family life, and other heteronormative sociocultural conventions of the time, but he also encouraged others to do so, beginning with his twelve male disciples. Christians, according to this narrator—"a bunch of people who claim to follow such a queer man" (312)—fail to recognize Christ's queerness, a point that echoes recent writings in queer theology.[68] Her observation exemplifies what Robert Goss, with reference to Foucault, calls "the insurrection of subjugated knowledge," which, he argues, is "the foundation of a thoroughly queer theology."[69]

Whereas churches in Kenya and elsewhere in Africa may rigidly stick to heteronormative conventions, making Christ into "a symbol of homophobic oppression and violence,"[70] these *SOOL* accounts reclaim Jesus Christ as a source and symbol of queer politics, laying a crucial foundation for the development of a grassroots African queer theology.

Toward a Queer Theology of Fruitfulness

As noted above, one tradition in African women's theology is the use of autobiographical narrative. A beautiful example of this is Mercy Oduyoye's 1999 essay "A Coming Home to Myself: A Childless Woman in the West African Space," a deeply personal reflection on Oduyoye's status as a married but childless African woman. Through an intertextual reading of this essay vis-à-vis the *SOOL* life stories, let us explore the common ground between feminist and queer methodology, politics, and theology in Africa.

Belonging to the Asante people in Ghana, who are traditionally matrilineal, Oduyoye married at a relatively late age into the patrilineal Yoruba people of Nigeria. Regardless of the differences in lineage system, both her blood relatives and her in-laws began to question her when, a few years into the marriage, she had not given birth. Neither their advice and prayers nor visits to medical doctors and traditional healers helped her conceive. While her husband demonstrated "exceptional faith" in the biblical "Abraham-and-Sarah paradigm" of long-awaited childbirth at a late age, Oduyoye reached the point where she "regretted the decision to get married when I was 'past my prime' and with less than a perfect womb" (she had fibroid tumors surgically removed). A self-proclaimed feminist, she found herself in the position of insisting that her husband have children with another woman so that he, at least, would not have to bear the stigma of childlessness—a stigma that "can be just as devastating for African men as for African women."[71]

As Oduyoye puts it, in Africa, "one is never really a full and faithful person until one has a child." While this is the case in African traditional cultures, she suggests that Christianity, with its insistence on the biblical command to be fruitful and multiply (Gen. 1:28), has only reinforced it. When Oduyoye got little support from the church, she realized, as she put it, that "I therefore had to work things out for myself, believing that I am no less in the image of God because I have not biologically increased and multiplied." Reading her own life story in relation to the biblical stories of women like Hannah and Elizabeth, she came to understand that there are other ways of being fruitful, that is, of working "to enhance and enrich humanity."[72]

> For me, then, childlessness in the West African space has been a challenge—to my womanhood, my humanity, and my faith. To say that I have overcome would be sheer arrogance, for we live by grace, and it is by the grace of God that I am who I am. It is for the church to acknowledge and raise up the diversity of God's gift and to celebrate all the ways of bringing forth life. My concern is for a theology of procreation that responds to this challenge, a theology and eschatology that will speak to both those who reproduce themselves biologically and those who do not, a theology that embraces forms of fruitfulness, biological and beyond.[73]

Clearly, Oduyoye's quest for a new theology of procreation, centered on a broader notion of fruitfulness, is born of her own experience as a childless African woman struggling with sociocultural pressures and norms relating to gender and sexuality.

Oduyoye's autobiographical account is relevant here for a number of reasons. Her account is one of the most intimate examples we have of storytelling as a method in, and source of, African theology. Methodologically, it exemplifies how a personal life story can be read as a theological text, and how in African feminist theology, women's struggles with cultural norms and expectations regarding gender and sexuality are the starting point for a prophetic critique of such norms, and for creative theological reflection. I have suggested that *SOOL*—although, unlike Oduyoye's essay, not intended as a theological text per se—can be engaged theologically, especially because many of the stories explicitly use religious language and touch on theological themes. Analyzing that language and those themes is key to reconstructing narrative African queer theologies. In other words, storytelling is a critical method for the development of an African queer theology, just as it has been for African feminist theology.

Oduyoye's essay addresses a theme that also runs through *SOOL*: the concern with procreation and the related sociocultural pressure to marry and have children. The *SOOL* statement quoted earlier that "African women are raised from childhood to belong to a man and to children" echoes Oduyoye's experience; even her maternal great-uncle, who had always supported her in her studies and was proud of her professional career, was happy when she finally got married, because in his view "an Asante woman must get married and be the vehicle for the reincarnation of her ancestors."[74] Although none of the narrators in *SOOL* invoke the belief in ancestors that reinforces the need for procreation in the traditional religious and cultural worldview, some of them express the desire for children, as in this statement: "I want to have a baby, it is good to have someone who will carry on your lineage" (139). Clearly, in modern Kenya as well as traditionally, there is strong sociocultural pressure on both women and men to have children. Apparently, what Oduyoye calls "the child factor in Africa" affects not only heterosexual married women like herself but also queer people who see no choice but to live up to parental expectations and cultural obligations. Moreover, queer people may be subjected to physical force, as in the account of arranged rape, narrated by a male-identifying transgender person. "My mother wanted me to get with a man so she could have a grand-child. She went out and found a man who was a family friend, then forced me to have sex with him. I got pregnant. My best friend advised me to get an abortion. I said to myself, 'Even if I am trans, trans people also have babies.' So I gave birth to a baby girl" (140). While a lot of attention, especially in South Africa, has been paid to sexual violence against lesbians who are subjected to "corrective rape," this account of an equally traumatic experience draws attention to what could be called "procreative rape"—a form of rape primarily inspired not by homo- or transphobic motivation per se but by the sociocultural pressure to procreate, if not voluntarily, then by force. Both forms of sexual violence, as well as the dehumanization of childless women addressed by Oduyoye, are of course driven by similar patriarchal and heteronormative prejudices.

An intertextual reading of Oduyoye's account and *SOOL* points to common ground for feminist and queer politics in Africa. Oduyoye herself identified this common ground in the early 1990s, in an essay in which she presents a critique of leading African theologian John Mbiti from Kenya, specifically his book *Love and Marriage in Africa*. She takes issue with the way in which Mbiti uncritically reinforces the traditional view of marriage and procreation as defining one's humanity, and she denounces the implications of this view for women in general and childless women in particular, as well as for gay and lesbian people. Oduyoye claims to be "rather horrified by Mbiti's demonization of homosexuals and 'able bodied persons' who stay out of the dominant definition of marriage," which, she says, also characterizes the broader African context. "Homophobia," she writes, "like the phobia of childlessness, is understandable in Africa for it cuts at the roots of Africa's main reasons for sustaining the heterosexual marriage institution—children. Hence, as long as procreation is linked directly with immortality and with the remembering of one's forbears, I do not see a way out." Oduyoye sees no option but to intervene in what she calls "dominant heterosexual orthodoxy."[75] Although she does not develop this point in much detail, the direction in which she points is relevant for feminist and queer politics and theology in Africa today.

Since the logic of the "child factor" is based on the traditional African linkage of fruitfulness with immortality, Oduyoye proposes an alternative, broader notion of fruitfulness as enriching and contributing to humanity, which she expresses poetically:

> *Increase in humanity.*
> *Multiply the likeness of God for which you have the potential.*
> *Multiply the fullness of humanity that is found in Christ.*
> *Fill the earth with the glory of God.*
> *Increase in creativity.*
> *Bring into being that which God can look upon and pronounce "good," even "very good."*[76]

Such a theology—or "liberating eschatology," as Oduyoye calls it—of fruitfulness can affirm the humanity of both those who do and those who do not reproduce biologically, and it acknowledges that people, regardless of their sexual orientation, gender identity, or marital status, can be fruitful and reach "fullness of life" in many different ways. This, she suggests, is what theologians should help the church to understand. Both Oduyoye's feminist storytelling and the lgbt storytelling in *SOOL* thus represent a liberating eschatology based on a queer aesthetics that calls "the natural into question," as José Esteban Muñoz puts it.[77] "The natural" refers here to the normative idea of biological reproduction as the only or best way for human beings to be fruitful, a view challenged by queer storytelling, which emphasizes "the diversity of God's gifts," in Oduyoye's words.[78] Indeed, *SOOL* provides abundant evidence of the many ways in which queer people in Kenya and elsewhere in Africa enhance and enrich humanity.

QUEER WORLD-MAKING

Storytelling of the kind found in *SOOL* allows Kenyan queers to creatively reimagine their pasts, and to imagine their futures and dream of a world to come in which they can be who they are and live their lives to the fullest—storytelling is a form of what Muñoz calls "cruising utopia," as it looks toward the horizon of an African queer future. This queer world, constructed and imagined through stories, is a world of possibility: there are multiple ways of Kenyan queer sexual being, social being, religious being. The intersections of Kenyan, Christian, and queer identities, *SOOL* suggests, are manifold. Queer politics cannot be reduced to one normative notion of queerness but must find ways of allowing and enabling this multiplicity. And African theology must acknowledge the diversity among "ordinary Africans," including queer Africans, when it seeks to develop a "theology from below." It must take into account both the struggles and the aspirations of queer folk as narrated in *SOOL* and similar anthologies.

As a world-making process, storytelling is also a form of building community. As Jackson puts it, "Storytelling is a form of restorative praxis—of sharing one's experiences with others, of finding common ground, of coming out of the closet, of restoring one's place in the public sphere."[79] *SOOL* demonstrates how such common ground and common language are being explored and developed. Both within and through the stories, the contours of an emerging Kenyan queer community become visible.

INTERLUDE 3

Positive

This book has become deeply intertwined with the story of my life, and not just my life but my body, too. During the process of research and writing, I learned that I was infected with HIV. On the basis of the blood test results, the excellent staff at the Leeds Centre for Sexual Health were able to reconstruct the transmission history and give a close estimate of the infection date. I probably contracted the virus in South Africa, during my research fellowship at the Stellenbosch Institute for Advanced Study (STIAS) in the period April–June 2016. Halfway through that period, I was ill for about a week. It started over the weekend, and that Sunday I wrote on Facebook (as one does when feeling miserable): "To anyone who envies me for my travels abroad, I want you to know that this weekend I've just been feeling a little (home)sick, cold and lonely," with the hashtags #WhyKeepUpAppearances?, #MissingMyHubby, and #Tomorrow WillBeBetter. Instead of feeling better the next day, however, I felt even more unwell. It took three more days before I went to see a doctor, according to whose diagnosis I had tonsillitis, for which he prescribed penicillin. I had to cancel the seminar I was supposed to give at STIAS that week. One good friend—or shall I be honest and say lover?—came to see me in the evenings. His attention and care helped me feel better. Only the next weekend did I feel my energies coming back slowly. In retrospect, of course, I see that my sickness probably had little to do with inflamed tonsils. It must have been the phase of seroconversion—the period, usually one to three weeks after the initial infection, when the body starts to develop HIV antibodies, accompanied by heavy flulike symptoms.

As I say, in all likelihood I contracted HIV in South Africa, ten years after I visited the country for the first time as a visiting student at the University of KwaZulu-Natal. During that first visit, I took classes in the master's program on theology, HIV, and AIDS, and I conducted research for my dissertation on the reflections of three southern African feminist theologians on religion, gender, and HIV. I also encountered the realities of the HIV epidemic with my own eyes through exposure trips to community-based organizations, both in KwaZulu-Natal and in Swaziland (two regions most heavily affected by the pandemic, which around that time was at its peak).

I contracted HIV eight years after my first peer-reviewed article appeared in a South African theology journal. The subject of the essay was the work of African theologians who seek to overcome the silence and stigma surrounding the epidemic by creatively employing the classic theological metaphor of the church as the body of Christ, as reflected in their claim that the body of Christ today is HIV-positive.[1]

I contracted HIV on the African continent while working on a research project dealing with queer activism and politics in Africa. I had not intended HIV to be a major theme of this project, but it became one of the subthemes of the book, for it appeared to be relevant in each of the case studies: both Binyavanga Wainaina (chapter 1) and the producer of the "Same Love" video, George Barasa (chapter 2), are openly HIV-positive; some of the narratives in *Stories of Our Lives* are about the realities of HIV (chapter 3); and in the circle of Cosmopolitan Affirming Church, HIV is a topic of discussion (chapter 4).

Does it make a difference to my research and writing that I am now HIV-positive? Does it make a difference that the virus transmitted to me most probably came from a black African male body? Does it make a difference that I contracted the virus on the continent that has been central in my writing about gender, sexuality, and, indeed, HIV and AIDS since the beginning of my academic career? Does it make a difference that I contracted the virus while on a fellowship at a prestigious institute whose slogan is "a creative space for the mind," with its emphasis on academia as an intellectual and perhaps disembodied pursuit? Does it make a difference that I contracted the virus while staying in Stellenbosch, a beautiful but rather conservative town dominated by Cape Dutch architecture and populated by a mostly white, Afrikaans-speaking, and Dutch Reformed community, its public space still defined by the urban-planning legacy of apartheid—and also a town where the crossing of both racial and sexual boundaries appears to be transgressive?

Without being able to answer these questions definitively, what I did realize, more or less immediately, is that my HIV status is political. The classic feminist slogan that the personal is political certainly applies to a bodily infection by a virus that, almost four decades after its discovery, is still associated with moral taboo and surrounded by silence—simply because it is sexually transmitted. I have read enough about the power of stigma to know that the only way to overcome it is by breaking the taboo and the silence—by being open and honest and sharing one's story, if one has the necessary personal courage and social support. Thanks to the latter, I believe I have gained the former.

It was in the process of reading *Stories of Our Lives* and thinking about how to use these Kenyan queer life stories in this book that I realized that I could not leave out my own story. For the sake of academic honesty and integrity, I had no choice but to disclose my status and explain how it connects me to the African continent, its history of disease, and its role in the global pandemic. For the sake of reciprocity with the people I got to know while researching this book, who shared with me their struggles, their hopes, and their stories of love and desire, sex and relationships, disease and vulnerability, I have no choice but to share my own story.

Of course, I *do* have a choice—no writer, academic or otherwise, is obliged to disclose intimate revelations about his or her life and body. And, of course, when writing about my status here, I can choose my words carefully and reveal information selectively. The decision to disclose is motivated by the deep insight, beautifully, almost poetically, captured by Judith Butler when she writes, "Each of us is constituted politically in part by virtue of the social vulnerability of our bodies—as a site of desire and physical vulnerability, as a site of a publicity at once assertive and exposed."[2] I discovered the physical vulnerability of my body when even my commitment to practicing safe sex could not prevent transmission of the virus. I experienced the social vulnerability of my body when, immediately after receiving the test results, I confronted the unavoidable question: to disclose or not to disclose? Butler's insight stresses the importance of assertively claiming our bodies as sites of publicity, of turning vulnerability into strength. It also emphasizes the need to let our bodies speak truth about desire and love, even if this truth transgresses (as it often does) heteronormative standards of monogamy and so-called decent sexual behaviors.

Butler's account of bodily vulnerability and the precariousness of life as essential to what human beings have in common, and therefore as one basis of community and solidarity, reminds me of the Apostle Paul's message that in the body of Christ (as a theologically imagined community), when one member suffers, all members suffer together (1 Cor. 12:26). Several African theologians have used this concept to argue that if one member is HIV-positive, all members are positive. The South African theologian Tinyiko Maluleke has evoked the words of the prophetic anti-apartheid *Kairos Document* to argue that the HIV epidemic constitutes a new *kairos*—in the sense of both "crisis" and "moment of truth"—for the church in southern Africa and indeed for the whole world.[3] In some of my early academic work, I engaged this idea of the body of Christ being HIV-positive, reflecting upon its ethical, political, and theological consequences as a metaphor of solidarity in contemporary global Christianity and in a globalizing, postcolonial, yet fragmented world.[4] Employing postcolonial theorist Homi Bhabha's notion of interstice, I have suggested that the body of Christ can be considered an interstitial or intervening space, giving birth to "interstitial intimacy," that is, an "intimacy that questions binary divisions through which . . . spheres of social experience are often spatially opposed"—to begin with, the division between those who are HIV-positive and those who are not.[5] Call it ironic, but several years after writing about this, another embodied (not metaphorically this time but literally) form of intimacy has now inscribed me and my body into the history of HIV in Africa and globally.

I wish to share this part of the story of my life because it has become so intricately connected to the life stories and bodily histories of Africans who are living with the virus or who have died as a result of its disruption of their immune systems. I wish to share this part of the story of my body because it is now tied so closely to the many HIV-infected and affected bodies inhabiting this continent—some of whom I have come to know intimately, have had pleasure with, have made love to. Love at a cost. To paraphrase Achille Mbembe, quoted earlier in this book, what initially was a theoretical, rather abstract recognition "of the body and flesh of 'the stranger' as flesh and body just like mine"—"the stranger" in this case referring to black African HIV-infected bodies—has now become a very real, embodied reality as well.[6]

Thanks to the significantly increased accessibility to antiretroviral treatment in most parts of Africa, the face of the HIV epidemic on the continent and its impact on the lives of those who are infected have changed dramatically. Every year, fewer people are dying from AIDS in Africa, and instead they are living with HIV. From a medical perspective, the virus may constitute less of a crisis these days, yet the stigma surrounding it still makes the epidemic a "moment of truth," both in Africa and elsewhere. This piece of writing is my moment of truth—for myself and for the African queer bodies and lives I write about in this book.

Marcella Althaus-Reid has referred to queer theologies as necessarily being embodied, first-person, "self-disclosing, autobiographical" theologies.[7] In the previous chapter I demonstrated how such theologies can be read in Kenyan queer life stories. But that does not require any disclosure of myself. Thus, in this interlude, I am sharing the story of my own body, and I would suggest that from a theological perspective, the body of Christ opens up the space for such vulnerable, embodied, and sexual storytelling. To conclude with the words of the theologian Shawn Copeland, "the only body capable of taking us all in as we are with all our different body marks is the body of Christ."[8]

CHAPTER 4

Kenyan Queer Christian Community

During my first trip to Kenya, in 2015, when I told lgbt activists and community members about my research interests, several people mentioned a "gay church" in Nairobi. My interest was sparked immediately, and I began searching for more information. I managed to establish contact with one of the church's leaders and was soon invited to attend a service. On the appointed Sunday afternoon, I encountered a group of about twenty-five young people in the office space of an lgbt rights organization, where they had gathered for worship. From that first visit I was struck by the warm welcome, informal style, and intimate setting of the service, which stood in a stark contrast to the ecstatic mass worship of the Pentecostal megachurch in central Nairobi that I had attended that morning. I remember my surprise at the rather traditional, evangelical type of theology reflected in the sermon delivered by the guest preacher, which I had not expected in a "gay church."

Whereas the previous chapters of this book focus on written and visual texts, this one addresses what might be described as a social text. It is about a group of Nairobi-based lgbt people who make up a Christian faith community, and who along the way have developed common ritual practices, theological language, and ethical orientation. In the field of queer studies in religion, considerable attention has been paid to lgbt churches, most notably to the Universal Fellowship of Metropolitan Community Churches, founded in the United States in 1968; since then it has developed a global presence. In her sociological study of two MCC congregations in the United States, Melissa Wilcox argues that these churches not only create an affirming space for lgbt Christians but also help re-create the world. "The symbols and sources of community available at MCC," she writes, "literally construct a new world in which the combination of Christian belief with LGBT identity is not only normative but also highly valued."[1] Graeme Reid makes a similar argument in his study of a South African MCC congregation led by charismatic minister Tsietsi Thandekiso (now deceased). Not only does this church reject the charge that homosexuality is incompatible with African cultures and help members develop an integrated cultural identity for gay and lesbian Christians in an African context; by adopting Christian, mostly Pentecostal-influenced rhetoric, style, and rituals, the church also provides a counternarrative to the popular claim that homosexuality is "un-Christian."[2] Apart from South Africa, with its unique history in matters of lgbt rights and faith, there are a few Christian churches, ministries, and individual pastors in other African countries who welcome and affirm lgbt people of faith and defend lgbt rights, but no substantial study of them has been done to date.[3] This case study of Nairobi's Cosmopolitan Affirming Church (CAC) aims to help fill this gap by examining how an lgbt Christian space is being created in contemporary Kenya.

This chapter offers a thick description of CAC, in particular of the religious symbols and theological sources through which the church negotiates lgbt identities and Christian faith in the Kenyan context. It is based on ethnographic fieldwork that began in August 2015 and continued during later visits, in February, March, and December 2016 and July 2018. During these visits I attended weekly church services and other church meetings, hung out with congregants, and made notes on my observations and conversations. In addition to many informal conversations with church members and leaders, I also conducted formal interviews with eleven people involved in or connected to the church. Between and after these periods "in the field," I conducted long-distance fieldwork enabled by social media. Of particular importance were the CAC WhatsApp group, which I joined in January 2016 and through which I have followed CAC conversations since then, and Facebook, where many CAC members sent me friendship requests that I accepted. The WhatsApp group gave me insight into discussions about a range of CAC topics, while Facebook and its Messenger app facilitated personal communication.

The data thus collected are the basis for the account presented in this chapter. My reading of CAC as a social "text" is interspersed with references to queer studies and religious studies literature, specifically literature on lgbt forms of Christianity and African and queer theologies. These references inform my reading of CAC as a queer Kenyan Christian space, and of the church's African Christian queer world-making potential. In an effort to avoid an idealized, flat, or static account, I acknowledge that CAC, like queer spiritual spaces more generally, are "transitory, liminal, provisional, preposterous, fragile, strategic, mutable, contested, negotiable and multifarious," in the words of Sally Munt.[4] In other words, I aim to show how CAC is a Kenyan queer Christian space *in the making*. And while CAC is a Kenyan initiative, the chapter also looks at the transatlantic connection between the church and an African American Christian organization, and examines the emergence of a pan-African movement that is progressively mobilizing around sexuality.

INTRODUCING COSMOPOLITAN AFFIRMING CHURCH

CAC was founded in September 2013, and its first service was held that November. "The Cosmopolitan Affirming family was started by a group of young and ambitious people who believed in a just and a more inclusive society," a statement on its Facebook page begins. "These young folks [five names are given] had a great desire to serve a God of their understanding—the God of love and inclusion. With support, blessings and anointing from Pastor Joseph Tolton of the Fellowship of Affirming Ministries (TFAM), CAC as commonly known was born with five laity leaders."[5] This introduction emphasizes the role of the five founding members of CAC—stressing both their youth and their status as laypeople—while mentioning the support they received from an ordained pastor, the American bishop Joseph Tolton. The Facebook page refers to "numerous challenges" the leadership team experienced along the way and mentions that three of its founders—including George Barasa, the producer of the "Same Love" video discussed in chapter 2—have since moved on to "engagements elsewhere."[6]

In 2014, while still involved in CAC, Barasa posted the following message on his Facebook page on March 26: "Cosmopolitan Affirming Church invites you all to worship with us this Sunday. For location/direction contact me personally via my inbox. For comments/suggestion below this post. Affirm your sexuality/spirituality." This message found its way into the media, with one online media outlet writing: "SHOCKER!! GAY gospel artist JOJI BARO opens a GAY CHURCH in Nairobi. There is MASSIVE recruitment of Youths into his Church..... Read the SHOCKING details here!!!!!!!!!!!!!!!"[7] This exaggerated and sensationalist statement is a typical instance of the tendency of Kenyan popular media to broadcast moral panic about homosexuality, following a broader pattern in Africa and other parts of the world when it comes to homosexuality and gay rights.[8] The allegation that this "gay church" is recruiting youths promotes the hackneyed myth that homosexuality is a threat to the family and the future of the nation, exploiting the well-worn media strategy of representing children "as a particular locus of social vulnerability" to homosexual predators.[9] In this case, the panic is amplified by the religious dimension, the idea of a "gay church" being even more frightening to most Kenyans than homosexuality in general, and apt to be regarded by many as an oxymoron. Somewhat shaken, no doubt, by this kind of media attention, CAC has since then maintained a relatively low profile and has received little attention from the Kenyan media. Instead of promoting an active public presence, church leaders focus strategically on building relationships with Kenyan lgbt organizations and with other churches and Christian organizations. This does not mean that the church operates in secret, however: it does have an active and visible online presence through its Facebook page and, since 2018, a website that gives the full names—and photos—of the current leaders, and also Twitter and Instagram accounts.[10]

From its founding in 2013, CAC has slowly grown in numbers. There is no membership register, but when I first attended the church, on August 9, 2015, about twenty-five people were present. During my 2016 fieldwork, the number of congregants was higher, usually more than thirty and occasionally as many as fifty, which by July 2018 seemed to have stabilized at around thirty-five attendants at a typical service. In the three-year period of my fieldwork there was considerable turnover in the membership; beyond a small group of hardcore members, many people attend CAC for a relatively short period and then leave for various reasons: some do not feel at home spiritually, some find the Sunday commute too onerous, and others leave Nairobi for work or studies elsewhere. But their participation in CAC, however brief, can still be meaningful, helping them to rethink and possibly reconcile their sexuality and faith.

Since its beginning, CAC has made use of several venues. Relocation has been necessary because of growth but also because of concerns about safety and security. When I first visited in 2015 and during my fieldwork in early 2016, the church was using the office space of the National Gay and Lesbian Human Rights Commission (NGLHRC), located in a relatively safe, low-density area a thirty-minute walk from Nairobi's central business district. But this space had its limitations—primarily, members complained, its distance from downtown Nairobi. In addition, on Sundays when attendance was high, the room was too small, and people had to sit on the stairs or stand in the corridor. Midway through 2016, CAC started renting a room in a commercial property in the business district, where they continue to worship. This location can be seen as both strategic and prophetic: in the midst of the buzz of downtown Nairobi, with all the noise of traffic, street vendors and street preachers, churches and mosques, there is also a gathering of lgbt Christians who meet to pray and praise their God, read and interpret the Bible, discuss matters of sexuality and faith, and share their life experiences. Their presence anticipates "the city yet to come," a city with freedom not only for the expression of religion but also for diverse sexualities.[11] In that sense, the weekly gatherings of CAC clearly present one of the "countervailing tendencies" and "dissonant times" typical of contemporary African urban worlds.[12]

Becoming a Church

An important milestone in the short history of CAC was the official installation of the three current leaders—two male, one female—in church ministry, on September 13, 2015. The leaders were anointed with oil and blessed by Bishop Tolton, after which they were vested with a stole. One of them was named lead minister, as he is most senior in age and has been involved in CAC from the beginning. Although it was emphasized that the installation ceremony should not be understood as an "ordination" but as an "elevation" into leadership and ministry,[13] its significance is illustrated by the use of a photo of this highly symbolic moment as the cover image on the church's Facebook page for quite some time. In 2018, a minister in training (male) was added to the leadership team. The elevation of ministers did not satisfy the Kenyan government's criteria for the registration of religious societies, but in 2018 CAC managed to register as a community-based organization instead, under the name Cosmopolitan Affirming Community. This added a cloak of legality to the organization and gave members more confidence in its statutory structures.[14]

Another important event was the first *kesha*, a prayer night typical of Pentecostal churches, that took place on January 29–30, 2016; other *keshas* have been held occasionally since then. In addition to prayer and worship, the first *kesha* included scripture readings, preaching, a motivational talk, encouragement from a prophetess, a dialogue on the so-called clobber passages (the texts in the Bible often used to argue against homosexuality), comedy and dance, and a "CAC Live" show (about which more below). The program concluded with a dance session called "dancing for Jesus." In the days leading up to the *kesha*, excitement in the WhatsApp group mounted. Members posted messages such as, "I won't miss this night of reunion with the Lord!" and "We are hours away from the divine intervention of the Holy Spirit into our lives." That these expectations were not too high was confirmed by the conversations in the group the day after the *kesha*, in which members testified that they had been touched and blessed, interpreting this as a sign that as a church, "this year we are going far." Whereas the installation of three lay leaders as ministers confirmed the formal character of CAC as a church, the *kesha* confirmed the spiritual nature of CAC, its ability to provide the religious experience and spiritual empowerment that are so important in popular forms of Christianity in Kenya.

What's in a Name?

The name Cosmopolitan Affirming Church helps us understand the mission and vision of the church. The meaning of "affirming" becomes clear from the church's Facebook page, which states, "The church affirms the Christian beliefs of faith and love, spirituality, community and prayer. It encourages all people from different backgrounds to worship together in the interfaith world regardless of state, economic status, gender or sexual orientation/preference." So "affirming" refers primarily to beliefs that are considered essential tenets of Christianity, listed here in a very general way, without any attempt at doctrinal precision. The implicit suggestion is that these beliefs entail and instill a sense of equality and unity, a fundamental commonality that transcends social position and identity, including sexual and gender identity. That is, it is not lgbt identities as such that are being affirmed, but the Christian belief in the equality of all human beings regardless of their sexual orientation or gender expression, which are thus affirmed indirectly.

It is striking that the word *interfaith* is used, for this suggests that CAC offers a space for interfaith worship, welcoming people from both Christian and non-Christian backgrounds, while simultaneously upholding "Christian beliefs," spreading "the gospel of Jesus Christ" and being "the body of Christ," exclusively Christian language and imagery. This emphasis on Christianity is apparent not only in the statement but also in CAC's worship and preaching. George Barasa, one of CAC's founders, explained that CAC was intended to be open to non-Christian believers—he specifically mentioned Kenyan lgbt activists and community allies who are Muslims and atheists, along with Ugandan lgbt refugees, some of whom are Muslims—and to "take care of their spiritual needs."[15] Other church leaders confirmed that several people from other or no faiths have been involved in CAC. Such participation is further enabled by the relatively open and informal structures of the church, e.g., the absence of a formal membership register, and by the fact that CAC is as much a social as a religious space. One participant who considered himself part of CAC, for instance, told me that he is "spiritual but not religious"; although he was baptized in the Anglican Church, he no longer considered himself a Christian. During Sunday services, he tended to walk out when the sermon began, as he had "had enough of preaching" and preferred to explore matters of spiritual truth on his own.[16] CAC's claim of openness to non-Christian believers notwithstanding, I found that the practice of worship and preaching reflected the assumption that attendants share a commitment to the Christian faith. I saw no attempt to make CAC an explicitly interreligious space, or any explicit gesture of inclusion toward people from other or no faith traditions, apart from the general statement that "all are welcome" and invited to "interact with the God of your understanding." It may be that in the few years of its existence, CAC has evolved from a faith-based support group for lgbt people into an lgbt-affirming Christian faith community.

The word *cosmopolitan,* according to one of the ministers, denotes "the unity in the belief in . . . the God of love despite our differences in denominational backgrounds, religious beliefs and practices, ways of worship or even country of origin."[17] This unity, he explained, is informed by the exclusion and discrimination that CAC members experienced in their previous "faith spaces," after which they had to rediscover and reclaim "the God of love." Thus *cosmopolitan,* in the CAC context, appears to be synonymous with *ecumenical,* indicating a sense of Christian unity that transcends confessional differences. Indeed, church members come from a wide range of denominational backgrounds, among them Anglican, Catholic, Presbyterian, Seventh Day Adventist, and Pentecostal. Yet the term *cosmopolitan* comes from a particular discourse (of cosmopolitanism) that has a broader scope than the religious field. As a political and philosophical term, it refers to a particular understanding of the world, and of humankind, as being united, and it inspires a particular kind of political engagement. According to Kwame Anthony Appiah, cosmopolitanism is buttressed by two intertwined concepts, the first being the idea that we have obligations to others—obligations beyond the ties of kinship or shared citizenship—and the second being that "we take seriously the value not just of human life, but of particular human lives, which means taking an interest in the practices and beliefs that lend them significance."[18] The meaning of *cosmopolitan* in the context of CAC reflects the latter notion in particular: lgbt human lives matter, and so do the faith practices and beliefs that lend these lives significance.

The Congregation

Demographically, the congregation is relatively young. At the time of my 2016 fieldwork, the youngest member was eighteen years old, while the oldest were in their mid- to late thirties; the majority were in their midtwenties. There was a clear gender imbalance, with about two-thirds of the congregation being male. Concerned about this, the leadership was working on getting more women involved in the church, with limited success. One apparent obstacle was that many potential female members wanted CAC to be less of a "churchlike" space and preferred more informal and conversational gatherings to formal worship with preaching.[19]

Some of the male members clearly enjoyed performing a certain level of gender fluidity and ambiguity, using the church as a safe space for cross-dressing. This was most evident in the drag-queen contest I observed during the Sunday service on February 21, 2016. This contest was introduced by the presenter as a way to address and challenge transphobia in the community—"community" referring to both the church and the wider Kenyan lgbt community. The contestants were frequently referred to as "transgenders," which may reflect a conflation of transgenderism with cross-dressing. Apart from this contest, several congregants I interviewed said things like, "I look like a man, but inside I feel more like a woman."[20] With one exception, however, they did not identify with the "transgender" label but tended to describe themselves as "a feminine gay man" or "a bottom." I overheard one heated discussion in which a congregant argued that CAC should not refer to itself as an lgbti community because, in his words, "we have no bisexuals, we have no transgenders, we have no intersex"—to which someone else responded, "eheh, you don't know!" For the purpose of this study, I am not interested in the exact representation at CAC of the various categories under the lgbti umbrella (these categories themselves are far from stable identifiers, as discussed in chapter 3). What matters is that the congregation has a queer makeup, with a substantial number of members dressing and performing bodily gestures in ways that are considered nonnormative and transgressive in Kenya, in styles that can be described in such terms as "effeminate gay," "butch lesbian," or "gender fluid."

As noted above, members come from a wide range of denominational backgrounds. Some still attend other churches in the morning and come to CAC afterward, while CAC has become the primary congregation for others. Congregants gave different reasons for their continued involvement in other churches. Some still live with their families and are expected to attend church with family members on Sunday mornings. Others felt that CAC, as much as they appreciated it, did not satisfy all their spiritual needs. For Pentecostals, this sense of lack typically related to the experience of ecstatic worship and charismatic practices such as deliverance that are common in Pentecostal churches. Catholics were likely to attend Mass, because receiving the Eucharist was essential to their understanding of Christian life. At the same time, these people did not want to miss CAC services, because, as one of them explained, "here I feel comfortable the way I am."[21] Yet these diverse denominational backgrounds also mean that people come to CAC with differing expectations of worship style, and CAC leaders sometimes struggle to satisfy everyone's preferences.[22]

With regard to socioeconomic background, the congregation is diverse. A majority have a relatively low level of education and professional training; they typically live in the slums on the outskirts of Nairobi, trying to make money in the informal sector, as most other Kenyans do. Some of them engage in sex work, incidentally or structurally, as a way to make ends meet. As one of the church members told me, "Life is so hard here, especially as time reaches when you are dry: no soap, no cooking oil, bills at the shop are increasing day and night, you get stressed all over. The only option you feel is to admit for a guy who could be your father to fuck you and at least give you, like, a thousand shilling. It really hurts and life damages on my heart."[23] A smaller number of congregants come from Kenya's middle classes and have more resources. They have typically attended high school and are now studying for academic or professional degrees, or, in a few cases, have secured formal employment. These differences in socioeconomic background are visible in CAC services, some members being smartly dressed while others lack the means to afford new clothes and fashion items (though they often manage to take care of their appearance). The church has long been planning economic-empowerment projects for its most disadvantaged members; with support from the Open Society Initiative for Eastern Africa in 2018, it opened an Arts and Beauty Shop in Eastlands, Nairobi, aiming to provide "craft skills and employment" for some members (unfortunately, running the shop turned out to be difficult, and it closed after a couple of months).

Ethnicity is an important, and often a divisive, factor in Kenyan society, but among the urban youth who attend CAC it does not appear to be a major issue. In the church's WhatsApp group, one will occasionally find a joke about the Kikuyu or Luo people, the main rival groups in Kenyan society. More frequently, though, in the group and in the church itself, there is emphasis on the need to end "tribalism" in Kenya, as in this post of June 6, 2016, written after a violent incident in Nairobi: "Dear Kenyans let's stand together and say NO to tribal violence and let's be one because nowadays a young Kikuyu guy is marrying a Luo girl, and the trend continues; it's only the big [people] out there who are fighting, but some of our youths are busy loving one another." CAC members told me that the shared experience of homophobia creates a sense of solidarity within the lgbt community that transcends ethnic background, though one of the ministers expressed his disappointment that, in spite of the church leadership's insistence on voting on the basis of policy and political ideology, CAC members appeared to vote in Kenya's 2017 elections mostly along ethnic lines.[24]

Owing to the participation of a considerable number of Ugandan lgbt refugees in CAC, nationality also appeared to be relevant. Since the introduction of Uganda's Anti-Homosexuality Bill in 2009 and the subsequent outburst of sociopolitical homophobia in the country, a significant number of Ugandan lgbt people have moved to Kenya. But their situation in Kenya is very precarious, as they are "enduring living conditions harsher than they might have imagined."[25] They face many challenges, for they are not allowed to work, struggle to make ends meet, and fear harassment from the police. On top of that, they do not find the Nairobi lgbt community particularly welcoming or supportive. As one of them told me, "There is the thing of Uganda-Kenya. The lgbti [people] in Kenya don't want you, the Ugandan lgbti, they don't associate with you, so you find that there is the thing of hatred."[26] Against this background, it is particularly significant that a group of Ugandan refugees had found their way to CAC and had been welcomed there. As CAC states on its Facebook page, "Cosmopolitan Affirming Church family opened wide its doors and provided a safe space for the refugees, many of whom were yearning for spiritual nourishment."

At the time of my 2016 fieldwork, "the Ugandans," as they were called, sometimes made up almost half the congregation during Sunday services. They were actively involved in running the church and had taken particular responsibility for worship. Although CAC advertises itself as providing "a safe space" for the refugees, the presence of a large contingent of Ugandans also appeared to cause tensions. Some Kenyan members felt that the church had been "taken over" by Ugandans. With the choir at times consisting mainly of Ugandans, some Kenyan church members complained about songs in the Luganda language. Some of the Ugandan members, for their part, expressed disappointment that the church did not provide them sufficient financial or practical support. These tensions exemplify one area in which CAC is a queer community still in the making. By 2018, few Ugandans remained in CAC; the most active Ugandan members had resettled in other countries, while others lived too far out of Nairobi to travel into the city for church on Sunday.

Even so, CAC maintained a relationship with the Nature Network, a Ugandan refugee group in Nairobi. On February 27, 2016, I was invited to attend the launch of the network, together with CAC ministers, and on July 29, 2018, I joined CAC during a joint worship service with the Nature Network in Matasia, on the outskirts of Nairobi. Looking back at the period during which CAC provided a shelter for Ugandan refugees, Minister Moses said that the church had proved its "right to exist"; it was one of the few lgbt organization in Kenya that welcomed them.[27]

THE AFRICAN AMERICAN CONNECTION

As noted above, Bishop Joseph Tolton is an African American pastor working with an organization called The Fellowship of Affirming Ministries (TFAM), where he is in charge of global ministries. TFAM has been described by Ellen Lewin, in the subtitle of her book about the organization, as a "black Pentecostal church coalition" centered on the idea of "radical inclusivity."[28] Indeed, the organization presents itself as "a multi-denominational group of primarily African American Christian leaders and laity" working "to support religious leaders and laity in moving toward a theology of radical inclusivity which, by its very nature, requires an equally radical social ministry reaching to the furthest margins of society to serve all in need without prejudice or discrimination."[29] The organization was founded, and is led to date, by Reverend Yvette Flunder, an openly lesbian African American pastor on the front lines of the fight for lgbt rights in the United States, especially in the black church.[30] Flunder, like Tolton, has deep roots in the black Pentecostal tradition—roots that both ministers combine with a commitment to social justice inspired by liberation theology. They specifically apply this commitment to the area of sexuality. Thus TFAM addresses the difficulty of reconciling "spiritual[ity], social justice, and political views about the place of gays and lesbians in the black community and in church life."[31] Moreover, its commitment to work in this area inspired a transatlantic crossing, an extension of TFAM's work to Africa.

As part of her ministry, Flunder became involved in addressing issues related to HIV and AIDS, first in the black community in the United States and later also in Africa, beginning in Zimbabwe. This was the origin of an Africa-focused ministry that expanded in 2009, when the Anti-Homosexuality Bill was introduced in the Ugandan Parliament. At the same time, Tolton got involved in the work of TFAM, embarking on a pro-lgbt Christian mission in Uganda and soon also in other African countries. Under the name The Fellowship Global (TFG), Tolton runs several programs that promote social justice and contribute to building an inclusive pan-African Christian faith movement. This vision is captured in rhetoric that combines the typical Pentecostal language of religious revival with progressive theological language of social justice and inclusivity, and which refers to Christianity, African traditions, and black history as key resources. "As heirs of the civil rights movement, African spirituality, Christian traditions, and prophetic witness," says its website, "we have a vision for a radically inclusive revival to usher in a new era of social justice."[32] One of TFG's programs is called the United Coalition of Affirming Africans (UCAA), which is active in Kenya, Rwanda, Uganda, and the Democratic Republic of the Congo, where it builds partnerships with local Christian clergy, supports faith-based lgbt advocacy, and provides theological training.

During a visit to Kenya in 2013, Tolton met with members of the Kenyan lgbt community, and the idea was born to start an inclusive church. With the moral, spiritual, and financial support of TFG, Cosmopolitan Affirming Church was established. Tolton visits Kenya several times a year to meet with the CAC leadership team, giving them theological training and guidance on the running and growth of the church. During these visits he also usually preaches at CAC and administers Holy Communion. Countering the possible criticism that CAC is an American-driven initiative, Tolton downplayed his own role by emphasizing that he had led no more than eight to ten Sunday services over two years, concluding, "So it's not me, it's the people on the ground who are running their church. God has given leaders on the ground to make it happen."[33] The CAC ministers, however, acknowledge the important role Tolton has played to date, both financially and in terms of providing moral, spiritual, and theological mentorship. He is also very popular among the members, who see in him a spiritual father figure as well as an inspiring and powerful preacher. Whenever Tolton preaches, CAC members typically post messages in the WhatsApp group, like these from February 14 and April 17, 2016: "the sermon was so touching . . . the bishop was on fire," "I feel so blessed by the word of today, thanks to the bishop."

TFAM activities in Africa are framed by TFG as an intervention in "the global economy of Christianity."[34] In TFG's understanding, the recent sociopolitical homophobia in various African countries is primarily the result of the active involvement and leadership of conservative American evangelicals. Having lost the "culture wars" over same-sex marriage and lgbt rights back home, these evangelicals are alleged to have shifted the focus of their political energies to Africa, making this continent the new battleground.[35] According to TFG, "colonialist laws and missionary mentalities have become the springboard for the export of homophobia by US-based Evangelicals like Scott Lively and Rick Warren."[36] Thus, explaining God's call to Bishop Flunder to intervene in the controversy around Uganda's Anti-Homosexuality Bill, Tolton invoked the typical Pentecostal trope of God's speaking directly to us: "It was during the crisis in Uganda in 2009 that the Lord spoke to her [Flunder] about the need for African Americans to be a part of that response, because Americans were implicated by the Ugandan bill because it was American money that supported the bill, and it was Americans who actually helped to design it."[37] Similarly, a TFG press release about Tolton's visit to several African countries in 2015 framed this tour as an attempt to "counteract" evangelical Christian antigay politics in Africa: "As black gay Christians who identify with Pentecostal worship and as people of social justice, we are countering the work of conservative, mostly white American evangelicals who are doubling down on their attempt of spiritual colonization of Africa."[38] This statement adds an explicitly racial dimension to the argument about U.S. conservatives' exportation of American culture wars. The culture wars are framed not just as a clash between American conservative and progressive Christians, but between *white* conservative evangelicals and *black* progressive Christians. The statement also implies a link between black American Pentecostalism and a radical gospel of social justice, contrasting it with white evangelicalism, which it links to a colonizing agenda.

Elaborating on the notion of spiritual colonization, Tolton described American evangelical theology as "dominionist"—as wanting to "conquer the world for Christ"—and referred to the Ugandan Anti-Homosexuality Act as a primary example of this.[39] In his opinion, American evangelicals have set their sights on Africa because they know that it is decisive for the future of Christianity. The TFG statement quotes the prominent American evangelical pastor Rick Warren as saying, "The future of Christianity is not Europe or North America, but Africa, Asia, and Latin America." Andrew Walls has made this point more eloquently, observing that African Christianity has become "a major component of contemporary representative Christianity, the standard Christianity of the present age, a demonstration model of its character," and arguing that it is even "potentially the representative Christianity of the twenty-first century."[40] This truth, which is reflected in the demographic shift in world Christianity and the rapidly growing number of Christians in Africa, is acknowledged not only by Warren and his evangelical compatriots but also by TFAM—and it motivates both sides to engage in a battle for the soul of Christianity in Africa. In Tolton's words, "there are two strains that are flowing throughout Christendom right now. We call one 'dominionism' and one 'discipleship.'"[41] Obviously, he associates TFAM and TFG with the latter, that is, with practicing discipleship through following Jesus and his radically inclusive ministry. This is the understanding of the Christian faith that TFG seeks to promote, laying the "groundwork for a pan African progressive Christian movement."[42] "We're very interested in a 'discipleship' strain of Christianity," Tolton continues, "the inclusive message of the Christ really becoming the dominant strain of Christianity. Because whatever strain of Christianity Africa embraces over the next fifty to a hundred years will be what Christendom is known as in the world, because this is the place where it will be defined."[43] The progressive and inclusive form of Christianity that TFAM seeks to promote is not only concerned with issues of sexual and gender diversity but has a broader sociopolitical agenda that addresses Africa's economic, social, and health concerns. The organization claims to have an "inter-sectional perspective of structural social change" that "pro-actively connects the LGBTI experience in Africa with the totality of the human experience in Africa."[44] This perspective is TFAM's response to the perceived link between American evangelicals' opposition to homosexuality and lgbt rights and their support of neoliberal socioeconomic policies. Pointing out that capitalism is inherently connected to patriarchy, homophobia, and racism, Tolton argues that both African Americans in the United States and lgbt people in Africa are the victims of the social, economic, and political agenda driven by American evangelicals of European descent. That they have "a common oppressor," he says, should motivate African Americans, and American lgbt people of color in particular, to support TFAM's work in Africa. In Tolton's vision, TFAM is spearheading a global queer movement with a radical political agenda, aiming to bring about "a fundamental structural change in how humanity understands itself . . . and ultimately undoing an unjust capitalist system that is deeply connected to, married to patriarchy."[45] TFAM's sociopolitical stance is consistent with the emerging discourse of African queer politics. For example, the African LGBTI Manifesto, which emerged from a roundtable session of African lgbti activists held in Nairobi in 2010, explicitly calls for an "African revolution" that liberates the continent and its people from centuries of political and economic oppression, and it underlines the need for justice and self-determination "at all levels of our sexual, social, political and economic lives."[46] Along the same lines, Sokari Ekine and Hakima

Abbas define the African queer political agenda as opposed to "oppressive hetero-patriarchal-capitalist frameworks," thus underlining the interconnections between capitalism, patriarchy, and heteronormativity.[47]

Observing that "there is not a tremendous African-American presence in Africa," TFAM believes that the current wave of sociopolitical homophobia in Africa provides African Americans with a new pan-African moment, that is, an opportunity to become engaged with the continent and people of Africa.[48] Whereas slavery, colonialism, and current socioeconomic policies have deliberately sought to divide the people of Africa and the diaspora, TFAM envisions a reengagement of African Americans and Africans on the continent, one that will be empowering for both and will pose a serious threat to the current economic system, which only serves the interests of American and African elites. Opposing the "dominionist Christianity" that is deeply invested in this system, TFAM seeks to ignite "a grassroots movement with a progressive faith frame"[49] that will bring about "a radically inclusive revival [and] usher in a new era of social justice."[50]

TFAM and TFG's vision of reshaping the global economy of Christianity provides the context for CAC's central role in a nascent pan-African movement that seeks to transform African Christianity. Indeed, the CAC's lead minister, together with Bishop Tolton, frequently convenes workshops for other religious leaders in Kenya and the wider East African region to promote an inclusive understanding of the Christian faith. Skeptical observers may view CAC, a small, lgbt-affirming church, as insignificant, but its members and allies see it as the beginning of something new and radical, with the potential to change the future of Christianity in Kenya and on the African continent.

MAKING A QUEER FAMILY

Given the diverse denominational, ethnic, and socioeconomic backgrounds of the CAC congregation, how does this group of people form a community, and what is the nature of this community? Obviously, CAC is a faith community, and the Sunday worship service is at the heart of congregational life. But the Sunday service is also a social event. The small size of the congregation and the informal style of the service allow members to catch up with one another before and after (and even during) the service. Some people arrive quite late, apparently more interested in the refreshments served after the service, yet, as one of the ministers told me, "at least they receive a blessing, and people come to Jesus in many different ways—if it is through a cup of tea, they come to Jesus through tea."[51] Occasionally, Sunday worship is replaced by a social gathering—one Sunday during my fieldwork there was a hike in the hills on the outskirts of Nairobi, and on two other Sundays members of CAC met for prayer and a picnic in Uhuru Park and at the Nairobi Arboretum, respectively. These social outings strengthen the bonds within CAC, and also build relationships with other lgbt activists and community members, who are invited to join. During the arboretum gathering, which had been organized by non-CAC members, tensions arose when a CAC minister, in a short speech, made an explicit reference to the centrality of religious faith at CAC, which led some of the non-CAC folks present to express discomfort and claim to feel excluded. This incident illustrates what can be called CAC's double marginalization: it is obviously marginalized by other Christian churches, which reject its affirmation of lgbt people and their rights, but it is also stigmatized in some lgbt activist circles for being a Christian church. Having learned by hard experience that institutional religion is no friend of theirs, many activists have adopted a negative attitude toward religion and faith and consequently also sometimes treat CAC with suspicion. CAC leaders told me of the difficulties they've encountered in attempts to collaborate with other Kenyan lgbt organizations, which tend to be less than welcoming to explicitly faith-based groups.[52]

Church as Family

As far as CAC's social and spiritual bonds are concerned, it is significant that members often refer to the church as a "family." The Facebook group uses the name "Cosmopolitan Affirming Family," and the church's WhatsApp group is called "CAC Family." Conversations within the group typically start with salutations like "Good morning, family," "Hello, family," or "Evening, family," and they often end with "Good night, family" or "God bless you all, dear family." The familial language, also used during church services, appears to be informed by the feeling of many members that CAC provides them with an "alternative family."[53] This sense of family is particularly important in light of members' common experience of being ostracized by their families and by society more generally—in the case of the Ugandan refugees, to the heartbreaking extent that they had to leave their home country. It is no surprise that finding a social and spiritual home in CAC would come as a relief and be felt as a great blessing. Even members who still had relatively good relationships with their parents or siblings told me that CAC is where they really feel at home, because they can freely express their queer selves there. As such, the church embodies alternative queer community-making expressed in terms of kinship, a process captured by one narrator in *Stories of Our Lives* (see chapter 3) as follows: "I'm seeing gay people forming stronger bonds amongst themselves than they have with their families. Friends are becoming the new family."[54] CAC, in other words, becomes a family of choice, on the basis of a common nonnormative sexuality or, better, on the basis of the common experience of being marginalized because of sexual orientation. The notion of the church as family also "reaffirms the moral wrongness" of the rejection that many members have experienced in their biological families.[55] In rare cases where biological family and church family overlap—such as on a Sunday when the mother of one of the members came to a CAC worship service—this is collectively celebrated as a unique and very special occasion.

CAC is an alternative family not only on the basis of sexual orientation but also on the basis of faith. One of the ministers, explaining why the church's WhatsApp group is called "CAC Family," emphasized this point. "For us," he wrote to the group on September 22, 2016, "as people of the same gender loving orientation and Christians for that matter, we are not united by the people we are attracted to, [by] our circumstances, or by family blood, but we are united by the DNA of Christ and his blood that was shed on Calvary." One might read this as a statement that the basis of community in CAC is narrow and exclusive, limited to those who hold a particular view of Christ's salvific role in humankind's redemption. But, as we have seen, CAC's congregants come from a wide range of Christian denominations—and some do not even identify as Christian—and the concept of faith at CAC is not exclusive but explicitly aspires to offer a radical, all-embracing welcome and to reflect the open and inclusive model of what in African cultures is often referred to as the "extended family."[56] The basis of queer community and kinship at CAC is the belief that "God's desire is [for] us to be a family" in which "there are no outsiders [but] all are insiders," because God is "the God of love and inclusion."[57] Thus CAC takes seriously the conviction that the Christian faith, in the words of Elizabeth Stuart, puts the church "under a direct mandate to be queer" in a radical sense.[58] Theologically speaking, CAC is a community not on the basis of individual choice or preference but on the basis of God's choice for humankind—in all its diversity—through creation and redemption. At CAC this mandate is upheld by the practice of welcoming people from different ethnic groups and nationalities, different class and religious backgrounds, and offering them refuge, unity, and affirmation. Living out this commitment in practice, of course, is not without tensions, some of which I observed myself, between Kenyan and Ugandan members, members of different ethnic groups, members who are relatively well off and those who are not, members with a more conforming and those with a more transgressive gender performance, and so on. Queer community, like any human community, is never fully achieved but is always a work in progress—progress that, speaking theologically, takes place against and is motivated by an "eschatological horizon," as I discuss below in more detail.[59]

Family of God

The faith-based notion of being family "in God" echoes a line of thinking about the church that is quite popular in African theology, especially in Catholic circles, where the church is commonly referred to as the "family of God."[60] Partly, this ecclesiology has developed out of the idea that the family metaphor is culturally appealing given the importance of family life in African contexts. Yet the metaphor is also considered meaningful in light of the social crises that affect contemporary African society, ranging from ethnic conflict and political instability to poverty, disease, and inequality. Pope John Paul II referred to the "gross violations of human dignity and rights" in many African countries when he said, "The Church as the Family of God in Africa must bear witness to Christ also by promoting justice and peace on the Continent and throughout the world. . . . In what concerns the promotion of justice and especially the defence of fundamental human rights, the Church's apostolate cannot be improvised."[61] The pope's statement notwithstanding, many lgbt people feel that the Catholic Church, like most other churches, has in fact improvised on the defense of human dignity and rights. This is what motivated the CAC founders to establish their own church, which was intended to be a radically inclusive family.

The notion of the church as family or household of God has also been embraced by African women theologians. In Mercy Oduyoye's words, this idea implies that "all human beings are the people of God. They belong to God's household housed on this planet and around God in the unseen realms. All of creation is cared for by God, the source of our being." On that basis, Oduyoye critiques church practices and structures that marginalize women and fail to acknowledge the unity and equality of humanity, and she expresses the hope "that God will liberate the church from gender dualism and make all real participants in this household of God." She suggests that women's organizations in the church can be seen as an anticipation of this reality, as church women affirm and nurture one another and "create for themselves a church within the Church."[62] CAC can also be seen as a "church within the Church," created by lgbt people of faith to affirm and nurture one another, while anticipating, hoping for, and working toward the liberation of the church as a whole from homophobia and heteronormativity. Spaces such as CAC thus have great symbolic and political importance, however small, and therefore perhaps seemingly insignificant, they may be. As Ashon Crawley points out with regard to black queer-affirming churches in the United States, "the point of the work was to create the space of possibility" and to show that "alternatives exist—*already*—against the normative modes under which we endure."[63] CAC offers just such a space of possibility, vis-à-vis both other Kenyan Christian churches and the Kenyan lgbt community, in its demonstration that a positive relationship between lgbt identities and Christian faith is possible.

PERFORMING QUEER WORSHIP

How, then, do CAC's Sunday worship services create such a space of possibility? Making use of a multipurpose space in a building that does not look like a typical church, CAC members endeavor every Sunday to make the space a sacred place. They don't do this by using traditional liturgical objects, which are practically absent at CAC services. There are no candles, altar cloths, or crucifixes, reinforcing the church's overall evangelical Protestant orientation. When the NGLHRC office was used for Sunday services, the "liturgical center"—a small space at the front of the room, around which white plastic garden chairs were arranged—featured only a small wooden table, where the worship leader and preacher put their Bible and notes. After moving to the premises in the central business district, the table was replaced by a lectern used for announcements, prayer, and preaching.

Before the sermon, the acting minister dons a liturgical stole over his or her casual dress. One member from a Catholic background told me how important this is to him for the making of sacred space: "I love when I see the leaders wear the stole, which also we do in the Catholic Church. It makes me feel like I'm in church."[64] Particularly significant, of course, is the fact that an lgbt-identifying person wears the stole. This liturgical vestment not only demonstrates the general truth that an "important locus of symbolism in Christian ritual is the leader"; in the context of an lgbt church, such decoration also "symbolically confers sacred status on a lesbian, gay, bisexual, or transgender body," and thus expresses God's acceptance of lgbt people more generally.[65]

The stole is the only traditional liturgical vestment used at CAC; more central to the sacralization of space is a discursive practice, often a prayer, in which the space is declared "not just an office, not just a house, but a meeting place to encounter you, oh Lord," as one of the CAC ministers put it during a service I attended in February 2016. That such statements are made several times during a typical service, and are repeated in one way or another almost every week, shows that the sacred nature of the space cannot be taken for granted but must be affirmed time and again. Frequently, such declarations come with a call upon the congregation to behave accordingly, that is, not to use their mobile phones or to walk in and out of the room during the service.

While sacred space-making is mostly discursive, one interesting material aspect deserves mention: the decoration of the place of worship. At NGLHRC, the windows of the room were dressed with rainbow-colored curtains. This is not surprising, given that it is the office space of an lgbt rights organization and that the rainbow is the international symbol of the lgbt movement. But the rainbow is also a biblical symbol referring to God's covenant with all creation. During Sunday worship, more than during the use of the office space on weekdays, both aspects of the rainbow symbol came to prominence, the twofold meaning being naturally integrated and the rainbow curtains symbolically expressing a strong sense of lgbt pride in the eyes of God. The main blind wall of the NGLHRC office space was painted red and had been decorated with human handprints of various sizes and in various colors, symbolizing diversity and solidarity. Furthermore, the office was decorated with a number of handcrafted African art objects, including a carved wooden statue of an ancestral figure that stood in the window with the rainbow curtains. This gave the space an African cultural touch, seamlessly and meaningfully combined with the global lgbt symbol. During Sunday worship, the statue also subtly represented indigenous religious culture in an otherwise Christian setting.

At the new premises in downtown Nairobi, a rainbow curtain continued to decorate the room, but without African art. The curtain, which was carefully hung on the wall prior to the service, served as "a potent reminder and a symbolic celebration" of the congregation's lgbt identity.[66] Adding a decorative expression of African identity or indigenous spirituality was apparently not considered a priority. Indeed, the recognition of African indigenous spirituality appeared to be controversial. In December 2016 I took part with other CAC members in a video conference with TFAM delegates in the United States, presided over by Bishop Tolton. The conference was opened not only with Christian prayer but also with a libation ritual for the ancestors, reflecting TFAM's claim of being heirs of both "African spirituality" and "Christian traditions."[67] After the meeting, I overheard several CAC members expressing their disapproval of this practice, using loaded words such as "animistic." One of the CAC ministers told me later that, inspired by the observation of a similar TFAM ritual at a previous meeting, he had once proposed that CAC pour libations to the ancestors during services—a proposal that had received an overwhelmingly negative response, on which basis he concluded that the congregation was "not yet ready" for such a ritual.[68] Blurring or crossing the boundaries between Christianity and indigenous religions was apparently too transgressive for most CAC members, who—influenced by colonial and neocolonial traditions of thought—conceive of Christianity as incompatible with indigenous religions. One of my interlocutors—a prominent lgbt activist with personal connections to CAC—gave this as a reason why he did not feel spiritually at home in the church. He had found "a sense of harmony" in indigenous religious practice after his grandmother had told him about traditional healers involved in same-sex sexual relations; subsequently, he felt that CAC was "too Christian" to make room for his religious experience.[69]

Informal, Intimate, and Embodied Worship

The Sunday services at CAC are rather informal in style. Services officially begin at 3:00 P.M., but a few early birds arrive beginning around 2:00 P.M. to arrange the chairs, put up the rainbow curtain, and catch up with one another. At around 3:00, one of the ministers takes the floor, welcomes everyone, and initiates a round of introductions. One Sunday, a first-time visitor introduced herself by name and said, "I'm born again and believe in Jesus as my lord and savior. Also I'm lesbian and couldn't believe that there's a church that would accept me as I am and where I can worship." These words convey a sense of the unique space that CAC provides—a space where people can express, and feel affirmed in, both their sexual orientation and their Christian identity, and can integrate the two. After the introductions, the floor is given to the choir. One choir member plays the role of worship leader, introducing the praise songs and speaking words of encouragement, faith, and prayer in order to lead the congregation into the presence of God. Singing is usually accompanied by hand clapping and bodily movement, reflecting the influence of the embodied and participatory Pentecostal-charismatic styles of worship that are so popular in Kenya and elsewhere in Africa.

After a round of worship and praise, one of the ministers will take the floor and lead the congregation in intercessory prayer, in which people pray aloud individually, sometimes speaking in tongues. This may take about ten minutes, after which the choir sings one or two more praise songs, occasionally a more traditional hymn. The preacher is then introduced and, following the scripture reading, delivers the sermon. Depending on the preacher, CAC sermons can vary widely in terms of both style and content. Some sermons have a rather conversational style, the preacher sharing his or her personal experiences and insights, while others strongly emphasize teaching, the preacher explaining scripture passages or topical themes. Still other sermons have a strong rhetorical character, emphasizing the need for religious commitment and Christian living, for example, or using prophetic language and imagery to present a religious or political vision. The different styles of preaching seem to reflect ministers' diverse denominational backgrounds, which range from Seventh Day Adventist, to Catholic, to Pentecostal.

In the early days, CAC tended to invite guest preachers from a small pool of lgbt-friendly clergy from various denominations in Nairobi. Once CAC had installed its own ministers, however, these leaders tended to take turns preaching, sometimes inviting gifted church members to give a sermon. Most CAC preachers take a rather spontaneous approach, preaching from a few written notes. They typically prepare themselves to preach through prayer and Bible study, and often refer to "what the Lord had been speaking" to them in the previous week, thus implicitly claiming to speak with divine authority. Occasionally, in lieu of a formal sermon, there is a group discussion about a biblical text or a topic relevant to the community.

The sermon is usually followed by one or two more songs and by prayer, with congregants sometimes asking for specific prayers or blessings. One Sunday I observed a deliverance ritual during this part of the service, when a congregant asked for protection from evil spirits and curses that he felt were affecting his life; two ministers laid their hands on him while invoking the power of Christ and calling on God and his angels to protect, strengthen, and guide the afflicted man. The ritual, a classic body technique in many Christian traditions, was much milder and more understated than the ecstatic deliverance practices common in Kenya's Pentecostal-charismatic churches; whereas the latter tend to be spectacular performances of spiritual power, the CAC ritual was much more intimate. Yet it did include the use of verbal prophesy that is typical of charismatic ritual language, and it had a similar effect on the person who was prayed over, who felt spiritually empowered and protected.[70]

The next part of the service often featured the "CAC Live" show, introduced early in 2016 with the aim of making services more varied and attractive. The show was invented and is presented by a church member with strong journalistic interests. He explained to me his reasons for coming up with the format of CAC Live:

> First, to promote talents among members and to show people that being a homosexual doesn't make someone inferior; it means we can do things which are wonderful and great. Second, to tell the stories of other LGBTIQ members throughout the world so that our members may not feel like we are alone, so that people know that the struggle is all over the world. Third is to tell our stories in our own perspective and dimension. It's not every day you hear gay related stories in the Kenyan media so it is up to us to tell our own stories. Fourth is to separate the truth from lies, in many instances we just hear the negative sides of our life stories in local and international media, but the fact is that we have a lot to offer to the world, so it is up to us to tell our achievements, success and courage. Fifth and lastly, if CAC Live doesn't tell the stories and interviews, nobody will.[71]

The content and structure of the show varies from week to week, but it may include an overview of some recent lgbt-related or more general news stories in Kenya, Africa, or globally, an interview with one of the members or guests (one Sunday I had the privilege of being interviewed myself), or a group discussion of a given topic. During the January 2016 *kesha* prayer night, CAC Live featured an interview with leading lgbt rights activist Eric Gitari, and a few weeks later the show centered on the "Same Love" video that had just been released (see chapter 2). Significantly, the show is considered part of the church service. Whereas in traditional Christian worship it is the element of intercessory prayer that links the church to the world, CAC Live presents an alternative way to bring the world "outside" into the church, facilitating in particular an engagement with the world of local and global lgbt activism and culture. The presenter quoted above, with his emphasis on telling *our* stories, suggests the empowering space that the show creates.

The CAC Live show is occasionally followed by a practice called "secret friend" in which congregants write their names on slips of paper and put them in a box, after which everyone draws a paper slip from the box. The next Sunday, they are supposed to bring a small gift for the person whose name they drew and present the gifts publicly. This practice is yet another way in which CAC seeks to cultivate a sense of community, solidarity, and friendship within the congregation. At the end of the service, while standing and holding hands, the congregation says aloud the words of the blessing and a prayer of dismissal. This is followed by a farewell ritual, in which all congregants hug one another before they slowly depart.

But the end of the service is not the only time that congregants embrace. One Sunday, I counted no fewer than five occasions on which members hugged one another, spontaneously or after instructions from the worship leader: first, upon arrival, as a form of greeting; second, at the start of the service; third, during the service as a way of exchanging Christmas greetings (it was the Sunday before Christmas); fourth, at the end of the service, as a way of sharing the Peace; fifth, after the service, in parting. Far from an obligatory ritual, the hugs were exchanged with great care, with bodies held firmly and close. Thomas Csordas writes about what he calls the "holy hug" as a practice typical of charismatic prayer meetings, describing it as "a bodily expression of both spontaneity and intimacy."[72] The repeated embraces at CAC seem to reinforce this spontaneous character. This may reflect, in part, contemporary youth culture, in which hugging is a common practice, including between people of the same gender. In the Kenyan context, such bodily contact, especially among men in public, must follow a culturally defined script in order not to appear too intimate and give rise to the suspicion of homosexuality. In the safe space of CAC, people can hug one another without having to worry about this. Yet there may be an even deeper meaning to the hugging at CAC. As Munt has observed, bodily touch is essential to the creation of queer spiritual space and reveals "the life drive" with which many queer spiritualities are fundamentally concerned; bodily touch allows queer people to find or create places where they can be "comfortably extant" and can "stretch themselves out into the unknown."[73] At CAC, all of this hugging seems to be a deeply affirmative bodily ritual, with queer bodies—seen as untouchable in society and subjected to gossip, ridicule, and violence—welcoming and embracing one another in the presence of God, and performing God's touching love with one another.

Dressed Like a Queen

One of the popular songs at CAC is "I Love the Way You Handle My Situations," which was sung in almost all the services I attended during my 2016 fieldwork. The lyrics were originally written by Robert Kayanja, a prominent Ugandan Pentecostal pastor. Whereas the lyrics of Kayanja's version consist of only two lines, however, the version sung by the CAC choir was much expanded.

> *I love the way you handle my situations,*
> *I love the way you fight for me.*

I love the way you treat me like a son
I love the way you fight for me.
I love the way you handle my situations,
I love the way you fight for me.
I love the way you treat me like a son,
I love the way you treat me like a king,
I love the way you handle my situations,
I love the way you fight for me.
I love the way you treat me when I'm down,
I love the way you fight for me.
I love the way you dress me like your only son,
I love the way you fight for me.
I love the way you handle my situations,
I love the way you fight for me.

These lyrics are particularly meaningful in the context of the struggles church members have experienced because of their sexuality and the challenges they still face in their everyday lives. In the context of CAC, this song becomes a song of empowerment and encouragement for lgbt people of faith, in much the same way that "Gospel songs are transformed into affirmations of black queer identity" in the United States, according to Roger Sneed.[74] Indeed, in the tradition of African American spirituals, this song exemplifies Ngũgĩ wa Thiong'o's point about the spiritual as an "aesthetic of resistance" with a "force of beauty and imagery of hope."[75]

Interestingly, on the Sunday of the drag-queen contest, the lead singer added two lines to the lyrics: "I love the way you treat me like a queen / I love the way you dress me like a queen." Several people in the congregation, not yet aware that the contest would take place later in the service, welcomed these lines with surprise and suppressed laughter. Only later in the service did the meaning of these lines become clear: they expressed the belief that one can cross-dress in the eyes of God—indeed, that cross-dressing can be a liturgical practice. Of course, there is a long history of ritual cross-dressing in Christian liturgy, which according to Lisa Isherwood can be seen as an expression of "the message of equality of the Christian gospel."[76] On this occasion, the traditional forms of ritual cross-dressing—priests' wearing of liturgical robes, for example—were replaced by modern drag practices inspired by popular queer culture.[77] The effect, however, was similar, presenting a form of "gender iconography, making visible the spaces of possibility which are closed off by dichotomous conceptualization."[78] Thus the drag-queen contest was not just "for fun," as I initially thought. Nor was it primarily about making a political statement about transphobia in the community, although it was introduced as such. Through the song, the drag-queen contest was made both a liturgical performance and a theological statement, implicitly claiming that God had dressed the participants—whether they identified as gay or transgender, male or female—as beautiful queens. The drag-queen contest thus illustrated Michael Warner's point that "religion makes available a language of ecstasy, a horizon of significance against which transgressions against the normal order of the world and the boundaries of self *can be seen as good things*."[79] The four contestants, some of whom initially seemed hesitant, unsure about whether the contest was appropriate in the church setting, were affirmed in their belief that indeed it was appropriate to dress in drag in church. The enthusiastic response of the congregation made them increasingly confident as the show proceeded. The song, then, was a song of queer empowerment, celebrating in an explicitly Christian language of faith the fluidity of gender and the aesthetics of cross-dressing and drag performances. Moreover, the song and the cross-dressing it referred to were a form of religious queer world-making. As José Esteban Muñoz points out, "the aesthetic, especially the queer aesthetic, frequently contains blueprints and schemata of a forward-dawning futurity." I would add that the drag-queen contest in the setting of this Christian worship service gave the congregation a glimpse of "the worlds proposed and promised by queerness," in this case a world where God dresses all lgbt people as queens, and where society treats and values them as such.[80] Moreover, as much as the drag-queen contestants were inspired by Western drag practices, they had also given their outfits and performances a distinct East African touch through their choice of jewelry and fabrics. Thus they contributed to East African queer world-making in a religious setting. The vision of an African and religious queer future mediated through this aesthetic was obviously appealing to CAC congregants. When the song was sung again a week later at the inauguration of the newly elected Miss CAC 2016, including the same invented lines, it was welcomed with enthusiastic cheering.

DEVELOPING QUEER THEOLOGY

The word "affirming" is at the heart of CAC's name and theology. What is the basis for this affirmative theology, and how is it applied to sexual orientation? And what is the broader theological narrative in which CAC frames and understands its ministry?

CAC's Facebook page opens, "In God's family, there are no outsiders. All are insiders. Black and white, rich and poor, gay/queer and straight, Muslim and Christian—all belong. God's desire is us to be a family." "God's family" apparently includes all of humankind; indeed, the statement later refers to "the unconditional love of God, which embraces all humanity," regardless of background, race, faith, sexual orientation, or gender expression. The word *embrace* indicates that this affirmation is not just rational but affectionate and embodied, as it is based on the love of God, which is believed to be unlimited and radical in its embrace of each person. Through God's love, human beings, as the children of God, are united in one family. This belief in God's inclusive love is empowering, for it allows lgbt people to resist popular religious narratives that use religious language to exclude and stigmatize them. In the words of a sermon at CAC on July 29, 2018, "The truth is that God is a God of love. Not a homophobic god, a transphobic god, a biphobic god, a queer-phobic god. He's a God of Love. That God is our advocate, siding with us in our struggle."

The Facebook statement also refers to "the gospel of Jesus Christ, the message of hope and inclusion of all people in the body of Christ." The suggestion, again, is that *all* people, regardless of their background, race, faith, or sexuality are part of what in Christian parlance is called "the body of Christ." This phrase is derived from the New Testament, 1 Corinthians 12:12–27 to be precise, where Paul writes metaphorically about the church as a body, specifically the body of Christ. The CAC statement interprets this metaphor in a radically inclusive way, claiming that the body of Christ is indiscriminate toward sexual orientation and other categories that are used to exclude people from mainstream churches. CAC thus acknowledges the belief that, in Thomas Bohache's words, "if the Church *is* the Body of Christ, then any/every *body* must be welcome" (emphasis in original).[81] In other words, the statement on the CAC Facebook page makes two important theological claims: it affirms (1) the full humanity and (2) the full Christianity of lgbt people of faith—they are fully and integrally part of both God's family of humankind and the church as the body of Christ. Although this is a theological given, it must be defended constantly and reclaimed over and over again from the dominant religious, social, and cultural powers. This struggle is at the heart of how CAC understands what it means to follow Jesus. A CAC sermon on February 21, 2016, used this language to describe this understanding: "As affirming Christians, we believe in the undiluted view of what it looks like to follow Jesus through inclusion, justice, community transformation, forgiveness, loyalty, and love that frees us from our obsession with dogma and debates that hinder us to be truly followers of Jesus Christ." This excerpt is typical of the foregrounding of orthopraxis (correct actions) over orthodoxy (correct beliefs) that is common in liberation theologies, and it reflects the related awareness that the "following of Jesus cannot be strictly personal but must involve a public, sociological conversion resulting in a transformation of a public situation," as Bohache puts it.[82]

The humanity and Christianity of lgbt people of faith must be affirmed repeatedly to counter the message, received from their families, churches, and communities, that lgbt people are less than human, cannot be Christian, and are irredeemable sinners who will go to hell. Many lgbt people internalize these beliefs, with detrimental effects for their self-esteem and their mental and spiritual well-being, and they may decide to break with their churches and communities in order to express their sexuality. The affirmative theology of CAC seeks to help them by reconciling their sexuality and faith, and by empowering them as lgbt people of faith. During the same sermon, the CAC preacher addressed those persons who had come to accept and internalize the rejection and negativity to which they had been subjected. "You know so many people in our community," he said, "they live such pathetic lives, because they've been made to believe that nothing good can come out of them. They have been called names, and they've got used to it, they're just fine. But it is time, it is time as a church, it is time as lgbt community, to stand and to say: We know our rights, we know who we are, we know what we do!" The preacher paused while the congregation applauded. He then emphasized that whatever names one is given by society—outcast, sinner, child molester—"when you have your faith in Christ, those are not your names." Faith in Christ defines one's true identity, he suggested, and helps us overcome victimization.

One crucial strategy that helps lgbt people accept and affirm their sexual orientation involves educating them about the Bible's so-called clobber passages (that is, the specific biblical verses used by Christian conservatives to condemn homosexuality). In a session during CAC's January 2016 *kesha,* the following texts were discussed: Genesis 1:27 and 19:18–20, Leviticus 18:22 and 20:13, Deuteronomy 23:17–18, Romans 1:26–27, and 1 Corinthians 1:10 and 6:9–11. In the session, the CAC lead minister taught that the Bible should not be read ahistorically, out of context, to cherry-pick passages that serve a narrow political or ideological purpose; he emphasized instead that Jesus Christ's message of love and affirmation is the norm through which the rest of the Bible should be interpreted. Rather than go into a detailed exegetical discussion of the specific texts and the antihomosexual arguments homophobic conservatives derive from them, the *kesha* session was used to downplay the relevance of these texts and to redirect people's attention to the inclusive love of Christ.[83] One of the people who attended the *kesha* summarized what he took from it as follows: "The Bible, yes, it's written, but it is written to a different community, it is a specific message to a specific community, to a specific audience, not our community. . . . And the funny thing is that Jesus Christ never mentioned the matter of homosexuality; he came and just preached love. So I believe it's very simple and clear: I am who I am."[84] CAC thus seeks to neutralize traditional Christian arguments against homosexuality and to assure people that their sexuality is not against God's will.[85] In the words of Sarojini Nadar, CAC addresses the "hermeneutical immobility" typical of Kenyan churches in general in relation to issues of sexuality, and it provides members with hermeneutical and theological tools for "more holistic, liberating ways of engaging with Scripture."[86]

This holistic approach to scripture is buttressed by CAC's understanding of creation. Many church members expressed the belief that their sexuality was integral to how God had created them—a belief that had grown and was affirmed through their involvement in CAC. "God created everyone in his image," one member explained. "He didn't create us homosexuals in the image of animals; God created us in his image, whereby we have to live. We came here to live exemplary [lives] and show the image of God through sharing love."[87] It was this insight, he continued, that prevented him from leaving his Christian upbringing behind, for he realized, as he said, that "I should continue serving God when I'm gay, too." Another church member alluded to Psalm 139 to argue that his sexual orientation was not a self-chosen "lifestyle" but something God-given: "God has plans for us, and also when I look at the Bible, it's already saying that he knew me even before I was in my mother's womb. That is very important."[88] This affirming theology reflects a form of essentialism that naturalizes homosexuality, confirming that it is as much an inborn trait as eye color. Such essentialism is not in fashion in contemporary queer theory, which prefers the idea that sexuality is socially and discursively constructed. Yet in religious contexts like CAC, essentialism based on the concept of God's creation appears to be strategic. As R. Stephen Warner writes in his study of the Metropolitan Community Church in the United States, "The power of gay Christian essentialism is that it invokes a powerful and benevolent God to proclaim the issue of homosexuality to be beyond human control . . . and demands, as a matter of simple justice, inclusion of gays."[89] This is exactly what CAC's creation-based theology seeks to do in the Kenyan context.[90] Interestingly, Warner suggests that this theology is apolitical, and that the strategy of Christian gay essentialism is "pluralist, not revolutionary," because it presents gay people as only "trivially different" from the rest of society (the only difference being that they sleep with people of the same sex). Whether this argument holds true in the U.S. context is beyond the scope of the present discussion, but in the Kenyan context, demanding justice and inclusion for lgbt people is in fact revolutionary. The argument that lgbt people are created in the image of God, and that their sexuality is part of God's design, radically challenges popular discourses that deny the humanity of people with nonnormative sexualities and gender identities. The queer struggle in Africa, as Sokari Ekine points out, is about "the power to determine who counts as human and what lives count as lives."[91] The belief that lgbt people are created in God's image as sexual and gendered beings is deeply political, and it empowers CAC members to reclaim their self-determination and to radically affirm the humanity of lgbt people in the eyes of God.

Rewriting the Book of Acts

Within CAC discourse, the theological importance of the church's contribution to the wider lgbt struggle in Kenya and Africa was captured in the phrase "rewriting the book of Acts." The New Testament book of the Acts of the Apostles tells about the emergence and early years of the Christian Church. "Rewrite the book of Acts" is a figure of speech that appears to have originated with TFAM founder Bishop Flunder,[92] and it was introduced in Kenya by Bishop Tolton in one of his sermons at CAC. As Tolton put it, "I told the congregation a couple of weeks ago that they are Acts, they are the book of Acts. The book of Acts is the book where the church emerged and figured out who and what they were going to be, and they [CAC members] are literally writing acts with their lives. With every step they take, they are writing the book of Acts again."[93]

This is a deeply significant claim. Tolton is suggesting that, like the early church two thousand years ago, CAC is currently "figuring out" its identity and mission, and that this will be decisive for nothing less than the nature and future of Christianity—in Kenya and possibly even more widely. This comparison with the early church—led by such legendary figures as the Apostle Paul—may seem overblown for a few dozen people worshipping in a rented space on Sunday afternoons. Yet we must consider the comparison in the context of TFG's vision, in which CAC is one crucial initiative in a broader project, still nascent, which will give rise to a new, progressive Christian movement in Africa destined to reshape the face of African and possibly even global Christianity. In the same way that the early church, according to the book of Acts, was inspired by the Holy Spirit and was part of God's plan for the world, so CAC is believed to be at the forefront of a movement driven by the Holy Spirit and crucial to realizing God's mission in Kenya, Africa, and the world at large. CAC's mission is to promote an understanding in the Kenyan lgbt community that Christian faith can be positively integrated with lgbt identities, on the one hand, and to teach other Kenyan Christian circles that lgbt people can be people of faith, too, and that an affirmative Christianity is possible. To this end, CAC leaders network with both other lgbt activists and other Christian ministers, and also hold workshops and joint celebrations. For example, in September 2016, CAC collaborated with TFG in organizing a conference in Nairobi for a group of "affirmative pastors." Eight months later, in May 2017, CAC organized a special service on the occasion of International Day Against Homophobia and Transphobia, to which it invited activists and pastors; in addition, CAC occasionally holds joint services with other churches with which it has built relationships. These may be small steps, but the narrative of Acts encourages the church to believe that small beginnings can have a major long-term impact.

Tolton's notion of rewriting the book of Acts had landed solidly in the CAC congregation, and it became an important subject of discussion. One CAC leader elaborated on the theme in a sermon on March 6, 2016, delivered a number of weeks after Tolton introduced it. He gave the notion an explicitly political edge, calling the congregation to unite in action and become a movement for change:

> It is time as a church to rewrite the book of Acts. It is time for us to change the constitution of Kenya as a church. It is time for us to fight all this discrimination, all this branding of names. We know our brand. It is time to stand and tell people: this is what we want, this is what we believe in—we believe in inclusion, we believe in liberation, we believe in freedom, justice, and equality. That is what we believe in. It is time to be counted, it is time to be in the process. . . . It is you, you, you, all of us, myself included, who need to be in this process.

The parallel drawn here between rewriting the book of Acts and changing the Kenyan constitution is telling, the suggestion being that Acts is being rewritten through work for legal change in order to achieve inclusion, liberation, freedom, justice, and equality for all Kenyans. It suggests that "rewriting the book of Acts" is as much a religious as a sociopolitical project—in fact, it is a political and theological metaphor that captures the significance of the movement for change in which CAC is involved. The phrase "change the constitution" should perhaps not be taken literally: Kenya adopted a new constitution in 2010 that contains what is widely considered an expansive and progressive human rights provision. What the preacher might have meant is that this constitutional provision should be used to effect further legal change—specifically, the revision of the penal code that currently criminalizes homosexuality. Indeed, CAC members have been actively involved in a petition that seeks to repeal section 162 of the penal code, which was heard by the High Court in Nairobi in 2018.

The project of legal, social, and political change in which CAC is involved was framed, in the same sermon, in an eschatological way. The scripture readings being taken from the book of Isaiah (chapter 65) and the book of Revelation (chapter 21), which both center on the vision of "a new heaven and a new world" that are symbolized by "the new Jerusalem," the preacher equated this eschatological vision with the queer struggle in Kenya:

> We are in the New Jerusalem—the New Jerusalem which signifies equality, the New Jerusalem which signifies inclusion, the New Jerusalem where there is space and joy. In our country today we are facing oppression as the lgbti community. We are being branded names; people don't want to see us; our family members don't want to be associated with us because they think we are outcasts. But God is telling you today that in the New Jerusalem, amen, there is equality, in the New Jerusalem there is inclusion, in the New Jerusalem there is restoration, in the New Jerusalem there is hope. God is good all the time. We are marching to the New Jerusalem. . . . Come and march. Come and let us journey together. Let us walk together because we are in the new heaven and the new earth.

The New Jerusalem in the Bible is a city of salvation and redemption, the image of God's new creation. In this sermon, it is equated with a place of sexual equality and inclusion, a place where queer people are no longer stigmatized and oppressed but can experience joy and fullness of life. The New Jerusalem, in other words, becomes a metaphor for the African queer city yet to come. The sermon demonstrates that a Christian concern for eschatology, in Susannah Cornwall's words, "is also, and simultaneously, a queer concern for a more just society."[94]

Interestingly, the preacher of this sermon presents an apparent paradox between "we *are in* the New Jerusalem" and "we *are marching to* the New Jerusalem." This echoes a tradition in Christian theology that emphasizes that salvation (also referred to in biblical language as the Kingdom of God, or "the new heaven and the new earth") is "already but not yet." This tradition has been referred to as "presentist-and-futurist eschatology,"[95] in that it reflects "a sense in which it [the Kingdom of God] is a present reality but another [sense] in which it has not yet come in all its fullness."[96] In liberation, queer, and other political theologies, this dual sense envisions "a God acting in history," a God acting on the side of human struggle for the fullness of life. It further entails a notion of prophecy as "discerning God's activity in the world now, the meaning of that activity for the community of faith, and the appropriate response."[97] The apparent paradox in the sermon, then, becomes a productive tension, on the one hand emphasizing a God who is "creating [the new earth] in this world today," and on the other hand emphasizing that "God is counting on you today," which culminates in a call upon the congregation to become part of God's movement for change. As the same minister preached a few weeks earlier, on February 21:

> God is calling you today: "Come my son, come my daughter. I want you to stand, I want you to seek after me, and I will show you the way." I want you as an lgbt person to be the prophet of this community. I want you to stand and fight against all this hatred labeled against our community. I want you to stand and speak against all this evil happening in our society—corruption, tribalism, nepotism, all this happening in our society. God is counting on you. God is believing that you are able, he has empowered you, he has given you this vision, he has commissioned you today to go and stand and seek after him. Amen? Amen! God is calling you today. Just stand and say: "Yes, I'm here, I want to seek after you; I want healing in my community, I want healing in my society; I want this to happen in our family; I want this to happen in this church, when we seek him." He's counting on you today. He's saying, "Come and stand." Be the prophet of our society. I believe in you. Do you receive it, brothers and sisters? Amen? Amen!

This was the end of the sermon, and the congregation received it with hearty applause. Obviously, they were inspired by the utopian vision enthusiastically sketched by the preacher—a prophetic vision of hope that functioned as both "a critical affect and a methodology," as it made the congregation part of an anticipatory performance.[98] The same theme of our becoming prophets came up later in my fieldwork, in a sermon delivered by another CAC minister on July 29, 2018. Talking about the biblical prophets who spoke truth to power, he said, "we are the prophets that speak truth to power today. Only the truth can set us free. We speak truth by telling our true narratives—resisting the things other people say about us and showing who we truly are."

Significantly, the political edge of CAC's theology is framed in a much broader way than just the struggle for lgbt human rights.[99] CAC members are called to stand up "against all evil" happening in Kenyan society. The issues alluded to here—corruption, tribalism, and nepotism—were not mentioned incidentally. In the sermon delivered on March 6, 2016, the same preacher went into more detail, discussing the problem of poor governance and weak democratic institutions, and he imagined the New Jerusalem as a place free not only from homophobia and transphobia but also from all the other social injustices negatively affecting Kenyans' lives. He urged members to register to vote in the upcoming 2017 presidential election. "Have you registered?" he asked. "Are you ready to vote for good governance, for morality, integrity among our leaders, or are you the kind of person asking: from what tribe is that person coming from?" The preacher explained to me that he considered it part of CAC's mission to address these kinds of issues. The church is supposed to be "an authority on morality" in society, he said, but the established churches misuse their position to discriminate against certain groups of people, and they also tend to maintain the tribalism that afflicts Kenya. "That's why," he concluded, "I feel that as CAC, we should also be at the forefront to speak against all these vices that are happening not only in our political systems, but in our institutions and all aspects that concerns humanity." Adding to this was his sense that because CAC is a young congregation, with members who have the potential to become future leaders in the country, "we should mentor them to be leaders who have the interest of the people at their hearts."[100]

CAC members, by becoming "agents of change" and taking part in the movement for equality, justice, and freedom in Kenya, become co-workers with God in realizing the eschatological vision. Indeed, as the preacher said in the sermon on July 29, 2018, "we are claiming freedom, not because it is our right, but because the word of the Lord speaks about it. Our freedom is a promise from God, and we claim that promise." Through their actions in this process, CAC members believe that they are rewriting the book of Acts. The minister who preached on this theme on March 6, 2016, added, "The book of Acts will always be written by the radical people, by the people who are ready for change, by the people who have a vision, amen, the people who really have the purpose, the people who are driven by a strong will, who are really self-motivated and are ready to take the challenge, amen. Oh my God. The new earth and the New Jerusalem is not for the cowards." The preacher acknowledged that members of the congregation might feel weak because of all the pressure they face in society, but he insisted that with God's help they would prevail. "As an LGBT member," he told them, "you are in a very hostile environment, and there is oppression, discrimination left, right and center. . . . But God is telling you today: 'You will withstand that pressure.' And that's why I think you are in Kenya, in this country, because God knew that you will withstand the pressure, because God knew that you will overcome the storm, because God knew that he is developing you for a greater task, God knows that he's preparing you for a greater future." It is clear that Warner's argument that a creation-based affirming theology is apolitical and not revolutionary does not hold true in the context of CAC. Rather than present lgbt people as only "trivially different" from the rest of society, CAC sees them as squarely in the vanguard of a movement for social and political change in Kenya. They are agents of change, and God is counting on them to succeed where political and religious leaders have failed. What we see in this theological vision is a notion of queerness similar to the one captured by José Esteban Muñoz when he writes, "Queerness is essentially about the rejection of a here and now and an insistence on potentiality or concrete possibility for another world."[101]

NAVIGATING AN ETHICS OF SEX AND RELATIONSHIPS

Its affirming theology might be politically revolutionary, but what about CAC's teaching on, and attitude toward, sexuality itself? Discussing the question of queer sexual ethics, Tolton told me that he and the people involved in TFG and the UCAA are still working on developing a sexual ethics. He asked rhetorically, "What would it be for us to write Acts and create a sexual ethic there that goes well beyond abstinence?"[102] Tolton did not elaborate further, but it seemed that he envisioned a sexual ethics that diverges, in progressive ways, from the mainstream Christian preoccupation with controlling and restricting sex through, for example, abstinence before marriage.

At CAC, I found that matters of love, relationships, and sex were issues of primary concern for many members and were discussed frequently, for instance, in the WhatsApp group. In one church service, I observed a lively debate about love and sex, initiated as part of the CAC Live show. I had been interviewed in the same show two weeks earlier, and, to my surprise, most of the questions concerned my intimate life (I had naively expected to be asked about my research and academic work). A few weeks earlier, when I introduced myself to the congregation, I had mentioned that my partner and I had been together for twelve years. Apparently, people found this fascinating, and several asked me afterward about "the secret" to such a long-term relationship, adding that they wanted the same for themselves. When I appeared on the CAC Live stage, the host demonstrated a similar fascination, asking for details about my wedding five years earlier and the challenges of marital life. One question was about how we deal with jealousy in our relationship, especially given that I travel a lot. What I learned from this and other conversations was that members generally desire a long-term relationship yet have very few examples of long-term same-sex relationships, and struggle with the challenge of commitment in their own relational and sexual lives.

The CAC Live show and, even more so, the WhatsApp group provide members with space in which to share the challenges they face, raise questions, seek advice and support, and discuss issues openly. One Sunday, for example, the CAC Live host initiated a discussion about whether it is acceptable to have sex with someone else when you or your partner are away from home for a long period of time. This and similar conversations centered on the relationship between love and sex. Such conversations were relatively open, and members expressed different opinions. At the same time, dominant voices in these discussions tended to shape the debates and lead them in a particular direction, by bringing in normative perspectives and sidelining other views. Take, for example, the discussion about the question of sexual appetite on the road, posed during the CAC Live show on March 6, 2016.

A. These things happen even in the other world, when a man leaves his wife for, say, a year.

B. But the truth is, it is rampant among the lgbti.

C. You know, it's all about someone's mentality. If I have a partner, what makes me a lesbian is that I am proud of my body, I love my body. That's why I love my fellow girl. If I were in a relationship, I would sex-chat with her; we would masturbate on Skype.

D. I support what she says. You can masturbate.

E. Come on, guys, let's get real. What if there's no Wi-Fi? We all have our sexual needs.

C. No! When you love one person, it is not a boxing match, it is not football or rugby, it is not a game. When my love would be away for a year, I am that kind of loyal. Why would I do something that doesn't mean anything? I am in a relationship with her. It's not that because she is away, I can sleep with my friend.

D. That thing of sleeping around is too much.

B. Research shows that HIV and AIDS and other STDs are rampant in the gay community. You can believe it or ignore it, but it's the truth. The reason is that we don't have discipline, we don't know what commitment is, we don't know what responsibility is. A lot of people, once they discover their sexuality, they think homosexuality is about alcohol, sex, et cetera. Some people are more mature, but overall that's the idea. People don't know how to stay in relationships. It's all about discipline. The reason we don't have discipline is that we don't have accountability. As straight people, the moment they begin dating or courting, their families will know, the church will know, their friends will know, and they will hold them accountable. In our case, because we date in secrecy, no one is watching you, no one is controlling you, and people end up doing what they want. As much as I want to say that some are honest, some are faithful, the fact of the matter is that we still live underground and we are still club kids who are irresponsible. That's why coming to a place like this, a church, sort of gives you that understanding, it teaches you those values that many other gay people don't have outside there. Your thinking should be different from those people out there, because you know the word of God and what is says on relationship, on courtship. When I hear all these different views, I wonder: why do you come here? Our mindset should be different. We are here because we want to be role models, when eventually Kenya reaches lgbt freedom, so we are building foundations—meaning we have to show commitment and be responsible.

In this discussion, participants A and E suggest that sex outside a committed relationship is common not only among gay people but also among heterosexuals, and is just a way of satisfying natural human desires. Yet they are more or less sidelined by participants B and C, who come up with longer, more developed arguments. C indirectly suggests that A and E lack character and do not respect their bodies. B not only refers to certain "research" in order to counter A's suggestion and claim to speak from a position of knowledge and authority, but he also frames the question as being one of morality, maturity, and faith. He brings in an explicitly normative perspective, suggesting that his take on the matter corresponds to what CAC as a church stands for (or should stand for) and is in line with "the word of God." Where A indicates that there is no real difference between how gay and straight people in relationships deal with sex, B argues that members of the lgbt community are much more likely to engage in sex outside the context of a relationship, framing this in a moralizing way as their lacking responsibility, self-discipline, and maturity.

What is interesting in B's contribution is his explanation for the sexual "irresponsibility" he observes in the gay community. Whereas straight relationships, in his account, are usually public—known by relatives, friends, and acquaintances—same-sex relationships tend to be secret, which means that the community cannot keep a controlling eye on them, which increases the chances of promiscuity. It is clear that B is not just talking about the case posed by the CAC Live presenter but about sexual relationships in general, which, in the gay community, he claims, tend to be promiscuous. He presents CAC as a space where members should develop a different attitude in sexual matters—one defined by responsibility and discipline, with sex enjoyed only in the context of a committed relationship—so that they can set an example for the wider Kenyan lgbt community.

A similar argument took place a few weeks later, in a WhatsApp group discussion on April 10, which included a more concrete proposal for how the church could regulate relationships (I have removed the names and substituted asterisks).

A. It was nice sharing about relationship and love today during the service and I was delighted on the way guys debated the topic hopefully we should have a session more about love, lust, and relationships. . . .
B. At this point we should be talking about abstaining till the right time when one is ready, then bring your partner, introduce them to the leaders then get blessings to go ahead. Right now we having secret affairs and we are proud to talk about them in church.
C. **** you can't be serious.
D. I agree with you **** just like the heterosexuals abstain we should too.
B. Yes, we are Christians. Introduce your fiancé to church elders so that they can counsel you and walk with you as you build your marriage. Right now we are all living in sin, except for those who are single and abstaining.

In light of Tolton's suggestion about the need to develop a sexual ethics that goes beyond a narrow focus on abstinence, it is remarkable that the norm of sexual abstinence is explicitly invoked here by B and endorsed by D. D is one of the CAC leaders, so this endorsement is granted extra weight. Even more interesting is D's explicit reference to heterosexuals' setting the example of abstinence for gays and lesbians. My purpose here is not to debate the point as such (although I'm not aware of any evidence that heterosexuals are particularly good at abstaining from premarital sex, extramarital sex, or any other kind of sex), but to examine the norm that is being introduced here. The model of heterosexual relationships that are made public and visible to the community (and thus subject to social control) is presented as exemplary for same-sex couples. It is a model based on courtship, in which the enjoyment of sex is postponed till the moment when—in the words of another contributor to the CAC Live discussion quoted above—"you have come to know that person, when you are confident enough to commit your life to this person." This contributor opposed this to the practice that he claims is common in the lgbt community: "Unfortunately, for us, dating means that [when] I buy you a drink, in the middle of the night you are going to have sex. That is wrong. But as Christians we should think about courtship."

In the WhatsApp conversation, the references to abstinence and courtship were not unanimously welcomed by all. Two members objected by raising practical difficulties. One of them was in the early stages of a relationship and asked how he was supposed to abstain when his partner "wants it so badly." He confessed that sex was "no. 1 on the list" of reasons why he had entered into the relationship in the first place. Other group members responded by giving him a range of advice: discuss the matter with his partner and reach an agreement; bring his partner to church; reconsider his priorities in the relationship. The second suggestion came from a group member who asked simply, "What do you mean by abstain? My community can't." Someone else clarified, "He is talking about the sex workers. They can't abstain since it's their livelihood." This comment did not receive any serious response, apart from one member writing that he would pray that the person concerned would soon give up his profession and find another livelihood. A few CAC members are known (more or less publicly) to be involved in sex work and thus most clearly diverge from the ethics of abstinence and courtship promoted in the church. The CAC leadership believes that these members should definitely be welcomed in church, because they understand the precarious life conditions that force some people to engage in sex work, among other reasons. Yet the leaders also find the presence of sex workers "confusing." On the one hand, they do not want to judge, but on the other hand, they believe that sex work is against the Christian principle that "sex is holy."[103] CAC struggles with this moral dilemma, and it will continue to do so as long as it upholds moral norms that encourage sex to be practiced only in the context of long-term committed relationships.

The leader who told me that sex is holy also said that the church seeks to promote the courtship model of relationships. Interestingly, he simultaneously expressed his discomfort with applying a heterosexual model. "So I really think," he told me, "as Christians, we should really take our time on learning someone before we go into sex or into sleeping with the other person because that is a mistake that us—and I really hate comparing us with straight people because we are different—but us as queer people should really understand, that it is important to wait."[104] As for why it is important to wait, he referred to issues of sexual health—in particular the risk of STDs, including HIV—and also to the possible psychological effects of engaging in sex too quickly. Yet it is not only these reasons that play a role. The primary reason is the belief, upheld in CAC, that the courtship model is based on the biblical concept and thus is the Christian norm. In the area of sexual ethics, CAC thus explicitly distinguishes itself from the rest of the Kenyan lgbt community and promotes a model derived from heterosexual marriage. Even though the CAC leader says that "queer people" are different from "straight people," it is not at all clear what this difference entails. With regard to sexual ethics, Stephen Warner's comment about MCC might in fact apply to CAC: instead of being revolutionary, CAC may subject queer people to heterosexual norms and present them as only "trivially different" from the rest of society. This is understandable in the context of a society that takes a generally negative view of lgbt people. As one CAC leader explained, "society sees homosexuals as sex beasts," and the church seeks to counter this stereotype by promoting a sexual ethics that makes lgbt people more acceptable to society.[105] This may also explain why prominent church members, in private conversations, often were open and honest about their dating and sex lives, including the use of hookup apps like Grindr, while publicly, in church, they adopted a more conservative Christian stance.

It is also understandable given the context of the HIV epidemic, and especially the risks for men who have sex with men. CAC is obviously concerned about the sexual health of its members. Information on protection against HIV and other STDs is frequently shared on the WhatsApp group by the church's health and advocacy officer. In addition to this basic sexual health information, the church seeks to provide moral guidance to its members, discouraging casual sex and promoting a "responsible" sexual lifestyle.

It is thus perhaps understandable why Tolton's question about how to craft a sexual ethics that goes beyond a narrow concern with abstinence has not yet been actively explored, let alone answered. CAC's moral discourse on sexuality and relationships reminds us that queer spiritual spaces are not necessarily transgressive in every respect. But before we disparage CAC for not being radically disruptive of "regimes of the normal"[106] when it comes to sexual ethics, we might want to examine the norm of queerness as transgressive and antinormative. As Munt writes, "by pushing queer as a radical message we can unerringly appear to be bullying people into what are, for them, unsustainable ontologies."[107] In the moral and romantic universe of many CAC members, long-term committed relationships are considered the ideal, but at the same time such partnerships appear to be out of reach for many of them, as a result of the cultural, economic, and social constraints on pursuing same-sex relationships in Kenya. In this context, the moral and spiritual community that CAC provides not only supports and nurtures these romantic aspirations but also provides space for sharing feelings of disappointment, frustration, and failure, along with advice, relationship counseling, and pastoral support.

ANOTHER CHRISTIANITY IS POSSIBLE

In the long history of creative local appropriations of Christianity in African contexts, CAC has written another chapter. It radically distinguishes itself from mainstream forms of Christianity in Kenya on one prominent issue in Kenyan and African Christian discourses and politics: the recognition of homosexuality and lgbt rights. Whereas popular forms of Christianity in Africa, especially Pentecostal-charismatic traditions, have denounced lgbt sexualities as "un-African" and "un-Christian," CAC presents a radical counternarrative, while also providing an affirming and empowering spiritual and social space for lgbt people of faith, including a group of lgbt refugees from Uganda. As small and relatively insignificant as the church may appear to be, the movement of which CAC is at the heart of has great ambitions. In TFG discourse, the goal of this movement is to reshape the nature and future of Christianity in a progressive and inclusive direction—in Kenya, in Africa, and indeed worldwide.

Some readers may be skeptical about the feasibility of this ambition. The lgbt-affirming, pan-African Christian movement that TFAM seeks to propel is still in an embryonic stage, and its human and financial resources might prove far too limited to make a difference in the global economy of Christianity. But the nascent movement does have the potential to challenge and decenter monolithic narratives about Christian-inspired homophobia in Africa. The recent controversies in African societies, and in African Christian circles, about homosexuality and lgbt rights reveal deeply rooted conflicting understandings of personhood, human dignity, and sexuality. Initiatives such as

CAC counterbalance hegemonic discourses and narratives, and they remind us that there are, indeed, multiple modernities and Christianities in contemporary Africa that are linked to transatlantic dynamics in complex ways. Even if, in the long run, CAC turns out to be only a footnote, the existence of the church is deeply important—not only for the congregants who are affirmed in their sexuality and faith but also for Kenyan lgbt community members and Kenyan Christians who hear about the church and who, willingly or unwillingly, discover that another form of Christianity is possible. Indeed, the presence of CAC as a Kenyan Christian queer space makes it clear beyond doubt: an alternative to a homophobic African Christianity, and to a secular Western queer culture, already exists. Bursting with possibility for both the future and the present, CAC is a beacon of hope.

INTERLUDE 4

Ambassador

"It's now for you darling to be an ambassador of the Kenyan LGBTIQ. Don't tell only the struggles but also share with people our achievements so far, our courage, our potential, and how we want to transform society in different fields." I received this message from one of my research participants on the evening before I left Kenya after my fieldwork visit in January–February 2016. I had established a close relationship with him, after I had met him in the context of Cosmopolitan Affirming Church (CAC). He was one of the youngest church members, and I had been impressed by his wide-ranging interests and strong opinions, which always made it a pleasure to talk with him about social and political issues. To be honest, I also found him rather cute—in the sense of endearing, charming, and lovable—and I enjoyed his cheerful company.

On the evening before my departure, he sent me this farewell message on WhatsApp, and it has become dear to me. His use of the word "darling" was an acknowledgment of the friendship we had established, and it expressed the mutual affection that had grown between us. When I introduced myself at my first CAC service, I had deliberately emphasized that I had been in a relationship with my partner for more than a decade and that we had been married for almost five years. This was my way of managing any possible expectations regarding my romantic or sexual availability. My young friend had shown great interest in my relational life. He asked for a picture and admired my husband's handsome good looks. He inquired about "the secret" of our long-term relationship, and also asked how I managed being away from home for long periods of time: Was I able to do without sex for so long? Had I ever "tasted" a Kenyan guy? He asked these questions playfully, and I responded to them in an equally playful manner. We continued to interact flirtatiously but also had more serious conversations, and I grew fond of him. So I was touched when he called me "darling" in his farewell message, as it confirmed that the fondness was mutual. Other research participants I befriended likewise addressed me as "dear" or, more intimately, as "my dear." This affective dimension of my relationships with research participants not only made the fieldwork more enjoyable but was also in keeping with the queer methodology underlying it. Acknowledging and appreciating this affective dimension is a way of challenging the conventions of traditional, more detached approaches to ethnographic research.[1]

My friend's farewell message also reflected a shift in the balance of power between me, as the researcher, and this church member, as one of my informants. This is what happens when, in a queer approach to ethnography that acknowledges relationality, the research field extends beyond formal research spaces (interviews, focus groups, etc.) to include informal spaces of what Kath Browne has called "*fieldworkings* as performativities and intersubjectivities between the researcher and participants."[2] Power, in this approach, becomes multidirectional, the researcher and those being researched exercising power over one another, becoming dependent on one another, and making use of one another (or, putting it more positively, serving one another's interests). Thus, instead of my one-directionally asking him questions and his satisfying my academic curiosity (and agreeing to participate in a research project that advances my career), this informant blurred the boundaries, making me and my work part of *his* project, the project of changing the international perception of the lgbt community in Kenya and elsewhere in Africa. When he called me an ambassador, he expressed trust in my research and in me personally. His farewell message also acknowledged a certain level of "sameness" that this participant perceived between me and himself and his community—a sameness based not only on our shared sexual orientation but also on a shared political and religious commitment. Of course, this notion of sameness is not unproblematic. For instance, insofar as it is based on a shared sexual orientation, it assumes a universally shared "gay identity" that fails to acknowledge our very different experiences of gayness—mine as a European gay man and his as a Kenyan gay man, with our different social environments. Even if this perceived sameness provided a basis for our evolving friendship, it does not deny the differences—in geographical location, socioeconomic class, cultural background, financial security, degree of legal rights and freedom, and so on—that separate us. These differences affect my ability to serve as an ambassador and to tell the stories of a Kenyan lgbt community of which I, in the end, may at most be a friend and ally, but not a member myself (even if, at my last Sunday service at CAC, in July 2018, the minister declared me a member of the congregation). At the same time, whatever exactly is meant by "ambassador" in this context, this participant *had observed me* and had concluded that I was in a position to represent the community I had been researching. He trusted me to tell truthful stories about CAC and its people.

I also love my young friend's message because of the sense of optimism it bespeaks. This optimism was widely shared among Kenyan lgbt people at the time of my fieldwork, and is captured in the statement of one of Kenya's most prominent gay activists, Eric Gitari, that his country is becoming "a regional leader in gay rights."[3] The optimism reflected here stands in stark contrast to the dominant narrative about homosexuality and lgbt rights in Africa, which continues to reinforce generalizing ideas about "African homophobia" and African queer victimhood. This research participant explicitly commissioned me to tell a much more nuanced alternative narrative—one that balances stories of lgbt struggle and victimization with stories about lgbt achievements, about the changes taking place in Kenya right now, about the remarkable courage of lgbt Kenyans and their significant potential to make further gains. Indeed, telling a nuanced story has been one of the major aims of this book, and I truly hope that my friend and his comrades consider my attempt successful.

But why did this participant feel that the Kenyan lgbt community needs an ambassador in the first place—and a white European ambassador at that? Can the community not speak for itself, and tell its own stories? In fact, initiatives such as the *Stories of Our Lives* project (chapter 3) show that the community is very capable of doing so. At the same time, it is undeniable that my position, status, and privilege enable me to share these stories in places where they otherwise would not easily be shared—in the lecture rooms of the university where I teach, in the conference rooms of international academic meetings where I present my research, in the journals in which I publish my work, in the pages of this book. I have tried to use this position in a way that does justice to the full range of the experiences of my informants and to their aspirations and hopes for the future. Thus the meaning of the word *ambassador*, in the young Kenyan's farewell message, comes very close, I believe, to what in the context of social research is called advocacy. "Research as advocacy" refers to a situation in which "the researcher role becomes merged with that of supporting the group being studied in a political or other sense," and it "is focused on changing the way others see or treat those being researched."[4] As much as I have understood my project in such terms from the beginning, the message from my participant friend underlined the importance and validity of this perspective, not only in my own eyes but *in the eyes of the research community*.

Conclusion

The preceding chapters have examined various cases of Kenyan, Christian, and queer arts of resistance, drawing attention to the creative and artistic expressions through which lgbt activists and communities in Kenya are engaging in queer politics. Inspired by a broad notion of African cultural production, I have used the term *arts of resistance* as a heuristic concept to examine a variety of art forms and genres, ranging from the literary, audio-visual, and social media texts used by Binyavanga Wainaina, to the music video "Same Love," produced by Art Attack, to the autobiographical storytelling adopted by The Nest in their *Stories of Our Lives* project, to the creative forms of community organizing around religious belief and practice in Cosmopolitan Affirming Church.

In the discussion of these various artistic expressions, my focus has been less on their aesthetic dimensions than on their political significance. My interest is not in "arts" as such, but in arts as activism, or *artivism*. This focus is inspired by James Scott's classic study *Domination and the Arts of Resistance*. Scott offers an astute analysis of the ways in which culture and religion operate as registers where patterns of social, economic, and political domination, subordination, and resistance are enacted. Focusing on heavily dominated groups of people, such as black slaves in America and the Dalits, or untouchables, in India, Scott distinguishes between the "public transcript" of the interactions between these subordinated groups and the groups dominating them, and the "hidden transcript" of discourses used by subordinated people when they are out of sight and hearing of the power holders. The hidden transcript consists "of those off stage speeches, gestures, and practices that confirm, contradict, or inflect what appears in the public transcript"; it is "the privileged site for nonhegemonic, contrapuntal, dissident, subversive discourse." Between these two transcripts, Scott observes a territory of what he calls "the arts of political disguise," by which he means "the manifold strategies by which subordinate groups manage to insinuate their resistance, in disguised forms, into the public transcript."[1] He discusses basic techniques of disguise, such as anonymity, euphemism, and grumbling, as well as more culturally elaborate forms of disguise, such as oral culture, folktales, and rituals of reversal such as carnival.

Scott's theoretical framework might seem of limited use to the analysis of the case studies of Kenyan lgbt activism in this book. Each of the case studies presents forms more of "public" than of "hidden" resistance. Wainaina and Art Attack actively make use of the opportunities opened up by the internet, inserting their literary and audio-visual artivist expressions into the public sphere through YouTube, Facebook, Twitter, and other online forums, while The Nest used the more traditional form of publishing a book (though the book is also available in an electronic format, is promoted on a website, and is accompanied by a film with the same title). Cosmopolitan Affirming Church can perhaps best be described as semipublic, as this group so far has operated more or less under the radar of the general Kenyan public, although it has a public social media presence and a website with contact details, and its members gather every Sunday in downtown Nairobi. The difference between the public forms of resistance featured in this book and the hidden or disguised forms of resistance that Scott discusses is in part a difference of sociohistorical context and related technical opportunities. Scott's examples are mostly historical, and his book came out when the internet was still in a very early stage of development. As the preceding chapters have demonstrated, lgbt activists and communities in Kenya, and more broadly in Africa, gratefully make use of online forms of communication, mobilization, and action. However, this difference also reveals the stage of lgbt activism and queer politics in Kenya, and the sociopolitical context in which they operate. The strategic use of highly public instead of hidden forms of resistance, and of explicit rather than disguised strategies of political action, indicates that the individuals and communities involved feel rather emboldened and empowered. Apparently, they are not as heavily dominated, or as systematically subordinated, as the people featured in Scott's study. After all, their forms of resistance are being facilitated by transnational actors in the form of mostly Western lgbt and human rights organizations and movements, on the one hand, and progressive forces and developments in Kenyan society, on the other. As much as each of the case studies contests a hegemonic public transcript of homophobia and heteronormativity in the Kenyan public sphere, within the same public sphere there also exist counter-hegemonic discourses that offer support and protection to lgbt activists and communities. Thus Scott's binary categories of dominator and subordinated are too simplistic; instead, we must "treat agency and resistance . . . as practices dialogically produced in the interaction between state and society situated within a global system of power relations."[2]

Although the case studies presented here do not involve hidden transcripts, Scott's account of arts of resistance can help us understand them. As Scott argues, "Resistance to ideological domination requires a counterideology—a negation—that will effectively provide a general normative form to the host of resistant practices invented in self-defense by any subordinate group."[3] In this conclusion, I aim to reconstruct the general contours and strategies of a counterideology or counternarrative that I see emerging from the case studies. I do this in relation to the three key words in the title of this book—Kenyan, Christian, and queer—in two combinations: Kenyan-queer and Christian-queer. In this way I aim to distinguish three modes of resistance—critique, appropriation, and transformation—that can be discerned from the artivist texts discussed in the preceding chapters. By *critique* I mean the critical questioning of particular discourses, institutions, and norms and their relation to power—in Foucauldian terms, critique as an intervention in the politics of truth. For Foucault, "critique is the movement through which the subject gives himself [*sic*] the right to question truth on its effects of power and question power on its discourses of truth." Interestingly, he also describes it as a form of art, that is, an "art of voluntary insubordination, that of reflected intractability."[4] The notion of appropriation is commonly used in postcolonial theory to denote "the ways in which the dominated or colonized culture can use the tools of the dominant discourse to resist its political or cultural control."[5] It thus refers to processes through which colonized, subjugated, or otherwise marginalized groups resist hegemonic uses of certain sociocultural symbols and practices, and reclaim these to articulate and affirm their own identities. Transformation, finally, builds on the constructive and creative edge of both critique and appropriation. It refers to the new narratives that emerge from and through the discourses and practices of resistance of marginalized communities. As Bill Ashcroft points out, "Creative artists often seem to express most forcefully the imaginative vision of a society. But artists, writers and performers only capture more evocatively that capacity for transformation which is demonstrated at every level of society. . . . The imaginative and the creative are integral aspects of that process by which identity itself has come into being."[6] The overall interest of this book is in the newly imagined and creatively constructed Kenyan, Christian, queer identities that emerge from the texts of Kenyan lgbt artivism under discussion.

KENYAN QUEER ARTS OF RESISTANCE

A mode of critique can be observed in the various ways in which the texts under discussion draw critical attention to the sociopolitical opposition to homosexuality and lgbt rights in Kenya and in Africa more generally. We can see this most directly in the "Same Love" video, which in its lyrics explicitly denounces "the new African culture" of homophobia; the lyrics are supported by images of Ghanaian and Ugandan homophobic newspaper headlines and Kenyan politicians and religious leaders participating in the Protect the Family March. Binyavanga Wainaina has also publicly condemned the ways in which public space, in Kenya and other African countries, has been occupied by conservative religious forces spreading the demon of homophobia wherever they go. In *Stories of Our Lives,* we find narrative criticisms of the same dynamics, as storytellers narrate their personal experiences of discrimination, exclusion, and marginalization in Kenyan society because of their sexual orientations and gender identities. Their anonymity protects them from the fear of retaliation; in Scott's words, it serves "to shield their identity while facilitating open criticism."[7] Recall, for instance, the narrator who, having shared his experiences of harassment, concluded by saying that "this was the real Kenya, and this is what gay people go through."[8] Thus, in this explicit mode of critique, the case studies contest the strategies through which "a variety of sexual experiences, expressions and desires [have been] excluded from the realm of respectable citizenship," with queer forms of sexuality widely depicted as "un-Kenyan" and "un-African," leading lgbt people to be criminalized and demonized.[9]

The case studies reveal not only how lgbt people critique such patterns of exclusion and persecution, but also how they appropriate language and symbols that reinforce their claims to Kenyan identity. We see this in *Stories of Our Lives* in the narrator who said, "I am a homosexual, and very proud of that, and I am a Kenyan";[10] and we see it in the "Same Love" scenes of queer love in popular recreational spots like Fourteen Falls Park, Paradise Lost Park, and the Nairobi Arboretum. Both the arboretum and Uhuru Park have important political meanings in the Kenyan public mind and are sites of citizenship, which makes their occasional use by Cosmopolitan Affirming Church for prayer picnics a deeply symbolic act. Along with Kenyanness as a narrative of nationality and citizenship, lgbt artivism in these ways reclaims a cultural and political sense of African identity and pride, a distinct rejection of the popular claim that homosexuality is "un-African." This reappropriation of Africanness can be observed in the "Same Love" video's use of the South African flag as a symbol of an African trajectory of liberation and diversity, and in Wainaina's self-fashioning as Afropolitan. Moreover, a pan-Africanist strategy, such as Wainaina's invocation of the legacy of Martin Luther King and James Baldwin, or the references in "Same Love" to the civil rights struggle, reclaims not just an African but a black pan-African identity. Since sexuality has become a site for the contestation of African authenticity, these rhetorical and symbolic strategies allow lgbt folk to inscribe themselves into narratives of Africanness. This is significant because it adds nuance to accounts of global lgbt activism and queer politics as driven by a mostly white and Western "gay international."[11] Inasmuch as Kenyans have appropriated modern, originally Western narratives of lgbt identity, the case studies also reflect allusions to African histories of homosexuality, histories that remind us of the complex and transitional nature of gender and sexual diversity in postcolonial Africa. Regardless of the specific ways of conceptualizing sexuality, a thread running through the case studies is the appropriation of a language of love. This not only challenges and resists the popular view of same-sex relationships as concerned only with sex (as an abominable or animalistic physical act), but also contests Western racist and colonialist narratives in which Africa, according to Achille Mbembe, "is never seen as possessing things and attributes properly part of 'human nature,'" in this case specifically the ability to experience and express love.[12]

Obviously, the boundary between appropriation and transformation is fluid. The queer appropriation of these symbols and narratives involves their creative reconstruction, yielding new understandings of Kenyan and African identity. In the words of Homi Bhabha, these are "counter-narratives" that "disturb those ideological manoeuvres through which 'imagined communities' are given essentialist identities."[13] Whereas in popular discourse these essentialist identities are centered around ahistorical and nativist claims of an authentic "African" sexuality that is purely heterosexual, queer counter-narratives open up alternative imagined communities. The stories told in this book—of gay romance in the Nairobi Arboretum, of lgbt Christian worship in downtown Nairobi, of the refusal in so many "stories of our lives" to be shamed, broken, and hidden away—reconstruct narratives of Kenyan and

African identity within an ethical and political framework of diversity, equality, and freedom. The pan-African tendencies that we observe here insert a particular sense of black African pride into this framework, with a progressive commitment to sexual and racial as well as economic justice. The case studies draw on a "utopian political imagination" that enables us "to glimpse another time and place."[14] Through a variety of symbolic and discursive performances, they hold out the possibility of a queer African future as a powerful alternative to the Afro-pessimist narrative of "African homophobia."

CHRISTIAN QUEER ARTS OF RESISTANCE

With regard to Christianity, the case study that most explicitly approaches critique as an art of resistance is embodied in Binyavanga Wainaina. Wainaina systematically and persistently denounces the role of Christianity in driving homophobic politics in Kenya and other African countries. Reminding the public that Christianity itself was a colonial invention in Kenya and much of Africa, he exposes and attacks its ongoing colonizing tendencies. Making contemporary Pentecostal movements a particular target, he turns the Pentecostal rhetorical trope of demonization on Christianity itself, and suggests that Africa needs deliverance from this hypocritical religiosity and its sociopolitical agenda. The other case studies mount similar critiques of conservative Christianity in Africa. The "Same Love" video includes images of an antihomosexuality march organized by Kenyan Christian organizations to illustrate that religion is a key driver in homophobia's becoming the "new African culture." Several of the narratives in *Stories of Our Lives* describe queer people's exclusion and marginalization in the church. Cosmopolitan Affirming Church puts the critique of Kenyan Christianity's role in homophobia into the broader picture of global Christianity, and blames white American conservative evangelical Christians for promoting a "dominionist" form of Christianity. It is notable that many of these critiques are not formulated on a strictly secular basis but actively draw on religious registers.[15] Lgbt people have creatively appropriated Christian beliefs, texts, and symbols to make the case that they too are beloved in God's eyes and have the same right to practice their Christian faith that their heterosexual brothers and sisters do. They prove that queer critique can in fact be Christian—thus challenging the dominant Western notion that queer politics must necessarily be secular. This highlights a critical feature of public religion in contemporary Africa: as a publicly available archive, it is engaged and utilized by both conservative and progressive actors involved in the wars over what can be called "public sexuality."[16]

Christianity as a public religion is clearly a key site for African queer imagination and politics, which draws our attention to appropriation as a mode of resistance. Wainaina, again, exemplifies this trend. Although he is perhaps the most radical critic of Christianity discussed in this book, he calls upon the essence of the Christian faith in his critique of the homophobic tendencies of Kenyan and African Christianity. He invokes the memory not only of King and Baldwin but of the radical Jesus to blast what he perceives as the corrupted gospel preached in many African churches today. Likewise, many of the *Stories of Our Lives* narrators appropriate language about God and Jesus Christ to oppose institutional Christian religion, while in "Same Love," a well-known biblical text is appropriated to critique churches that preach hatred. Perhaps the most extensive appropriation takes place in the context of Cosmopolitan Affirming Church—a community that reclaims not only Christian beliefs, practices, texts, and symbols, but also the organizational form of "church."

The Bible and the Christian faith, then, are appropriated as "the master's tools," as Audre Lorde puts it, with which activists try to dismantle "the master's house"—in this case, the house of homo- and transphobia in a Christian guise.[17] Although Lorde (writing in a different context) suggests that such a strategy will prove fruitless, the Kenyan queer actors appear to believe otherwise. They have added another chapter to the long history of Christianity as a site of agency and resistance in Africa. In this history, colonial political subjugation and racial domination were originally the critical issues; in more recent decades, the issues have centered around the struggle for democracy, gender equality, and social and economic justice, while in the chapter currently being written, postcolonial homophobia is of major concern. Given that Christianity is such an important resource for Kenyan lgbt activists, it is striking that it has received little attention in the emerging field of African queer studies. In Kenya and elsewhere in Africa, perhaps even more than in North America or Europe, religious discourse might be "the secret that queer theory has hidden (in plain sight) from itself."[18] In order to be relevant in African contexts, then, queer studies will need to make a decolonizing and postsecular intervention, and must acknowledge and understand religion as a critical, creative, and constructive site of lgbt activism and queer politics.

Scott points out that "inasmuch as the major historical forms of domination have presented themselves in the form of a metaphysics, a religion, a worldview, they have provoked the development of more or less equally elaborate replies in the hidden transcript." He refers to black slave religion in America, which "was not merely a negation of the style of official services" that the enslaved had to attend but also "contradicted its content."[19] A similar process can be discerned in contemporary homophobia and heteronormativity, and its concrete effects on the lives of lgbt people in Kenya and elsewhere in Africa. Not only have they appropriated Christian beliefs and symbols, but they have transformed the essence and meaning of Christian faith itself. We see this in Wainaina's claims about "the real Jesus," about whom he has learned thanks to Martin Luther King and James Baldwin, and whom he sets against the false Jesus that he hears preached about in churches across the continent. The "Same Love" video's concluding statement that "love is God and God is love" transforms a homophobic God into a God who not only accepts and affirms same-sex love but is the source of the human capacity to make love. *Stories of Our Lives* presents plenty of examples of alternative interpretations of biblical texts and understandings of God and Christ. Not surprisingly, we find the most elaborate example of the appropriation and transformation of Christian beliefs and practices in Cosmopolitan Affirming Church. In its weekly worship services and other gatherings, the CAC community shows us that another form of Christianity is possible in Kenya, and that African Christianity can be transformed in a progressive, lgbt-affirming direction. Whereas the study of queer Christianities so far has been concerned with Western contexts, this book draws attention to the nascent beginnings of an African queer Christian movement as a "lived religion in transgressive forms" emerging on Kenyan soil.[20] This development is particularly crucial in that African Christianity, in the words of Andrew Walls, has become "a major component of contemporary representative Christianity, the standard Christianity of the present age, a demonstration model of its character."[21] As valid as Walls's point is, the present study shows that African Christianity is far from homogenous, and that there is a potential for divergent future trajectories. Engaging with the work of Edward Antonio, Emmanuel Katongole, Sarojini Nadar, Mercy Oduyoye, and other African theologians in the fields of Christianity, gender, and sexuality has allowed an exploration of this potential, demonstrating that theology can serve as an art of resistance and offer a vision of "abundant life for all."[22] These theologies represent and reinforce the hope that "another world is possible," and that such a queer world can be imagined from black, African, and Christian perspectives.[23]

The creative appropriation and transformation of Christianity by Kenyan lgbt actors appears to be inspired by a pan-African vision; three of the case studies explicitly demonstrate a transatlantic engagement with the African American civil rights movement and black prophetic Christianity. This book has thus unexpectedly moved into the emerging field of Africana religious studies, a field concerned with the religious cultures of and relationships between African and African-descended people.[24] Although sexuality has not yet figured prominently in Africana religion research, the case studies presented here draw attention to the ways in which activism around sexuality in contemporary Africa has provided momentum for creative and innovative exchanges between African lgbt actors and African American social movements and traditions of thought, especially in a Christian frame of reference. Thus the various arts of resistance studied in this book represent the possibility of a black, pan-African, and Christian form of queer imagination and politics, as an alternative to widespread homophobic forms of Christianity, popular antigay pan-Africanist discourses, and influential (typically white Euro-American) secular forms of lgbt activism. This, in turn, might open up critical avenues for rethinking the nature and future of Christianity and of activism around queer sexualities in Kenya, other African contexts, and beyond.

In the process of writing this book, I have also sought to engage in arts of resistance myself. Accounting for my ethnographic self, I have resisted dominant norms of detached and disembodied scholarship. For better or worse, I have tried to provide insight into the messiness of my fieldwork practice, the relational and embodied nature of my academic research, and the enmeshment of my private, professional, and political selves. This is my attempt at scholarly honesty and integrity, and above all at addressing and interrogating the various forms of othering potentially at issue in a project like this one. I recognize that it is my relatively privileged position as an academic with a secure position in a British university that enables me to resist and transgress certain academic conventions. Yet I hope that this openness will encourage others, and that this book will contribute to queer world-making in academia, specifically in the fields of African studies and religious studies, and to deeply humane scholarship that acknowledges and affirms our common, embodied human nature in all its complexity.

Notes

INTRODUCTION

1. Isaac Ongiri, "Gay Rights 'Non-issue,' Kenyan President Uhuru Kenyatta Says Ahead of Obama Visit," *Daily Nation*, July 21, 2015, http://www.nation.co.ke/news/Gay-rights-non-issue-Uhuru-Obama/1056-2801274-10eqhyx/index.html.

2. Joe Williams, "Obama Will Raise Gay Rights Issues Despite Kenya's Threats," *Pink News*, July 8, 2015, http://www.pinknews.co.uk/2015/07/08/obama-will-raise-gay-rights-issues-despite-kenyas-threats/.

3. *Daily Nation*, "Uhuru Kenyatta Dismisses Gays Rights as a Non Issue in Kenya," July 25, 2015, https://youtu.be/mFLd13yf5AE.

4. Kidala Vincent, "Notification of Peaceful Procession," Republican Liberty Party, July 13, 2015, http://houseofuzy.blogspot.com/2015/07/5000-naked-women-to-show-obama.html.

5. Maupeu, "Political Activism in Nairobi," 399.

6. For a reconstruction of the origins of this idea, see Epprecht, *Heterosexual Africa*.

7. Awondo, "Politicisation of Sexuality."

8. Scott Mills, *Uganda: The World's Worst Place to Be Gay?*, film documentary (London: BBC, 2011).

9. Otu, "LGBT Human Rights Expeditions." See also Awondo, Geschiere, and Reid, "Homophobic Africa"; Thoreson, "Troubling the Waters."

10. Hendriks, "Queer(ing) Popular Culture," 1.

11. Ombagi, "Nairobi Is a Shot of Whisky," 1.

12. Ekine, "Contesting Narratives of Queer Africa," 85.

13. See Currier, *Out in Africa*; Lorway, *Namibia's Rainbow Project*; Nyeck and Epprecht, *Sexual Diversity in Africa*.

14. Currier and Cruz, "Civil Society and Sexual Struggles," 338.

15. This sense of optimism is reflected, for instance, in Epprecht, *Sexuality and Social Justice*.

16. Currier and Migraine-George, "Queer Studies/African Studies," 292.

17. Obadare and Willems, *Civic Agency in Africa*. The concept of "arts of resistance" is derived from Scott, *Domination and the Arts of Resistance*.

18. Sandoval and Latorre, "Chicana/o Artivism," 82. For an example in an African context, see Artivists 4 Life, Robinson, and Cambre, "Youth Artivism in Uganda."

19. Asante, *It's Bigger Than Hip Hop*, 203.

20. Hellweg, "Same-Gender Desire," 890.

21. Eng, Halberstam, and Muñoz, "What's Queer About Queer Studies," 1.

22. Currier and Migraine-George, "Queer Studies/African Studies," 284.

23. Epprecht, *Heterosexual Africa*, 17, 16.

24. Mohanty, "Under Western Eyes."

25. Epprecht, *Heterosexual Africa*, 14.

26. Tellis and Bala, *Global Trajectories of Queerness*.

27. See, for example, Ekine and Abbas, *Queer African Reader*; Matebeni, *Reclaiming Afrikan*; Sandfort et al., *Boldly Queer*.

28. E.g., Martin and Xaba, *Queer Africa*; Mwachiro, *Invisible*.

29. Currier and Migraine-George, "Queer Studies/African Studies," 289.

30. Ekine and Abbas, "Introduction," 3.

31. Currier and Migraine-George, "Queer Studies/African Studies"; Macharia, "Archive and Method."

32. Spurlin, *Imperialism Within the Margins*, 29, 17.

33. Epprecht, *Sexuality and Social Justice*, 24.

34. Zabus, *Out in Africa*, 5.

35. Currier and Migraine-George, "Queer Studies/African Studies," 290, 291.

36. Macharia, "Archive and Method," 145.

37. For more on these ideas, see Wariboko, *Charismatic City*; Mendieta and VanAntwerpen, *Power of Religion*.

38. Casanova, *Public Religions*, 5.

39. Casanova, "Public Religions Revisited."

40. See, for instance, Ellis and Ter Haar, *Worlds of Power*.

41. Van Klinken, "Gay Rights, the Devil," 522.

42. Mbembe, *On the Postcolony*, 93.

43. Larkin and Meyer, "Pentecostalism, Islam, and Culture," 287.

44. Shankar, "Civil Society and Religion," 27.

45. Burchardt, "Equals Before the Law," 239.

46. Mbiti, *African Religions and Philosophy*, 1.

47. Ellis and Ter Haar, *Worlds of Power*, 2.

48. Shankar, "Civil Society and Religion," 34.

49. Wilcox, "Outlaws or In-Laws," 73.

50. Comstock and Henking, "Introduction," 11.

51. Wilcox, "Outlaws or In-Laws," 74.

52. Jenzen and Munt, "Queer Theory," 47.

53. Wilcox, "Outlaws or In-Laws," 74.

54. Spurlin, *Imperialism Within the Margins*, 29.

55. Wilson, "Socio-Political Dynamics," 545.

56. Wilcox, "Outlaws or In-Laws," 94.

57. See Boisvert and Johnson, *Queer Religion*, vol. 2.

58. Epprecht, *Sexuality and Social Justice*, 67.

59. Nyanzi, "Queering Queer Africa," 67.

60. Van Klinken and Otu, "Ancestors, Embodiment."

61. See, for instance, Gaudio, *Allah Made Us*; Muparamoto, "Enduring and Subverting Homophobia."

62. Adejunmobi, "Provocations," 61, 59.

63. Ekotto and Harrow, "Introduction," 3–4.

64. Muñoz, *Cruising Utopia*, 135.

65. Macharia, "Archive and Method," 140.

66. Halberstam, *Female Masculinity*, 13.

67. Chitando, Adogame, and Bateye, "Introduction," 9.

68. For an introduction to African theology, see Parratt, *Reinventing Christianity*. For an overview of recent developments, see Stinton, *African Theology on the Way*.

69. See Martey, *African Theology*; Mugambi, *Christian Theology and Social Reconstruction*; Oduyoye, *Introducing African Women's Theology*.

70. Van Klinken and Gunda, "Taking Up the Cudgels."

71. Njoroge, "Beyond Suffering and Lament," 119.

72. Dube, *HIV and AIDS Bible*, 40.

73. Phiri, "Born This Way." See also Van Klinken and Phiri, "'In the Image of God.'"

74. Gunda, *Bible and Homosexuality*; Togarasei and Chitando, "'Beyond the Bible.'"

75. Bongmba, "Hermeneutics and the Debate"; Bongmba, "Homosexuality, Ubuntu, and Otherness."

76. West, "Queer Theological Pedagogy," 216.

77. Hackett, "Field Envy," 99.

78. Coffey, *Ethnographic Self*, 9.

79. Conquergood, "Rethinking Ethnography," 181.

80. For more on this subject, see Kulick and Willson, *Taboo*; and Markowitz and Ashkenazi, *Sex, Sexuality, and the Anthropologist*.

81. Hoel, "Embodying the Field"; Hoel, "Taking the Body Seriously"; Gilliat-Ray, "Body-Works and Fieldwork."

82. Orsi, *Between Heaven and Earth*, 14.

83. Mbembe, *On the Postcolony*, 2.

84. Coffey, *Ethnographic Self*, 1.

85. Butler, *Precarious Life*, xx.

86. Spivak, "Can the Subaltern Speak," 297; Rao, *Third World Protest*, xx.

87. Gifford, *Christianity, Politics, and Public Life*, 249, 112, 135.

88. Parsitau and Mwaura, "God in the City," 99.

89. Deacon and Lynch, "Allowing Satan In," 126.

90. Deacon, "Kenya"; Bompani, "For God and for My Country"; Van Klinken, "Gay Rights, the Devil."

91. Karanja quoted in Catherine Karongo, "NCCK Says No to Push for Gay Marriages," *Capital News*, May 11, 2012, https://www.capitalfm.co.ke/news/2012/05/ncck-says-no-to-push-for-gay-marriages/. For the 2012 report, see Kenya National Commission on Human Rights, "Realising Sexual and Reproductive Health Rights in Kenya: A Myth or Reality?," April 2012, http://www.knchr.org/portals/0/reports/reproductive_health_report.pdf.

92. Lydia Matata, "Kenya: MPs, Religious Leaders to Hold Anti-Gay Protest on Monday,"

Star, July 4, 2015, https://allafrica.com/stories/201507040102.html.

93. Ndzovu, "Un-Natural, Un-African."

94. Ocholla, "Kenyan LGBTI Social Movement."

95. Mburu, "Awakenings," 189.

96. Kenyatta, *Facing Mount Kenya*, 156.

97. Quoted in Baraka and Morgan, "'I Want to Marry,'" 25.

98. Samuel Karanja, "William Ruto Vows to Defend Kenya Against Homosexuality," *Daily Nation*, July 5, 2015, http://www.nation.co.ke/news/politics/William-Ruto-Gay-Rights-Homosexuality/1064-2775872-cpjhn6z/index.html.

99. Musila, "Phallocracies and Gynocratic Transgressions."

100. Macharia, "Queer Kenya," 273.

101. Murunga, "Elite Compromises," 159.

102. Eric Gitari, "Kenya Leads in LGBT Equality in the Region," *Star*, April 1, 2016, https://www.the-star.co.ke/news/2016/04/01/kenya-leads-in-lgbt-equality-in-the-region_c1317474.

103. *Daily Nation*, "Kenyatta Dismisses Gays Rights." See also Christiane Amanpour, "President: Gay Rights 'of No Importance' in Kenya," CNN, April 20, 2018, https://edition.cnn.com/videos/world/2018/04/20/kenya-uhuru-kenyatta-gay-rights-intv-amanpour-intl.cnn/video/playlists/africa/.

104. Gitari, "Kenya Leads in LGBT Equality."

105. Macharia, "Queer Kenya."

106. Mwangi, "Queer Agency," 94.

107. For more on this idea, see Njogu and Oluoch-Olunya, *Cultural Production*.

108. Esther, interview by author, Mombasa, March 15, 2016.

109. Minister Moses, interview by author, Nairobi, July 23, 2018.

CHAPTER 1

1. Msibi, "Lies We Have Been Told," 72.

2. Adebanwi, "Writer as Social Thinker."

3. Mateveke, "Critique and Alternative Imaginations."

4. Baderoon, "'I Compose Myself,'" 903.

5. Knighton, "Refracting the Political," 33.

6. "Binyavanga Wainaina, Kenyan Author, Comes Out as Gay to Challenge Homophobic Laws," *HuffPost*, January 21, 2014, https://www.huffingtonpost.com/2014/01/21/gay-kenyan-author-_n_4639443.html.

7. Julius Sigei, "Binyavanga Drops Gay Bombshell," *Daily Nation*, January 21, 2014, http://www.nation.co.ke/news/Binyavanga-drops-gay-bombshell/-/1056/2155250/-/ev2e1vz/-/index.html.

8. Ekine, "Beyond Anti-LGBTI Legislation," 19.

9. Sigei, "Binyavanga Drops Gay Bombshell."

10. Mwachiro, "Lost Chapter Found."

11. "Wainaina Declares: 'I Am Gay, and Quite Happy,'" *Mail and Guardian*, January 22, 2014, https://mg.co.za/article/2014-01-22-wainaina-declares-i-am-gay-and-quite-happy.

12. Binyavanga Wainaina, "I Am a Homosexual, Mum," Africa Is a Country, 2014, http://chimurengachronic.co.za/i-am-a-homosexual-mum-by-binyavanga-wainaina/.

13. Binyavanga Wainaina (@BinyavangaW), Twitter, January 20, 2014, 10:41 P.M.

14. Binyavanga Wainaina, "Bring Me the Obedient Children," part 1 of *We Must Free Our Imaginations (1/6)* January 21, 2014, https://www.youtube.com/watch?v=8uMwppw5AgU&t=94s.

15. "Kalota who lived in my home, the sweetest young man. 23 years old, too ashamed to ask for a HIV test..died Dec 2012. Died of shame." Binyavanga Wainaina (@BinyavangaW), Twitter, January 21, 2014, 7:47 A.M.

16. Okey Ndibe, "The Binyavanga Wainaina Interview (Part 1)," This Is Africa, April 10, 2014, https://thisisafrica.me/binyavanga-wainaina-interview-part-1/.

17. The Anti-Homosexuality Act passed in the Parliament of Uganda on December 20, 2013, while the Same-Sex Marriage (Prohibition) Act in Nigeria was signed into law by President Goodluck Jonathan on January 14, 2014.

18. Reuters, "Kenyan Writer Binyavanga Wainaina Comes Out and Vows to Challenge Homophobia in Africa," ITN, January 31, 2014, http://www.itnsource.com/en/shotlist/RTV/2014/01/31/RTV310114006/.

19. Halperin, *Saint Foucault*, 30.

20. Knighton, "Refracting the Political," 33.

21. Binyavanga Wainaina, "How to Write About Africa," Granta, January 19, 2006, https://granta.com/how-to-write-about-africa/.

22. See Tim Adams, "Binyavanga Wainaina Interview: Coming Out in Kenya," *Guardian*, February 16, 2014, https://www.theguardian.com/books/2014/feb/16/binyavanga-wainaina-gay-rights-kenya-africa.

23. Knighton, "Refracting the Political," 44.

24. Mbembe, "African Modes of Self-Writing," 263.

25. "Valentine Njoroge and Binyavanga Wainaina (Being Gay in Kenya)," *Jeff Koinange Live*, KTN News Kenya, January 29, 2014, https://www.youtube.com/watch?vCANd4G_ewBY.

26. Binyavanga Wainaina, Facebook, April 20, 2017, https://www.facebook.com/binyavanga.wainaina/posts/10154346462387343.

27. "I'm HIV+ and Happy, Says Binyavanga Wainaina," *Daily Nation*, December 8, 2016, https://www.nation.co.ke/news/I-m-HIV--and-happy-says-Binyavanga-Wainaina/1056-3479162-9bpnfm/index.html.

28. "A year later, I can begin to unpack the deep, toxic lesbophobia that enables gay men and straight men to bond in mutual misogyny to hurl 'lesbian' at women who speak out about sexual violence"; "Misogyny makes strange bedfellows. The spectacle of The Only Gay Man In Kenya (TOGMIK), ganging up with some of Kenya's most virulently homophobic public agitators, to jointly attack Kenyan women." Shailja Patel (@ShailjaPatel), Twitter, November 12, 2017, 11:53 P.M. and 12:18 A.M., respectively.

29. Johnson and Anderson, "Revealing Prophets," 6.

30. Kenya is not unique here. For example, observers have described Zimbabwe as "under the grip of a prophetic craze," especially owing to the emergence of young Pentecostal prophets. See Chitando, Gunda, and Kügler, "Introduction," 9.

31. Johnson and Anderson, "Revealing Prophets," 17, 19.

32. Okey Ndibe, "The Binyavanga Wainaina Interview (Part 2)," This Is Africa, April 10, 2014, https://thisisafrica.me/binyavanga-wainaina-interview-part-2/.

33. Binyavanga Wainaina, "This Ecstasy of Madness," part 2 of *We Must Free Our Imaginations (2/6)*, January 21, 2014, https://www.youtube.com/watch?v=SQrln8pogNw&t=68s.

34. Binyavanga Wainaina, "A Letter to All Kenyans from Binyavanga Wainaina or Binyavanga wa Muigai," *Brittle Paper*, October 25, 2017, https://brittlepaper.com/2017/10/kenyas-presidential-election-binyavanga-wainaina-essay/.

35. Shulman, *American Prophecy*, 132.

36. "That name Baldwin, is black, African, ours, the world's. don't fear those who put our values in the center of changing the world." Binyavanga Wainaina (@BinyavangaW), Twitter, March 9, 2014, 10:42 P.M.

37. "The Baldwin who was a 'gay icon of freedom,' an icon of many now forgotten freedoms. U don't get to just choose. now. coz it is separate." Binyavanga Wainaina (@BinyavangaW), Twitter, March 26, 2014, 1:44 A.M.

38. "James Baldwin wrote new scriptures." Binyavanga Wainaina (@BinyavangaW), Twitter, February 7, 2014, 12:48 A.M.

39. Heschel, *Prophets*, 10.

40. Halperin, *Saint Foucault*, 62.

41. Ekine and Abbas, "Introduction," 3.

42. Quoted in Mwachiro, "Lost Chapter Found," 99.

43. The Kikuyu are one of the ethnic groups of Kenya. In this book I spell it with a K, except in some quotations where the original text spells it with a G as Gikuyu.

44. Wainaina, *One Day I Will Write*, 160, 161.

45. For this talk, see Binyavanga Wainaina, "Conversations with Baba," TEDxEuston: Inspiring Ideas About Africa, December 6, 2014, https://www.youtube.com/watch?v=z5uAoBu9Epg.

46. I use the term *Afropolitan* to refer to a particular pan-African fashion and lifestyle, cultivated, for example, by the magazine the *Afropolitan*. Perhaps not coincidentally, that magazine included Wainaina in its list of "Seven of Africa's Brightest Stars" in 2015. Heather Clancy, "Africa Winners," *Afropolitan*, December 25, 2015, http://www.afropolitan.co.za

/articles/africa-winners-3445.html. On gay men's style and effeminacy, see Halperin, *How to Be Gay*.

47. Johnson and Anderson, "Revealing Prophets," 19. For the contest between "true" and "false" prophets, see Vengeyi, "Zimbabwean Pentecostal Prophets."

48. Wainaina, *One Day I Will Write*, 231–32.

49. David Owuor, *Prophecy of the 2007 Horrific Bloodshed in Kenya and Its Stunning Fulfillment*, posted January 22, 2010, https://www.youtube.com/watch?v=nK5EXFe8-nU.

50. "Kenyan Preacher Calls for Church's Repentance," *NewsHub*, September 17, 2014, https://bw.newshub.org/kenyan-preacher-calls-church-s-repentance-3702373.html#.

51. David Owuor, "His Sons No More," *Highway of Holiness*, n.d., http://www.highwayofholiness.us/his-sons-no-more/.

52. Parsitau, "Prophets, Power, Authority."

53. Quoted in Michael Wesonga, "Prophet David Owuor: President Uhuru Kenyatta Called Me over Insecurity," *Standard*, April 21, 2014, https://www.standardmedia.co.ke/?articleID=2000109861.

54. Parsitau, "Embodying Holiness," 181.

55. Burgess, "Pentecostals and Political Culture," 35.

56. "My mum's ex pastor, Mark Kariuki, the most visible anti-homosexuality campaigner in Kenya for years is quiet. I wonder who he is paying?" Binyavanga Wainaina (@BinyavangaW), Twitter, February 24, 2014, 9:11 A.M.

57. EAK, *Kenya Let's Pray*, 1, 19–20, 24, 30.

58. Sadgrove et al., "Morality Plays and Money Matters," 121.

59. See Van Klinken, "Homosexuality, Politics."

60. Kalu, *African Pentecostalism*, 219.

61. Ndibe, "Wainaina Interview (Part 1)." For the TED talk, see n. 45 above.

62. Quoted in Mbugua Ngunjiri, "My Beef with the Church—Binyavanga," SDE City News, 2014, https://www.sde.co.ke/thenairobian/article/2000114669/my-beef-with-the-church-binyavanga.

63. See, for instance, Bediako, *Christianity in Africa*.

64. Antonio, "Introduction," 11.

65. West, *Stolen Bible*, chapter five.

66. Lindhardt, "Introduction"; Meyer, "Christianity in Africa."

67. Ngũgĩ, *Decolonising the Mind*, 2, 26.

68. Ndibe, "Wainaina Interview (Part 2)."

69. Ngunjiri, "My Beef with the Church."

70. Ndibe, "Wainaina Interview (Part 2)."

71. Senyonjo, *All God's Children*, 82.

72. Mombo, "Kenya Reflections," 152.

73. Binyavanga Wainaina, "The Jesus of James Baldwin and Martin Luther King," Facebook, May 4, 2015, https://www.facebook.com/binyavanga.wainaina/posts/10152746795847343.

74. "Goerge Bushe's [*sic*] pastor has had more influence on the imagination of Africans than Martin Luther King and James Baldwin." Binyavanga Wainaina (@BinyavangaW), Twitter, January 24, 2014, 3:55 P.M.

75. For further reading about James Baldwin's relevance for African American Christian and queer thinking, see Hardy, *James Baldwin's God*, and Kornegay, *Queering of Black Theology*.

76. For more on that process, see Kee, *Rise and Demise*.

77. Soyinka, *Of Africa*, 129, 131.

78. In this way, Pentecostalism continues and at the same time transforms (through a Christian dualism) traditional African ontologies in which the spirit world is believed to be closely associated with, and to have direct effects on, the human realm. For a discussion of this dynamic, see Lindhardt, "Continuity, Change, or Coevalness."

79. Maxwell, "'Delivered from the Spirit,'" 361.

80. Hackett, "Discourses of Demonization," 62.

81. Van Klinken, "Gay Rights, the Devil."

82. Wainaina, *One Day I Will Write*, 65–66.

83. "My mother died partly because—as child of Pastor Mark 'Demon Remove' Kariuki, she stopped to believe her diabetes was real." Binyavanga Wainaina (@BinyavangaW), Twitter, January 27, 2014, 11:58 A.M.

84. Wainaina, *We Must Free Our Imaginations (2/6)*.

85. See Murray and Roscoe, *Boy-Wives and Female Husbands*.

86. Ngũgĩ, *Re-Membering Africa*, 28.

87. Bady, "'African Homosexual Deamon.'"

88. For more on this mutually beneficial relationship, see Kaoma, "Marriage of Convenience."

89. Bady, "'African Homosexual Deamon.'"

90. Ward, "Marching or Stumbling," 132.

91. Ndibe, "Wainaina Interview (Part 1)."

92. He uses and identifies with both terms in the 2014 *We Must Free Our Imaginations* video series, although earlier, in his 2012 keynote lecture at the African Studies Association UK conference at the University of Leeds, he dissociated himself from the term *Afropolitanism*. See Stephanie Bosch Santana, "Exorcizing Afropolitanism: Binyavanga Wainaina Explains Why 'I Am a Pan-Africanist, Not an Afropolitan' at ASAUK 2012," *Africa in Words*, February 8, 2013, https://africainwords.com/2013/02/08/exorcizing-afropolitanism-binyavanga-wainaina-explains-why-i-am-a-pan-africanist-not-an-afropolitan-at-asauk-2012/.

93. Muñoz, *Cruising Utopia*, 96.

INTERLUDE 1

1. Folarin, "Miracle," 11, 16, 19, 20.

2. Homewood, "'I Was on Fire,'" 251.

3. Tomlinson, *Ritual Textuality*, 4.

4. Hoel, "Taking the Body Seriously."

CHAPTER 2

1. Currier and Migraine-George, "Queer Studies/African Studies," 292.

2. Macklemore and Ryan Lewis, featuring Mary Lambert, "Same Love," October 2, 2012, https://www.youtube.com/watch?v=hlVBg7_o8no.

3. Art Attack, "Same Love (Remix)," February 15, 2016, https://www.youtube.com/watch?v=8EataOQvPII.

4. Art Attack, "Why We Made a Song About Homosexuality," NoStringsNG, March 7, 2016, http://nostringsng.com/podcast-let-homosexuals-be-art-attack/.

5. See Dhaenens, "Reading Gay Music Videos."

6. Starlit Media, "Is Noti Flow Lesbian? Watch What She Had to Say (#SameLove)," March 1, 2016, https://www.youtube.com/watch?v=YUrZ5H3iFXU.

7. Noti Flow, "Birthday Cake," March 13, 2016. The YouTube link is no longer active, but see http://trendkenyaonline.blogspot.com/2016/03/noti-flows-birthday-cake-music-video-now-on-youtube-watch-dirty-scenes-here.html.

8. Tonny Ndungu, "Kenyan Rapper Stars in Controversial, Steamy Video About Gay People," Tuko, 2016, https://tuko.co.ke/95894-kenyan-rapper-stars-in-a-controversial-steamy-gay-music-video.html.

9. See, for example, Tonny Ndungu, "Kenyan Gay Gospel Singer Who Is HIV Positive Stops Taking His ARV's," Tuko, 2016, https://tuko.co.ke/114242-kenyan-gay-gospel-singer-stops-taking-his-arv-medication-months-after-attempting-suicide.html.

10. CabuGah, "The Story of Joji Baro—The Gay Gospel Artist," *Nairobi Wire*, September 18, 2013, http://nairobiwire.com/2013/09/the-story-of-joji-baro-gay-gospel-artist.html.

11. "Here's First Kenyan Artist to Declare He's Gay," Ghafla, June 20, 2013, http://www.ghafla.com/heres-first-kenyan-artist-to-declare-hes-gay-find-out-who/.

12. John Nalianya, "Kenya: Priest Taught Me Gay Sex—Bungoma Man," *Star*, May 14, 2011, http://allafrica.com/stories/201105160826.html.

13. CabuGah, "Story of Joji Baro."

14. "Meet the People Fighting Homophobia and Transphobia in Africa," *HuffPost*, February 29, 2016, https://www.huffingtonpost.com/entry/love-is-not-a-crime-photography-exhibition-highlight-africas-lgbt-activists_us_56d0c4cbe4b03260bf76e2eb?34i2uik9.

15. CabuGah, "Story of Joji Baro."

16. George Barasa, "I mark ten years of my ministerial work as a gospel musician," Facebook, December 7, 2016.

17. CabuGah, "Story of Joji Baro."

18. George Barasa, interview by author, Nairobi, February 22, 2016.

19. Art Attack, "Why We Made a Song."

20. Sandoval and Latorre, "Chicana/o Artivism," 83.

21. Mwangi, "Queer Agency," 93.

22. Kenya reportedly has experienced the highest growth rates of smartphone use and internet penetration in Africa. See Bloggers

Association of Kenya, *The State of Blogging and Social Media in Kenya, 2015 Report*, 2, http://www.monitor.co.ke/wp-content/uploads/2015/06/The-State-of-Blogging-and-Social-Media-in-Kenya-2015-report.pdf.

23. Art Attack, "Why We Made a Song."

24. Barasa, interview by author, Nairobi, December 9, 2016.

25. Ezekiel Mutua, "Statement by the Kenya Film Classification Board on the YouTube Circulation of 'Same Love Remix' Music Video" (Nairobi: Kenya Film Classification Board, 2016), http://www.kfcb.co.ke/images/docs/press_statement_same_love_music_video.pdf (accessed October 13, 2016; no longer available).

26. Hassan Ndzovu discusses a similar conflation by the majority leader in the Kenyan Parliament, Aden Duale. See Ndzovu, "Un-Natural, Un-African," 82.

27. See, for example, Anthony Langat, "Ban on Sexy Music Video Raises Gay Rights Campaign Profile in Kenya," Reuters, March 10, 2016, http://www.reuters.com/article/kenya-gay-campaign-idUSL5N16H28N. This Reuters article was reprinted in the Kenyan newspaper the *Star* and on the South African news website TimesLive.

28. The exact numbers as of May 16, 2016, were 261,181 viewings, 2,468 likes, 805 dislikes, and 1,472 comments. By the time this book was in production, as of late September 2018, these numbers had increased to 322,951 viewings, 2,900 likes, 949 dislikes, and 1,527 comments.

29. Elizabeth Daley, "Kenyan Creators of Banned 'Same Love' Remix Are 'Living in Fear,'" *Advocate*, February 24, 2016, http://www.advocate.com/world/2016/2/24/watch-kenyan-creators-banned-same-love-remix-are-living-fear.

30. Art Attack, "Why We Made a Song."

31. George Barasa, conversation with author, July 14, 2018.

32. Audrey Mbugua (@AudreyMbugua), Twitter, February 23, 2016, 4:49 A.M.

33. "Kenyans must shout a Big NO to irresponsible Activism: especially the practice of homosexualizing TRANSGENDER PEOPLE. We AINT gays." Audrey Mbugua (@AudreyMbugua), Twitter, February 23, 2016, 5:39 A.M.

34. "@gathara @EzekielMutua @InfoKfcb Don't trivialize what these propaganda does to transgender people. It has even resulted to death." Audrey Mbugua (@AudreyMbugua), Twitter, February 23, 2016, 5:15 A.M.

35. Audrey Mbugua, "The Evils of Transgender Stereotyping." For the blog post, see https://transgender.or.ke/wp-content/uploads/2017/09/The-Evils-of-Transgender-Stereotyping.pdf.

36. Petition of Eric Gitari to the registrar of the High Court of Kenya, August 27, 2013 (petition no. 440), http://kenyalaw.org/caselaw/cases/view/108412/.

37. Audrey Mbugua Ithibu, executive director of Transgender Education and Advocacy, to the executive director, NGO Coordination Board, ref. Transgender Insights on the National Gay and Lesbian Human Rights Commission Application for Registration, Nairobi, November 16, 2013.

38. Eric Gitari, interview by author, Nairobi, March 11, 2016.

39. High Court of Kenya, judgment regarding petition no. 440 of 2013, dated, delivered, and signed at Nairobi, 24 April 2015, articles 142 and 144.

40. Mbugua's siding with NGOCB was particularly ironic given the rejection of her own application for the registration of TEA a few years earlier—a decision she successfully petitioned against in the High Court.

41. Bugz Maingi (@BugzMaingi), Twitter, February 23, 2016, 5:16 A.M.

42. Quoted in Martin Oduor, "Homosexual Beef! Gay Singer Joji Baro Strips Transgender Audrey Mbugua Following Yesterday's Heartbreaking Incident," Ghafla, February 24, 2016, http://www.ghafla.co.ke/blogs/music/7753-homosexual-beef-gay-singer-joji-baro-strips-transgender-audrey-mbugua-following-yesterday-s-heartbreaking-incident (accessed August 9, 2018). See also http://www.ghafla.com/homosexual-beef-gay-singer-joji-baro-strips-transgender-audrey-mbugua-following-yesterdays-heartbreaking-incident/.

43. See "African Conversations on Gender Identity."

44. Asante, *It's Bigger Than Hip Hop*, 205.

45. Tang, "Rapper as Modern Griot," 82.

46. Ntarangwi, *East African Hip Hop*, 12.

47. Ibid., 115.

48. Meyer, *Sensational Movies*, 15.

49. Vernallis, "Music Video's Second Aesthetic," 438.

50. Parsitau, "Gospel Music in Africa."

51. Chitando, *Singing Culture*, 14.

52. On hip-hop music in Kenya and its relationship to gospel music and to religion, see Kidula, "Local and Global," 172–73; Ntarangwi, *Street Is My Pulpit*.

53. Antonio, "Introduction."

54. See, for example, Mutambara, "African Women Theologies."

55. See Van Klinken and Gunda, "Taking Up the Cudgels."

56. The lyrics were published on the news website Kuchu Times. See "Kenyan Music Video Featuring Real Life Gay Couples Becomes Trendsetter," Kuchu Times, February 17, 2016, https://www.kuchutimes.com/2016/02/kenyan-music-video-featuring-real-life-gay-couples-becomes-trendsetter/. I have edited these published lyrics slightly, following my own transcription of the song. Lyrics used by permission of George Barasa on behalf of Art Attack.

57. Moore, *Sunshine and Rainbows*, 22–23.

58. Matebeni, "How ~~NOT~~ to Write," 63.

59. Puar, *Terrorist Assemblages*.

60. Mwikya, "Uganda Homophobia Spectacle."

61. Art Attack, "Why We Made a Song."

62. Macharia, "Archive and Method," 140.

63. Ngũgĩ, *River Between*, 1.

64. Kamau-Goro, "Rejection or Reappropriation," 72.

65. Monte, "Land in Kenyan Song," 15.

66. Geczy and Karaminas, *Queer Style*, 93.

67. Richard Kamau, "'I Am Not a Lesbian. I'm Bisexual'—Noti Flow," *Nairobi Wire*, April 13, 2015, http://nairobiwire.com/2015/04/i-am-not-a-lesbian-im-bisexual-noti-flow.html.

68. Theophano, "Pornographic Film and Video," 237.

69. Sedgwick, *Epistemology of the Closet*, 3.

70. Stoyan Zaimov, "Obama Needs to 'Shut Up and Go Home' with His 'Gay Agenda,' Says Politician at Kenyan March to 'Protect the Family,'" *Christian Post*, July 7, 2015, https://www.christianpost.com/news/obama-needs-to-shut-up-and-go-home-with-his-gay-agenda-says-politician-at-kenyan-march-to-protect-the-family-141252/.

71. George Barasa, "Recognising my boss Kasha Jacqueline Bombastic Nabagesera is the least I could do," Facebook, February 15, 2016.

72. In this, "Same Love" follows a strategy that has also been used by gay rights proponents in the United States who have claimed the legacy of Martin Luther King to support their case. This strategy is not uncontested, however, as gay rights opponents have claimed that the late civil rights leader would actually be on their side. For a study of these conflicting claims about King and gay rights, see Long, *Martin Luther King, Jr.*

73. Meyer, *Sensational Movies*, 84, 109.

74. See Shepherd, "Rank, Gender, and Homosexuality," 254.

75. On Christianity and its intersections with public and popular culture in Africa, see Englund, *Christianity and Public Culture*.

76. Gunda, *Bible and Homosexuality*, 22.

77. West, *Stolen Bible*.

78. E.g., 1 John 4:8 (NIV): "Whoever does not love does not know God, because God is love."

79. As such, the video resembles a move made by Zambian gay men who replaced the term "men who have sex with other men" with "men who love other men." See Van Klinken, "Queer Love in a 'Christian Nation.'"

80. Thomas and Cole, "Introduction," 3.

81. Vaughan, *Curing Their Ills*, 129.

82. These are the words of a Zambian Pentecostal bishop, quoted in Van Klinken, "Homosexual as the Antithesis," 133.

83. Thomas and Cole, "Introduction," 5.

84. Butler, *Precarious Life*, 2.

85. Muñoz, *Cruising Utopia*, 167.

86. Ibid.

87. See Vaughan, "Discovery of Suicide."

88. Mbembe, *On the Postcolony*, 27.

89. Mbembe, *Critique of Black Reason*, 176.

90. Cheng, *Radical Love*, 94–95.

91. Barasa, interview, December 9, 2016. For Fanon's reflections, see *Black Skin, White Masks*.

92. Wilcox, *Coming Out in Christianity*, 85.

93. Hayes and Roth, "Introduction," 2.

94. Sartre, "Genocide," 16.

95. See Card, "Genocide and Social Death."

96. For critical discussion of such claims, see, for instance, Drescher, "Atlantic Slave Trade"; Millet, *Victims of Slavery*.

97. The term "queer genocide" is incidentally used in popular writings about lgbt issues in Africa. See, for instance, "Queer Holocaust: Ghana's Government to Arrest All Gays as Spies," *Gaire*, July 22, 2011, http://www.gaire.com/e/f/view.asp?parent=1712041. See also Waites, "Genocide and Global Queer Politics."

98. Mbembe, *On the Postcolony*, 8.

99. Faupel, *African Holocaust*.

100. For a discussion of the martyrs of Uganda and how their story is used in contemporary sexual politics in Uganda, see Otu, "Saints and Sinners"; Rao, "Re-Membering Mwanga."

101. Van Klinken, "Gay Rights, the Devil."

102. Starlit Media, "Is Noti Flow Lesbian?"

103. Garvey, "Purpose of Creation," 29.

104. Martin Luther King Jr., "I Have a Dream . . . " (1963), 6, https://www.archives.gov/press/exhibits/dream-speech.pdf.

105. Michael Long argues that lgbt liberation logically follows from King's philosophical and theological beliefs, and from his "embrace of the *principle of personality*. For King, this principle means that *all* people are equal, free, and bound together, and that each and every person deserves the civil and human rights that make for creative life." Long, *Martin Luther King, Jr.*, 111.

106. Ntarangwi, *East African Hip Hop*, 2.

107. Ibid., 20.

108. Ngũgĩ, *Re-Membering Africa*, 77, 80.

109. Macharia, "Archive and Method," 142–43.

110. For more on this point, see Massoud, "Gay Rights in South Africa."

111. Ngũgĩ, *Re-Membering Africa*, 28.

112. Dhaenens, "Reading Gay Music Videos," 536.

113. Ibid.

114. Barasa, interview, December 9, 2016.

115. Maupeu, "Political Activism in Nairobi," 402.

116. See Morris and Sloop, "'These Lips Have Kissed,'" for an elaboration of this point.

117. Ishtar MSM, "The Power in Being Versatile," Facebook, March 21, 2016, https://www.facebook.com/Ishtar.MSM/posts/1265676826793030.

118. Hendriks, "SIM Cards of Desire," 230.

119. Barasa, interview, December 9, 2016.

120. Berlant and Warner, "Sex in Public," 553, 559, 554.

121. Ibid., 548, 558.

122. Warner, "Publics and Counterpublics," 112.

123. Berlant and Warner, "Sex in Public," 562, 565.

124. Homewood, "'I Was on Fire,'" 247, 248.

125. Orobator, *Theology Brewed in an African Pot*, 54.

126. Maina, *Historical and Social Dimensions*, 35.

127. See the classic study of the distinction between *agape* and *eros*, Anders Nygren's *Agape and Eros*. Others have argued that the meanings of both words in Greek overlap much more heavily than Nygren suggests.

128. Antonio, "'Eros,' AIDS, and African Bodies," 185, 186–87, 189–90, 183, 193, 195. For the study by Caldwell, Caldwell, and Quiggin, see "Social Context of AIDS."

129. Barasa, interview, December 9, 2016.

130. See Althaus-Reid, *Queer God*; Pinn, *Embodiment and the New Shape*.

131. See Van Klinken and Gunda, "Taking Up the Cudgels."

INTERLUDE 2

1. See, for example, Kulick and Willson, *Taboo*; Markowitz and Ashkenazi, *Sex, Sexuality, and the Anthropologist*.

2. See Gilliat-Ray, "Body-Works and Fieldwork."

3. For a sensitive treatment of these dynamics, see Hoel, "Taking the Body Seriously."

4. Bolton, "Tricks, Friends, and Lovers," 140.

CHAPTER 3

1. Njoki (member of The Nest), interview by author, Nairobi, March 4, 2016.

2. *Stories of Our Lives—An Anthology Film*, directed by Jim Chuchu (Nairobi: The Nest 2014).

3. Letter from the KFCB, quoted on the website of The Nest Collective, "Stories of Our Lives—An Anthology Film," http://www.thisisthenest.com/sool-film/.

4. Plummer, *Cosmopolitan Sexualities*, 161.

5. The Nest, *Stories of Our Lives*, 319 (hereafter cited parenthetically in the text).

6. Njoki, interview.

7. Plummer, *Cosmopolitan Sexualities*, 162.

8. Stone-Mediatore, *Reading Across Borders*, 150.

9. Jackson, *Politics of Storytelling*, 17.

10. Stone-Mediatore, *Reading Across Borders*, 150.

11. John, WhatsApp message to author, April 15, 2016.

12. Jackson, *Politics of Storytelling*, 15.

13. Plummer, *Cosmopolitan Sexualities*, 162.

14. Nadar, "'Stories Are Data with Soul,'" 23.

15. Njoki, interview.

16. Katongole, "African Renaissance," 32, 35.

17. Katongole has dismissed the suggestion that lgbt rights are among the most pressing moral issues for the church in Africa. See Katongole, "Church of the Future."

18. About the question of naming African women's theologies, see Nadar, "Her-Stories and Her-Theologies," 140.

19. Oduyoye, *Introducing African Women's Theology*, 10.

20. Phiri, Govinden, and Nadar, "Introduction," 6, 7.

21. See Nadar, "Her-Stories and Her-Theologies."

22. See Dube, "Talitha Cum Hermeneutics."

23. Oduyoye and Amoah, "Christ for African Women."

24. Moyo, "Singing and Dancing."

25. There are a few notable exceptions, such as Oduyoye's account, discussed later in this chapter.

26. Macharia, "Stories of Our Lives: Memories."

27. Ibid.

28. Binnie, *Globalization of Sexuality*, 3.

29. Boellstorff and Leap, "Introduction," 2.

30. For a discussion of this trend and of these developments in the academy, see, for example, Jagose, *Queer Theory*.

31. Butler, *Gender Trouble*, 42.

32. Plummer, *Telling Sexual Stories*, 82.

33. Epprecht, *Hungochani*, 37.

34. Sedgwick, *Epistemology of the Closet*, 3.

35. Foucault, *Will to Knowledge*, 27.

36. Tamale, "Researching and Theorising," 13; Nyanzi, "When the State Produces Hate," 179.

37. Baderoon, "'I Compose Myself,'" 908.

38. Plummer, *Telling Sexual Stories*, 49–50.

39. Plummer, *Intimate Citizenship*, 13.

40. Ibid., 101.

41. See Grossi, "Romantic Love."

42. Thomas and Cole, "Introduction," 5, 12.

43. Spronk, "Media and the Therapeutic Ethos," 187.

44. Thomas and Cole, "Introduction," 16.

45. Isin and Nielsen, "Introduction," 4.

46. Binnie, *Globalization of Sexuality*, 91.

47. Weston, "Get Thee to a Big City," 274.

48. For a (largely heterosexual-focused) account of the sexual economy in Mombasa and coastal Kenya more generally, see Meiu, *Ethno-Erotic Economies*.

49. For more on this history, see Aldrich, *Colonialism and Homosexuality*.

50. Porter, "Talking at the Margins"; Amory, "Mashoga, Mabasha, and Magai."

51. Spronk, "Media and the Therapeutic Ethos," 185.

52. Scott Mills, *Uganda: The World's Worst Place to Be Gay?*, film documentary (London: BBC, 2011).

53. See Munro, *South Africa and the Dream*.

54. Spronk, "Sex, Sexuality, and Negotiating Africanness," 502.

55. In Kenya, primary education begins at the age of six. The first year is known as standard 1 (the equivalent of first grade in the United States), and primary school goes up to standard 8.

56. Ganzevoort, "Introduction," 1.

57. See Ganzevoort, Van der Laan, and Olsman, "Growing Up Gay and Religious."

58. See Kangwa, "Theology of Retribution."

59. Moon, *God, Sex, and Politics*, 180, 182.

60. Cheng, *Radical Love*, 45.

61. Althaus-Reid, *Queer God*, 65. The narrator's statement reflects T-theology's tendency to masculinize God, which needs to be interrogated from a queer perspective.

62. Warner, *Church of Our Own*, 199.

63. Cheng, *Radical Love*, 97.

64. Oduyoye and Amoah, "Christ for African Women," 43–44.

65. West, *Stolen Bible*, 555.

66. Oduyoye, *Introducing African Women's Theology*, 58.

67. Gifford, "Ritual Use of the Bible," 179.

68. See, for example, Althaus-Reid, *Queer God*; Bohache, *Christology from the Margins*.

69. Goss, *Queering Christ*, 237.

70. Ibid., 165.

71. Oduyoye, "Coming Home to Myself," 111, 112.

72. Ibid., 113, 116, 118.

73. Ibid., 119.

74. Ibid., 110. In a matrilineal society such as the Asante, maternal great-uncles play an important role.

75. Oduyoye, "Critique of Mbiti's View," 354, 355, 361.

76. Oduyoye, "Coming Home to Myself," 118.

77. Muñoz, *Cruising Utopia*, 138.

78. Oduyoye, "Coming Home to Myself," 119.

79. Jackson, *Politics of Storytelling*, 23.

INTERLUDE 3

1. For more on this concept, see Van Klinken, "Body of Christ Has AIDS."

2. Butler, *Precarious Life*, 20.

3. See Maluleke, "Challenge of HIV/AIDS."

4. Van Klinken, "When the Body of Christ Has AIDS."

5. Bhabha, *Location of Culture*, 19.

6. Mbembe, *On the Postcolony*, 2.

7. Althaus-Reid, *Queer God*, 8.

8. Copeland, *Enfleshing Freedom*, 83.

CHAPTER 4

1. Wilcox, *Coming Out in Christianity*, 34.

2. For more on Thandekiso's church, see Reid, *Above the Skyline*.

3. For an overview, see Chitando and Mapuranga, "Unlikely Allies"; Van Klinken, "Christianity in Africa."

4. Munt, "Queer Spiritual Spaces," 20.

5. "About Cosmopolitan Affirming Church Kenya," Facebook, https://www.facebook.com/Cosmopolitan-Affirming-Church-Kenya-990143787709693/info/?tab=page_info.

6. Barasa left because he felt he needed a broader platform for his activism in order to have more impact. George Barasa, interview by author, Nairobi, February 22, 2016.

7. "Shocker!! Gay Gospel Artist Joji Baro Opens a Gay Church in Nairobi," Jobs and Career in Kenya, March 27, 2014, http://www.jobskenyahapa.com/shocker-gay-gospel-artist-joji-baro-opens-gay-church-nairobi-massive-recruitment-youths-church-read-shocking-details/.

8. Nyabuga, "Things Fall Apart," 292. See also Herdt, "Introduction."

9. Sadgrove et al., "Morality Plays and Money Matters," 121.

10. Cosmopolitan Affirming Community, https://cac-kenya.com/. In this chapter, nonetheless, I refer to the ministers with pseudonyms. For both Twitter and Instagram, CAC uses the handle @CAC_Ke.

11. See Simone, *City Yet to Come*.

12. Simone and Pieterse, *New Urban Worlds*, 2.

13. Ordination requires formal theological training.

14. Minister Moses, interview by author, Nairobi, July 23, 2018.

15. George Barasa, Facebook message to author, April 12, 2016.

16. Emmanuel, interview by author, Nairobi, March 14, 2016.

17. Minister Moses, WhatsApp message to author, April 12, 2016.

18. Appiah, *Cosmopolitanism*, xv.

19. Minister Susan, interview by author, Nairobi, March 8, 2016.

20. Joseph, interview by author, Nairobi, February 26, 2016.

21. Ibid.

22. Minister Moses, interview.

23. Kelvin, personal conversation with author on WhatsApp, July 17, 2017.

24. Minister Bryan, WhatsApp message to author, August 11, 2017.

25. Isaac Otidi Amuke, "Like the Weather (Part 1)," Commonwealth Writers, July 27, 2015, http://www.commonwealthwriters.org/facing-the-mediterranean-part-1/.

26. Ronnie, interview by author, Nairobi, February 23, 2016.

27. Minister Moses, interview.

28. See Lewin, *Filled with the Spirit*.

29. Yvette Flunder, "The Purpose of the Fellowship," Fellowship of Affirming Ministries, http://www.radicallyinclusive.com/the-purpose-of-the-fellowship.

30. See Flunder, "Healing Oppression Sickness."

31. Barnes, "Alpha and Omega," 155.

32. Fellowship Global, "About Us," http://thefellowshipglobal.org/about-us/.

33. Bishop Joseph Tolton, interview by author, Nairobi, February 24, 2016.

34. Fellowship Global, "Empowering Progressive Clergy in Africa," http://thefellowshipglobal.org/wp-content/uploads/2014/05/Empowering-Progressive-Clergy-in-Africa.pdf.

35. See Kaoma, "Marriage of Convenience."

36. Fellowship Global, "United Coalition of Affirming Africans," http://thefellowshipglobal.org/the-programs/empowering-progressive-clergy-in-africa/.

37. Tolton, interview.

38. Fellowship Global, "Black Pastors Launch African Tour to Counteract Rick Warren's Anti-Gay Movement," Believe Out Loud, April 7, 2015, http://www.believeoutloud.com/latest/black-pastors-launch-african-tour-counteract-rick-warren's-anti-gay-movement.

39. Tolton, interview.

40. Walls, *Cross-Cultural Process*, 119, 85.

41. Tolton, interview.

42. TFG, "Empowering Progressive Clergy."

43. Tolton, interview.

44. TFG, "Empowering Progressive Clergy."

45. Tolton, interview.

46. "African LGBTI Manifesto."

47. Ekine and Abbas, "Introduction," 3.

48. Tolton, interview. On neo-pan-Africanism, see Nathan, "Blessed Be the Tie."

49. TFG, "United Coalition of Affirming Africans."

50. TFG, "About Us."

51. Minister Bryan, interview by author, Nairobi, July 22, 2018.

52. Minister Moses, interview.

53. Reid, *Above the Skyline*, 102.

54. The Nest, *Stories of Our Lives*, 233.

55. Lewin, *Filled with the Spirit*, 169.

56. Chukwu, *Church as the Extended Family*.

57. "About Cosmopolitan Affirming Church" (see n. 5).

58. Stuart, "Sacramental Flesh," 75.

59. Ibid., 65.

60. For more on this concept, see Orobator, *Church as Family*.

61. John Paul II, "Post-Synodal Apostolic Exhortation."

62. Oduyoye, *Introducing African Women's Theology*, 79, 83, 84.

63. Crawley, *Black Pentecostal Breath*, 31.

64. John, interview by author, Nairobi, February 28, 2016.

65. Wilcox, *Coming Out in Christianity*, 134.

66. Ibid., 132.

67. TFG, "About Us." On the inclusion of Yoruba indigenous religious practices in TFAM, see Lewin, *Filled with the Spirit*, 152.

68. Minister Moses, interview by author, Nairobi, March 4, 2016.

69. Eric Gitari, interview by author, Nairobi, March 11, 2016.

70. For more on prophetic speech and charismatic deliverance rituals, see Csordas, *Language, Charisma, and Creativity*, in particular chapters 6 and 7.

71. John, WhatsApp message to author, April 15, 2016.

72. Csordas, *Language, Charisma, and Creativity*, 69.

73. Munt, "Queer Spiritual Spaces," 25.

74. Sneed, *Representations of Homosexuality*, 145.

75. Ngũgĩ, *Re-Membering Africa*, 32.

76. Isherwood, "Introduction," 4.

77. The influence of modern drag culture is also visible in discussions in the CAC WhatsApp group about the American reality TV series *RuPaul's Drag Race*. As one group member said of RuPaul and the contestants on his show, "they are the legends who have paved a way for us to express our sexualities freely without shame. The show empowers you as a gay person." CAC WhatsApp group, April 20, 2016.

78. Isherwood, "Introduction," 4.

79. Warner, "Tongues Untied," 229.

80. Muñoz, *Cruising Utopia*, 1.

81. Bohache, "Opening the Body of Christ," 122.

82. Bohache, *Christology from the Margins*, 96.

83. As the leader in charge of the session explained, discussing the clobber passages "proved tricky due to what the congregation including myself had internalized about such texts from our previous churches and also due to lack of deeper theological contextualization of the same." It was for this reason that he decided to focus on "the inclusive love of Christ." WhatsApp message from Minister Moses, April 20, 2016.

84. John, interview.

85. For a similar pattern, see Reid, *Above the Skyline*, 43.

86. Nadar, "On Being Church," 21. Nadar writes here about churches in Africa in relation to issues of gender, but her words can easily be applied to matters of sexual orientation.

87. Kelvin, interview by author, Nairobi, February 26, 2016.

88. John, interview.

89. Warner, *Church of Our Own*, 199.

90. Cf. Reid, *Above the Skyline*, 114–15.

91. Ekine, "Contesting Narratives of Queer Africa," 80.

92. Lewin, *Filled with the Spirit*, 149.

93. Tolton, interview.

94. Cornwall, *Controversies in Queer Theology*, 241.

95. Phan, "Roman Catholic Theology," 221.

96. Walls, "Introduction," 13.

97. Mary Engel and Susan Thistlethwaite, quoted in Westhelle, "Liberation Theology," 319.

98. Muñoz, *Cruising Utopia*, 4.

99. For a parallel, see Reid, *Above the Skyline*, 44–45.

100. Minister Bryan, interview by author, Nairobi, March 10, 2016.

101. Muñoz, *Cruising Utopia*, 1.

102. Tolton, interview.

103. Minister Bryan, interview, March 10, 2016.

104. Ibid.

105. Minister Susan, interview.

106. Warner, "Introduction," xxvi.

107. Munt, "Queer Spiritual Spaces," 23.

INTERLUDE 4

1. For an account of queer fieldwork approaches, see Rooke, "Queer in the Field."

2. Browne, "Negotiations and Fieldworkings," 134.

3. Quoted in Anne Dubuis, "Kenya Could Become the Next Country in Africa to Legalize Homosexuality," *Vice News*, May 9, 2016, https://news.vice.com/article/kenya-could-become-the-next-country-in-africa-to-legalize-homosexuality.

4. David and Sutton, *Social Research*, 605.

CONCLUSION

1. Scott, *Domination and the Arts of Resistance*, 4–5, 25, 136.

2. Willems and Obadare, "Introduction," 7.

3. Scott, *Domination and the Arts of Resistance*, 118.

4. Foucault, "What Is Critique," 47.

5. Ashcroft, Griffiths, and Tiffin, *Post-Colonial Studies*, 16.

6. Ashcroft, *Post-Colonial Transformations*, 5.

7. Scott, *Domination and the Arts of Resistance*, 140.

8. The Nest, *Stories of Our Lives*, 238.

9. Ndjio, "Sexuality and Nationalist Ideologies," 120.

10. The Nest, *Stories of Our Lives*, 227.

11. See Massad, "Re-Orienting Desire."

12. Mbembe, *On the Postcolony*, 1.

13. Bhabha, *Location of Culture*, 213.

14. Muñoz, *Cruising Utopia*, 96.

15. Cf. Asad et al., *Is Critique Secular?*

16. For the notion of public sexuality, see Nelson, "Where Are We," 102–3.

17. Lorde, "Master's Tools."

18. Wilcox, "Outlaws or In-Laws," 94.

19. Scott, *Domination and the Arts of Resistance*, 115, 116.

20. This is the subtitle of Talvacchia, Pettinger, and Larrimore, *Queer Christianities*.

21. Walls, *Cross-Cultural Process*, 119.

22. Oduyoye, *Introducing African Women's Theology*, 86.

23. For examples of such theologies, see Hopkins and Lewis, *Another World Is Possible*.

24. See Diakité and Huck, "Africana Religious Studies."

Bibliography

Abbey, Rose Teteki. "I Am the Woman." In *Other Ways of Reading: African Women and the Bible*, edited by Musa W. Dube, 23–26. Atlanta: Society of Biblical Literature, 2001.

Adebanwi, Wale. "The Writer as Social Thinker." *Journal of Contemporary African Studies* 32, no. 4 (2014): 405–20.

Adejunmobi, Moradewun. "Provocations: African Societies and Theories of Creativity." In *Rethinking African Cultural Production*, edited by Frieda Ekotto and Kenneth W. Harrow, 52–77. Bloomington: Indiana University Press, 2015.

"African Conversations on Gender Identity and ICD Classifications." In Ekine and Abbas, *Queer African Reader*, 431–39.

"African LGBTI Manifesto/Declaration." In Ekine and Abbas, *Queer African Reader*, 52–53.

Aldrich, Robert. *Colonialism and Homosexuality*. London: Routledge, 2003.

Althaus-Reid, Marcella. *The Queer God*. London: Routledge, 2003.

Amory, Deborah P. "*Mashoga, Mabasha*, and *Magai*: 'Homosexuality' on the East African Coast." In Murray and Roscoe, *Boy-Wives and Female Husbands*, 67–87.

Antonio, Edward P. "'Eros,' AIDS, and African Bodies: A Theological Commentary on Deadly Desires." In *The Embrace of Eros: Bodies, Desires, and Sexuality in Christianity*, edited by Margaret D. Kamitsuka, 181–96. Minneapolis: Fortress Press, 2010.

———. "Homosexuality and African Culture." In *Aliens in the Household of God: Homosexuality and Christian Faith in South Africa*, edited by Paul Germond and Steve De Gruchy, 295–316. Cape Town: David Philip, 1997.

———. "Introduction: Inculturation and Postcolonial Discourse." In *Inculturation and Postcolonial Discourse in African Theology*, edited by Edward P. Antonio, 1–28. New York: Peter Lang, 2006.

Appiah, Kwame Anthony. *Cosmopolitanism: Ethics in a World of Strangers*. London: Penguin, 2006.

Artivists 4 Life, Leslie Robinson, and Maria-Carolina Cambre. "Youth Artivism in Uganda: Co-Creators of Our Own Becoming." In *African Youth Cultures in a Globalized World: Challenges, Agency, and Resistance*, edited by Paul Ugor and Lord Mawuko-Yevugah, 75–94. Abingdon: Routledge, 2016.

Asad, Talal, Wendy Brown, Judith Butler, and Saba Mahmood. *Is Critique Secular? Blasphemy, Injury, and Free Speech*. New York: Fordham University Press, 2013.

Asante, M. K., Jr. *It's Bigger Than Hip Hop: The Rise of the Post-Hip-Hop Generation*. New York: St. Martin's Griffin, 2008.

Ashcroft, Bill. *Post-Colonial Transformation*. London: Routledge, 2001.

Ashcroft, Bill, Gareth Griffiths, and Helen Tiffin. *Post-Colonial Studies: The Key Concepts*. 2nd ed. London: Routledge, 2007.

Awondo, Patrick. "The Politicisation of Sexuality and Rise of Homosexual Movements in Post-Colonial Cameroon." *Review of African Political Economy* 37, no. 125 (2010): 315–28.

Awondo, Patrick, Peter Geschiere, and Graeme Reid. "Homophobic Africa? Toward a More Nuanced View." *African Studies Review* 55, no. 3 (2012): 145–68.

Baderoon, Gabeba. "'I Compose Myself': Lesbian Muslim Autobiographies and the Craft of Self-Writing in South Africa." *Journal of the American Academy of Religion* 83, no. 4 (2015): 897–915.

Bady, Aaron, ed. "'African Homosexual Deamon'—Binyavanga's Brief Treatise on Demonology." *Brittle Paper: An African Literary Experience*, January 8, 2014. https://brittlepaper.com/2014/01/african-homosexual-deamon-binyavangas-treatise-demonology/.

Baraka, Nancy, and Ruth Morgan. "'I Want to Marry the Woman of My Choice Without Fear of Being Stoned': Female Marriages and Bisexual Women in Kenya." In *Tommy Boys, Lesbian Men, and Ancestral Wives: Female Same-Sex Practices in Africa*, edited by Ruth Morgan and Saskia Wieringa, 25–50. Johannesburg: Jacana, 2005.

Barnes, Sandra L. "'The Alpha and Omega of Our People': A Sociological Examination of the Promise and Problems of the Contemporary Black Church." In *Free at Last? Black America in the Twenty-First Century*, edited by Juan Battle, Michael Bennett, and Anthony J. Lemelle, 149–72. Abingdon: Routledge, 2017.

Bediako, Kwame. *Christianity in Africa: The Renewal of a Non-Western Religion*. Edinburgh: Edinburgh University Press, 1995.

Berlant, Lauren, and Michael Warner. "Sex in Public." *Critical Inquiry* 24, no. 2 (1998): 547–66.

Bhabha, Homi K. *The Location of Culture*. London: Routledge, 2010.

Binnie, Jon. *The Globalization of Sexuality*. London: Sage Publications, 2004.

Boellstorff, Tom, and William L. Leap. "Introduction: Globalization and 'New' Articulations of Same-Sex Desire." In *Speaking in Queer Tongues: Globalization and Gay Language*, edited by William L. Leap and Tom Boellstorff, 1–22. Urbana: University of Illinois Press, 2004.

Bohache, Thomas. *Christology from the Margins*. London: SCM Press, 2008.

———. "Opening the Body of Christ." In *Queering Christianity: Finding a Place at the Table for LGBTQI Christians*, edited by Robert E. Shore-Goss, Thomas Bohache, Patrick S. Cheng, and Mona West, 121–25. Santa Barbara: ABC-Clio, 2013.

Boisvert, Donald L., and Jay Emerson Johnson, eds. *Queer Religion*. Vol. 2, *LGBT Movements and Queering Religion*. Santa Barbara: Praeger, 2012.

Bolton, Ralph. "Tricks, Friends, and Lovers: Erotic Encounters in the Field." In Kulick and Willson, *Taboo*, 140–67.

Bompani, Barbara. "'For God and for My Country': Pentecostal-Charismatic Churches and the Framing of a New Political Discourse in Uganda." In *Public Religion and the Politics of Homosexuality in Africa*, edited by Adriaan van Klinken and Ezra Chitando, 19–34. Abingdon: Routledge, 2016.

Bongmba, Elias K. "Hermeneutics and the Debate on Homosexuality in Africa." *Religion and Theology* 22, nos. 1–2 (2015): 69–99.

———. "Homosexuality, *Ubuntu*, and Otherness in the African Church," *Journal of Religion and Violence* 4, no. 1 (2016): 15–37.

Browne, Kath. "Negotiations and Fieldworkings: Friendship and Feminist Research." *ACME: An International Journal for Critical Geographies* 2, no. 2 (2003): 132–46.

Burchardt, Marian. "Equals Before the Law? Public Religion and Queer Activism in the Age of Judicial Politics in South Africa." *Journal of Religion in Africa* 43, no. 3 (2013): 237–60.

Burgess, Richard. "Pentecostals and Political Culture in Sub-Saharan Africa: Nigeria, Zambia, and Kenya as Case Studies." In *Global Pentecostal Movements: Migration, Mission, and Public Religion*, edited by Michael Wilkinson, 17–42. Leiden: Brill, 2012.

Butler, Judith. *Gender Trouble: Feminism and the Subversion of Identity*. 2nd ed. London: Routledge, 2006.

———. *Precarious Life: The Power of Mourning and Violence*. New York: Verso, 2004.

Caldwell, John C., Pat Caldwell, and Pat Quiggin. "The Social Context of AIDS in Sub-Saharan Africa." *Population and Development Review* 15, no. 2 (1989): 185–234.

Card, Claudia. "Genocide and Social Death." *Hypatia* 18, no. 1 (2003): 63–79.

Casanova, José. *Public Religions in the Modern World*. Chicago: University of Chicago Press, 1994.

———. "Public Religions Revisited." In *Religion: Beyond a Concept*, edited by Hent de Vries, 101–19. New York: Fordham University Press, 2008.

Cheng, Patrick S. *Radical Love: An Introduction to Queer Theology*. New York: Seabury, 2011.

Chitando, Ezra. *Singing Culture: A Study of Gospel Music in Zimbabwe*. Uppsala: Nordiska Afrikainstitutet, 2002.

Chitando, Ezra, Afe Adogame, and Bolaji Bateye. "Introduction." In *African Traditions in the Study of Religion in Africa*, edited by Ezra Chitando, Afe Adogame, and Bolaji Bateye, 1–16. Farnham: Ashgate, 2012.

Chitando, Ezra, Masiiwa Ragies Gunda, and Joachim Kügler. "Introduction." In *Prophets, Profits, and the Bible in Zimbabwe*, edited by Ezra Chitando, Masiiwa Ragies Gunda, and Joachim Kügler, 9–14. Bamberg: University of Bamberg Press, 2013.

Chitando, Ezra, and Tapiwa Praise Mapuranga. "Unlikely Allies? Lesbian, Gay, Bisexual, Transgender, and Intersex (LGBTI) Activists and Church Leaders in Africa." In *Christianity and Controversies over Homosexuality in Contemporary Africa*, edited by Ezra Chitando and Adriaan van Klinken, 171–83. London: Routledge, 2016.

Chukwu, Donatus Oluwa. *The Church as the Extended Family of God: Toward a New Direction for African Ecclesiology*. Bloomington: Xlibris, 2011.

Coffey, Amanda. *The Ethnographic Self: Fieldwork and the Representation of Identity*. London: Sage Publications, 1999.

Comstock, Gary D., and Susan E. Henking. "Introduction." In *Que(e)rying Religion: A Critical Anthology*, edited by Gary D. Comstock and Susan E. Henking, 11–16. New York: Continuum, 1997.

Conquergood, Dwight. "Rethinking Ethnography: Towards A Critical Cultural Politics." *Communication Monographs* 58, no. 2 (1991): 179–94.

Copeland, M. Shawn. *Enfleshing Freedom: Body, Race, and Being*. Minneapolis: Fortress Press, 2010.

Cornwall, Susannah. *Controversies in Queer Theology*. London: SCM Press, 2011.

Crawley, Ashon T. *Black Pentecostal Breath: The Aesthetics of Possibility*. New York: Fordham University Press, 2017.

Csordas, Thomas J. *Language, Charisma, and Creativity: The Ritual Life of a Religious Movement*. Berkeley: University of California Press, 1997.

Currier, Ashley. *Out in Africa: LGBT Organizing in Namibia and South Africa*. Minneapolis: University of Minnesota Press, 2012.

Currier, Ashley, and Joella M. Cruz. "Civil Society and Sexual Struggles in Africa." In *The Handbook of Civil Society in Africa*, edited by Ebenezer Obadare, 337–60. New York: Springer, 2013.

Currier, Ashley, and Thérèse Migraine-George. "Queer Studies/African Studies: An (Im)possible Transaction?" *GLQ: A Journal of Lesbian and Gay Studies* 22, no. 2 (2016): 281–305.

David, Matthew, and Carole D. Sutton. *Social Research: An Introduction*. 2nd ed. London: Sage Publications, 2011.

Deacon, Gregory. "Kenya: A Nation Born Again." *PentecoStudies* 14, no. 2 (2015): 219–40.

Deacon, Gregory, and Gabrielle Lynch. "Allowing Satan In? Moving Toward a Political Economy of Neo-Pentecostalism in Kenya." *Journal of Religion in Africa* 43, no. 2 (2013): 108–30.

Dhaenens, Frederik. "Reading Gay Music Videos: An Inquiry into the Representation of Sexual Diversity in Contemporary Popular Music Videos." *Popular Music and Society* 39, no. 5 (2016): 532–46.

Diakité, Dianne M. Stewart, and Tracey E. Huck. "Africana Religious Studies: Toward a Transdisciplinary Agenda in an Emerging Field." *Journal of Africana Religions* 1, no. 1 (2013): 28–77.

Drescher, Seymour. "The Atlantic Slave Trade and the Holocaust: A Comparative Analysis." In *Is the Holocaust Unique? Perspectives on Comparative Genocide*, 3rd ed., edited by Alan S. Rosenbaum, 103–24. Boulder: Westview Press, 2009.

Dube, Musa W. *The HIV and AIDS Bible: Selected Essays*. Scranton: University of Scranton Press, 2008.

———. "Talitha Cum Hermeneutics of Liberation: Some African Women's Ways of Reading the Bible." In *The Bible and the Hermeneutics of Liberation*, edited by Alejandro F. Botta and Pablo R. Andinach, 133–46. Atlanta: Society of Biblical Literature, 2009.

Edelman, Lee. *No Future: Queer Theory and the Death Drive*. Durham: Duke University Press, 2004.

Ekine, Sokari. "Beyond Anti-LGBTI Legislation: Criminalization and the Denial of Citizenship." In *Decolonizing Sexualities: Transnational Perspectives, Critical Interventions*, edited by Sandeep Bakshi, Suhraiya Jivraj, and Silvia Posocco, 19–31. Oxford: Counterpress, 2016.

———. "Contesting Narratives of Queer Africa." In Ekine and Abbas, *Queer African Reader*, 78–91.

Ekine, Sokari, and Hakima Abbas. "Introduction." In Ekine and Abbas, *Queer African Reader*, 1–5.

———, eds. *Queer African Reader*. Dakar: Pambazuka Press, 2013.

Ekotto, Frieda, and Kenneth W. Harrow. "Introduction: Rethinking African Cultural Production." In *Rethinking African Cultural Production*, edited by Frieda Ekotto and Kenneth W. Harrow, 1–16. Bloomington: Indiana University Press, 2015.

Ellis, Stephen, and Gerrie ter Haar. *Worlds of Power: Religious Thought and Political Practice in Africa*. London: Hurst, 2004.

Eng, David L., Judith Halberstam, and José Esteban Muñoz. "What's Queer About Queer Studies Now?" *Social Text* 23, nos. 3–4 (2005): 1–17.

Englund, Harri, ed. *Christianity and Public Culture in Africa*. Athens: Ohio University Press, 2011.

Epprecht, Marc. *Heterosexual Africa? The History of an Idea from the Age of Exploration to the Age of AIDS*. Athens: Ohio University Press, 2008.

———. *Hungochani: The History of a Dissident Sexuality in Southern Africa*. Montreal: McGill-Queen's University Press, 2004.

———. *Sexuality and Social Justice in Africa: Rethinking Homophobia and Forging Resistance*. London: Zed Books, 2013.

Evangelical Alliance of Kenya. *Kenya Let's Pray!* Nairobi: Evangelical Alliance of Kenya, 2014.

Fanon, Frantz. *Black Skin, White Masks*. Translated by Charles Lam Markmann. London: Pluto Press, 2008.

Faupel, J. F. *African Holocaust: The Story of the Uganda Martyrs*. 3rd ed. Nairobi: Paulines, 2007.

Flunder, Yvette. "Healing Oppression Sickness." In Talvacchia, Pettinger, and Larrimore, *Queer Christianities*, 115–24.

Folarin, Tope. "Miracle." In *A Memory This Size and Other Stories: The Caine Prize for African Writing, 2013*, 10–21. Oxford: New Internationalist Publications, 2013.

Foucault, Michel. "What Is Critique?" In *The Politics of Truth*, edited by Sylvère Lotringer and translated by Lysa Hochroth and Catherine Porter, 41–81. Los Angeles: Semiotext(e), 2007.

———. *The Will to Knowledge*. Vol. 1 of *The History of Sexuality*. Translated by Robert Hurley. London: Penguin, 1998.

Ganzevoort, Ruard R. "Introduction: Religious Stories We Live By." In *Religious Stories We Live By: Narrative Approaches in Theology and Religious Studies*, edited by Ruard R. Ganzevoort, Maaike de Haardt, and Michael Scherer-Rath, 1–17. Leiden: Brill, 2013.

Ganzevoort, Ruard R., Mark van der Laan, and Erik Olsman. "Growing Up Gay and Religious: Conflict, Dialogue, and Religious Identity Strategies." *Mental Health, Religion, and Culture* 14, no. 3 (2011): 209–22.

Garvey, Marcus. "Purpose of Creation." In *The Philosophy and Opinions of Marcus Garvey: Africa for the Africans*, compiled by Amy Jacques, 29. London: Routledge, 1967.

Gaudio, Rudolf Pell. *Allah Made Us: Sexual Outlaws in an Islamic African City*. Malden, Mass.: Wiley-Blackwell, 2009.

Geczy, Adam, and Vicki Karaminas. *Queer Style*. London: Bloomsbury, 2013.

Gifford, Paul. *Christianity, Politics, and Public Life in Kenya*. London: Hurst, 2009.

———. "The Ritual Use of the Bible in African Pentecostalism." In *Practicing the Faith: The Ritual Life of Pentecostal-Charismatic Christians*, edited by Martin Lindhardt, 179–97. New York: Berghahn Books, 2011.

Gilliat-Ray, Sophia. "Body-Works and Fieldwork: Research with British Muslim Chaplains." *Culture and Religion* 11, no. 4 (2010): 413–32.

Goss, Robert E. *Queering Christ: Beyond Jesus Acted Up*. Cleveland: Pilgrim Press, 2002.

Grossi, Renata. "Romantic Love as a Political Strategy." In *The Radicalism of Romantic Love*, edited by Renata Grossi and David West, 175–90. Abingdon: Routledge, 2017.

Gunda, Masiiwa Ragies. *The Bible and Homosexuality in Zimbabwe: A Socio-Historical Analysis of the Political, Cultural, and Christian Arguments in the Homosexual Public Debate, with Special Reference to the Use of the Bible*. Bamberg: University of Bamberg Press, 2010.

Hackett, Rosalind I. J. "Discourses of Demonization in Africa and Beyond." *Diogenes* 50, no. 3 (2003): 61–75.

———. "Field Envy, or the Perils and Pleasures of Doing Fieldwork." *Method and Theory in the Study of Religion* 13, no. 1 (2001): 98–109.

Halberstam, Judith. *Female Masculinity*. Durham: Duke University Press, 1998.

Hall, Donald E. *Reading Sexualities: Hermeneutic Theory and the Future of Queer Studies*. Abingdon: Routledge, 2009.

Halperin, David M. *How to Be Gay*. Cambridge: Harvard University Press, 2012.

———. *Saint Foucault: Towards a Gay Hagiography*. Oxford: Oxford University Press, 1995.

Hardy, Clarence E. *James Baldwin's God: Sex, Hope, and Crisis in Black Holiness Culture*. Knoxville: University of Tennessee Press, 2003.

Hayes, Peter, and John K. Roth. "Introduction." In *The Oxford Handbook of Holocaust Studies*, edited by Peter Hayes and John K. Roth, 1–22. Oxford: Oxford University Press, 2010.

Hellweg, Joseph. "Same-Gender Desire, Religion, and Homophobia: Challenges, Complexities, and Progress for LGBTIQ Liberation in Africa." *Journal of the American Academy of Religion* 83, no. 4 (2015): 887–96.

Hendriks, Thomas. "Queer(ing) Popular Culture: Homo-Erotic Provocations from Kinshasa." *Journal of African Cultural Studies* 31, no. 1 (2017): 71–88.

———. "SIM Cards of Desire: Sexual Versatility and the Male Homoerotic Economy in Urban Congo." *American Ethnologist* 43, no. 2 (2016): 230–42.

Herdt, Gilbert. "Introduction: Moral Panics, Sexual Rights, and Cultural Anger." In *Moral Panics, Sex Panics: Fear and the Fight over Sexual Rights*, edited by Gilbert Herdt, 1–46. New York: New York University Press, 2009.

Heschel, Abraham Joshua. *The Prophets*. Vol. 1. New York: Harper and Row, 1962.

Hoel, Nina. "Embodying the Field: A Researcher's Reflections on Power Dynamics, Positionality, and the Nature of

Research Relationships." *Fieldwork in Religion* 8, no. 1 (2013): 27–49.

———. "Taking the Body Seriously, Taking Relationalities Seriously: Methodological Reflections for an Embodied and Relational Approach to Ethnographic Research in the Study of (Lived) Religion." In *Beyond Insider/Outsider Binaries: New Approaches in the Study of Religion*, edited by George D. Chryssides and Stephen E. Gregg. London: Equinox, 2019.

Homewood, Nathanael. "'I Was on Fire': The Challenge of Counter-Intimacies Within Zimbabwean Christianity." In *Public Religion and the Politics of Homosexuality in Africa*, edited by Adriaan van Klinken and Ezra Chitando, 243–59. Abingdon: Routledge, 2016.

Hopkins, Dwight N., and Marjorie Lewis, eds. *Another World Is Possible: Spiritualities and Religions of Global Darker People.* London: Equinox, 2009.

Isherwood, Lisa. "Introduction." In *Trans/formations*, edited by Lisa Isherwood and Marcella Althaus-Reid, 1–12. London: SCM Press, 2009.

Isin, Engin F., and Greg M. Nielsen. "Introduction: Acts of Citizenship." In *Acts of Citizenship*, edited by Engin F. Isin and Greg M. Nielsen, 1–12. London: Zed Books, 2008.

Jackson, Michael. *The Politics of Storytelling: Variations on a Theme by Hannah Arendt*. 2nd ed. Copenhagen: Museum Musculanum Press, 2013.

Jagose, Annamarie. *Queer Theory: An Introduction*. New York: New York University Press, 1996.

Jenzen, Olu, and Sally R. Munt. "Queer Theory, Sexuality, and Religion." In *The Ashgate Research Companion to Contemporary Religion and Sexuality*, 45–58. Farnham: Ashgate, 2012.

John Paul II. "Post-Synodal Apostolic Exhortation Ecclesia in Africa of the Holy Father John Paul II to the Bishops, Priests and Deacons, Men and Women Religious and All the Lay Faithful to the Church in Africa and Its Evangelizing Mission Towards the Year 2000." Libreria Editrice Vaticana, 1995. http://w2.vatican.va/content/john-paul-ii/en/apost_exhortations/documents/hf_jp-ii_exh_14091995_ecclesia-in-africa.html.

Johnson, Douglas H., and David M. Anderson. "Revealing Prophets." In *Revealing Prophets: Prophecy in Eastern African History*, edited by Douglas H. Johnson and David M. Anderson, 1–27. London: James Currey, 1995.

Kalu, Ogbu U. *African Pentecostalism: An Introduction*. Oxford: Oxford University Press, 2008.

Kamau-Goro, Nicholas. "Rejection or Reappropriation? Christian Allegory and the Critique of Postcolonial Public Culture in the Early Novels of Ngũgĩ wa Thiong'o." In *Christianity and Public Culture in Africa*, edited by Harri Englund, 67–85. Athens: Ohio University Press.

Kangwa, Jonathan. "The Role of the Theology of Retribution in the Growth of Pentecostal-Charismatic Churches in Africa." *Verbum et Ecclesia* 37, no. 1 (2016): 1–9.

Kaoma, Kapya J. "The Marriage of Convenience: The U.S. Christian Right, African Christianity, and Postcolonial Politics of Sexual Identity." In *Global Homophobia: States, Movements, and the Politics of Oppression*, edited by Meredith L. Weis and Michael J. Bosia, 75–102. Urbana: University of Illinois Press, 2013.

Katongole, Emmanuel M. "'African Renaissance' and the Challenge of Narrative Theology in Africa." *Journal of Theology for Southern Africa* 102 (November 1998): 29–39.

———. "The Church of the Future: Pressing Moral Issues from Ecclesia in Africa." In *The Church We Want: African Catholics Look to Vatican III*, edited by Agbonkhianmeghe E. Orobator, 161–74. Maryknoll: Orbis Books, 2016.

Kee, Alistair. *The Rise and Demise of Black Theology*. London: SCM Press, 2008.

Kenyatta, Jomo. *Facing Mount Kenya*. 1938. New York: Vintage, 1965.

Kidula, Jean Ngoya. "The Local and Global in Kenyan Rap and Hip Hop Culture." In *Hip Hop Africa: New African Music in a Globalizing World*, edited by Eric Charry, 171–86. Bloomington: Indiana University Press, 2012.

Klinken, Adriaan van. "'The Body of Christ Has AIDS': A Study on the Notion of the Body of Christ in African Theologies Responding to HIV and AIDS." *Missionalia* 36, nos. 2–3 (2008): 319–36.

———. "Christianity in Africa: LGBT Affirming." In *Global Encyclopedia of Lesbian, Gay, Bisexual, Transgender, and Queer History*, edited by Howard Chiang, Anjali Arondekar, Marc Epprecht, Jennifer Evans, Ross G. Forman, Hanadi Al-Samman, Emily Skidmore, and Zeb Tortorici, 324–26. New York: Charles Scribner's Sons, 2019.

———. "Gay Rights, the Devil, and the End Times: Public Religion and the Enchantment of the Homosexuality Debate in Zambia." *Religion* 43, no. 4 (2013): 519–40.

———. "The Homosexual as the Antithesis of 'Biblical Manhood'? Heteronormativity and Masculinity Politics in Zambian Pentecostal Sermons." *Journal of Gender and Religion in Africa* 17, no. 2 (2011): 126–42.

———. "Homosexuality, Politics, and Pentecostal Nationalism in Zambia." *Studies in World Christianity* 20, no. 3 (2014): 259–81.

———. "Queer Love in a 'Christian Nation': Zambian Gay Men Negotiating Sexual and Religious Identities." *Journal of the American Academy of Religion* 83, no. 4 (2015): 947–64.

———. "When the Body of Christ Has AIDS: A Theological Metaphor for Global Solidarity in Light of HIV and AIDS." *International Journal of Public Theology* 4, no. 4 (2010): 446–65.

Klinken, Adriaan van, and Masiiwa Ragies Gunda. "Taking Up the Cudgels Against Gay Rights? Trends and Trajectories in African Christian Theologies on Homosexuality." *Journal of Homosexuality* 59, no. 1 (2012): 114–38.

Klinken, Adriaan van, and Kwame Edwin Otu. "Ancestors, Embodiment, and Sexual Desire? Wild Religion and the Body in the Story of a South African Lesbian Sangoma." *Body and Religion* 1, no. 1 (2017): 70–87.

Klinken, Adriaan van, and Lilly Phiri. "'In the Image of God': Reconstructing and Developing a Grassroots African Queer Theology from Urban Zambia." *Theology and Sexuality* 21, no. 1 (2015): 36–52.

Knighton, Rachel. "Refracting the Political: Binyavanga Wainaina's *One Day I Will Write About This Place*" *African Literature Today* 32 (2014): 33–46.

Kornegay, E. L., Jr. *A Queering of Black Theology: James Baldwin's Blues Project and Gospel Prose*. New York: Palgrave Macmillan, 2013.

Kulick, Don, and Margaret Willson, eds. *Taboo: Sex, Identity, and Erotic Subjectivity in Anthropological Fieldwork*. Abingdon: Routledge, 1995.

Larkin, Brian, and Birgit Meyer. "Pentecostalism, Islam, and Culture: New Religious Movements in West Africa." In *Themes in West Africa's History*, edited by Emmanuel Kwaku Akyeampong, 286–312. Oxford: James Currey, 2006.

Lewin, Ellen. *Filled with the Spirit: Sexuality, Gender, and Radical Inclusivity in a Black Pentecostal Church Coalition*. Chicago: University of Chicago Press, 2018.

Lindhardt, Martin. "Continuity, Change, or Coevalness: Charismatic Christianity and Tradition in Tanzania." In *Pentecostalism in Africa: Presence and Impact of Pneumatic Christianity in Postcolonial Societies*, edited by Martin Lindhardt, 163–90. Leiden: Brill, 2015.

———. "Introduction: Presence and Impact of Pentecostal/Charismatic Christianity in Africa." In *Pentecostalism in Africa: Presence and Impact of Pneumatic Christianity in Postcolonial Societies*, edited by Martin Lindhardt, 1–53. Leiden: Brill, 2015.

Long, Michael G. *Martin Luther King, Jr., Homosexuality, and the Early Gay Rights Movement: Keeping the Dream Straight?* New York: Palgrave Macmillan, 2012.

Lorde, Audre. "The Master's Tools Will Never Dismantle the Master's House." In *This Bridge Called My Back: Writings by Radical Women of Color*, 4th ed., edited by Cherrie Moraga and Gloria Anzaldúa, 94–101. New York: Kitchen Table Press, 2015.

Lorway, Robert. *Namibia's Rainbow Project: Gay Rights in an African Nation*. Bloomington: Indiana University Press, 2015.

Macharia, Keguro. "Archive and Method in Queer African Studies." *Agenda* 29, no. 1 (2015): 140–46.

———. "Queer Kenya in Law and Policy." In Ekine and Abbas, *Queer African Reader*, 273–89.

———. "Stories of Our Lives: Memories." New Inquiry, October 2, 2015. https://thenewinquiry.com/blog/stories-of-our-lives-memories/.

Maina, Wilson Muoha. *Historical and Social Dimensions in African Christian Theology: A Contemporary Approach*. Eugene: Wipf and Stock, 2009.

Maluleke, Tinyiko S. "The Challenge of HIV/AIDS for Theological Education in Africa: Towards an HIV/AIDS Sensitive Curriculum." *Missionalia* 29, no. 2 (2001): 125–43.

Markowitz, Fran, and Michael Ashkenazi, eds. *Sex, Sexuality, and the Anthropologist*. Urbana: University of Illinois Press, 1999.

Martey, Emmanuel. *African Theology: Inculturation and Liberation*. Maryknoll: Orbis Books, 1993.

Martin, Karen, and Makhosazana Xaba. *Queer Africa: New and Collected Fiction*. Braamfontein: MaThoko's Books, 2013.

Massad, Joseph A. "Re-Orienting Desire: The Gay International and the Arab World." In *Desiring Arabs*, 160–90. Chicago: University of Chicago Press.

Massoud, Mark F. "The Evolution of Gay Rights in South Africa." *Peace Review* 15, no. 3 (2003): 301–7.

Matebeni, Zethu. "How ~~NOT~~ to Write About Queer South Africa." In Matebeni, *Reclaiming Afrikan*, 61–63.

———, ed. *Reclaiming Afrikan: Queer Perspectives on Sexual and Gender Identities*. Cape Town: Modjaji Books, 2014.

Mateveke, Pauline. "Critique and Alternative Imaginations: Homosexuality and Religion in Contemporary Zimbabwean Literature." In *Public Religion and the Politics of Homosexuality in Africa*, edited by Adriaan van Klinken and Ezra Chitando, 213–28. Abingdon: Routledge, 2016.

Maupeu, Hervé. "Political Activism in Nairobi: Violence and Resilience of Kenyan Authoritarianism." In *Nairobi Today: The Paradox of a Fragmented City*, edited by Hélène Charton-Bigot and Deyssi Rodriguez-Torres, 381–405. Dar es Salaam: Mkuki na Nyota Publishers, 2010.

Maxwell, David. "'Delivered from the Spirit of Poverty?': Pentecostalism, Prosperity, and Modernity in Zimbabwe." *Journal of Religion in Africa* 28, no. 3 (1998): 350–73.

Mbembe, Achille. "African Modes of Self-Writing." Translated by Stephen Randall. *Public Culture* 14, no. 1 (2002): 239–73.

———. *Critique of Black Reason*. Translated by Laurent Dubois. Durham: Duke University Press, 2017.

———. *On the Postcolony*. Translated by A. M. Berrett, Janet Roitman, and Murray Last. Berkeley: University of California Press, 2001.

———. "On the Postcolony: A Brief Response to Critics." Translated by Nima Bassiri and Peter Skafish. *African Identities* 4, no. 2 (2006): 147–78.

Mbiti, John S. *African Religions and Philosophy*. 2nd ed. London: Heinemann, 1990.

———. *Love and Marriage in Africa*. London: Longman, 1973.

Mburu, John. "Awakenings: Dreams and Delusions of an Incipient Lesbian and Gay Movement in Kenya." In *Different Rainbows*, edited by Peter Drucker, 179–92. London: Millivres, 2000.

Meiu, George Paul. *Ethno-Erotic Economies: Sexuality, Money, and Belonging in Kenya*.

Chicago: University of Chicago Press, 2017.
Mendieta, Eduardo, and Jonathan VanAntwerpen, eds. *The Power of Religion in the Public Sphere*. New York: Columbia University Press, 2011.
Meyer, Birgit. "Christianity in Africa: From African Independent to Pentecostal-Charismatic Churches." *Annual Review of Anthropology* 33 (2004): 447–74.
———. *Sensational Movies: Video, Vision, and Christianity in Ghana*. Berkeley: University of California Press, 2015.
Millet, Kitty. *The Victims of Slavery, Colonization, and the Holocaust: A Comparative History of Persecution*. London: Bloomsbury, 2015.
Mohanty, Chandra Talpade. "Under Western Eyes: Feminist Scholarship and Colonial Discourses." In *Third World Women and the Politics of Feminism*, edited by Chandra Talpade Mohanty, Ann Russo, and Lourdes Torres, 51–80. Bloomington: Indiana University Press, 1991.
Mombo, Esther. "Kenya Reflections." In *Other Voices, Other Worlds: The Global Church Speaks Out on Homosexuality*, edited by Terry Brown, 142–53. New York: Church Publishing, 2006.
Monte, Ernest Patrick. "Representations of Land in Kenyan Song." *Critical African Studies* 10, no. 1 (2018): 14–30.
Moon, Dawne. *God, Sex, and Politics: Homosexuality and Everyday Theologies*. Chicago: University of Chicago Press, 2004.
Moore, Clive. *Sunshine and Rainbows: The Development of Gay and Lesbian Culture in Queensland*. St. Lucia: University of Queensland Press, 2001.
Morris, Charles E., and John M. Sloop. "'What Lips These Lips Have Kissed': Refiguring the Politics of Queer Public Kissing." *Communication and Critical/Cultural Studies* 3, no. 1 (2006): 1–26.
Moyo, Fulata L. "'Singing and Dancing Women's Liberation': My Story of Faith." In *Her-Stories: Hidden Histories of Women of Faith in Africa*, edited by Isabel A. Phiri, Devaraksham Betty Govinden, and Sarojini Nadar, 389–408. Pietermaritzburg: Cluster, 2002.
Msibi, Thabo. "The Lies We Have Been Told: On (Homo) Sexuality in Africa." *Africa Today* 58, no. 1 (2011): 54–77.
Mugambi, Jesse N. K. *Christian Theology and Social Reconstruction*. Nairobi: Acton, 2003.
Muñoz, José Esteban. *Cruising Utopia: The Then and There of Queer Futurity*. New York: New York University Press, 2009.
Munro, Brenna M. *South Africa and the Dream of Love to Come: Queer Sexuality and the Struggle for Freedom*. Minneapolis: University of Minnesota Press, 2012.
Munt, Sally R. "Queer Spiritual Spaces." In *Queer Spiritual Spaces: Sexuality and Sacred Places*, edited by Kath Browne, Sally R. Munt, and Andrew K. T. Yip, 1–33. Farnham: Ashgate, 2010.
Muparamoto, Nelson. "Enduring and Subverting Homophobia: Religious Experiences of Same-Sex Loving People in Zimbabwe." In *Christianity and Controversies over Homosexuality in Contemporary Africa*, edited by Ezra Chitando and Adriaan van Klinken, 143–56. London: Routledge, 2016.
Murray, Stephen O., and William Roscoe, eds. *Boy-Wives and Female Husbands: Studies in African Homosexualities*. New York: St. Martin's Press, 1998.
Murunga, Godwin R. "Elite Compromises and the Content of the 2010 Constitution." In *Kenya: The Struggle for a New Constitutional Order*, edited by Godwin R. Murunga, Duncan Okello, and Anders Sjogren, 144–62. London: Zed Books, 2014.
Musila, Grace A. "Phallocracies and Gynocratic Transgressions: Gender, State Power, and Kenyan Public Life." *Africa Insight* 39, no. 1 (2009): 39–57.
Mutambara, Maaraidzo. "African Women Theologies Critique Inculturation." In *Inculturation and Postcolonial Discourse in African Theology*, edited by Edward P. Antonio, 173–91. New York: Peter Lang, 2006.
Mwachiro, Kevin. *Invisible: Stories from Kenya's Queer Community*. Nairobi: Goethe Institut, 2014.

———. "A Lost Chapter Found: Interview with Binyavanga Wainaina." In Sandfort et al., *Boldly Queer*, 97–101.
Mwangi, Evan. "Queer Agency in Kenya's Digital Media." *African Studies Review* 57, no. 2 (2014): 93–113.
Mwikya, Kenne. "The Media, the Tabloid, and the Uganda Homophobia Spectacle." In Ekine and Abbas, *Queer African Reader*, 141–54.
Nadar, Sarojini. "Her-Stories and Her-Theologies: Charting Feminist Theologies in Africa." *Studia Historiae Ecclesiasticae* 35 (December 2009): 135–150.
———. "On Being Church: African Women's Voices and Visions." In *On Being Church: African Women's Voices and Visions*, edited by Isabel A. Phiri and Sarojini Nadar, 16–28. Geneva: World Council of Churches, 2005.
———. "'Stories Are Data with Soul': Lessons from Black Feminist Epistemology." *Agenda* 28, no. 1 (2014): 18–28.
Nathan, Roland A. "Blessed Be the Tie That Binds: African Diaspora Christian Movements and African Unity." In *The Africana World: From Fragmentation to Unity and Renaissance*, edited by Mammo Muchie, Sanya Osha, and Matlotleng P. Matlou, 275–86. Pretoria: Africa Institute of South Africa, 2012.
Ndjio, Basile. "Sexuality and Nationalist Ideologies in Post-Colonial Cameroon." In *The Sexual History of the Global South: Sexual Politics in Africa, Asia, and Latin America*, edited by Saskia Wieringa and Horacio Sivori, 120–43. London: Zed Books, 2013.
Ndzovu, Hassan J. "Un-Natural, Un-African, and Un-Islamic: The Three Pronged Onslaught Undermining Homosexual Freedom in Kenya." In *Public Religion and the Politics of Homosexuality in Africa*, edited by Adriaan van Klinken and Ezra Chitando, 78–91. Abingdon: Routledge, 2016.
Nelson, James B. "Where Are We? Seven Sinful Problems and Seven Virtuous Possibilities." In *Sexuality and the Sacred: Sources for Theological Reflection*, edited by Marvin Mahan Ellison and Kelly Brown Douglas, 95–104. Louisville: Westminster John Knox Press.
The Nest Collective. *Stories of Our Lives*. Nairobi: Nest Arts Company, 2015.
Ngũgĩ wa Thiong'o. *Decolonising the Mind: The Politics of Language in African Literature*. London: Heinemann, 1986.
———. *Re-Membering Africa*. Nairobi: East African Educational Publishers, 2009.
———. *The River Between*. London: Heinemann, 1965.
Njogu, Kimani, and G. Oluoch-Olunya, eds. *Cultural Production and Social Change in Kenya*. Nairobi: Twaweza, 2007.
Njoroge, Nyambura J. "Beyond Suffering and Lament: Theology of Hope and Life." In *Shaping a Global Theological Mind*, edited by Darren C. Marks, 113–20. Aldershot: Ashgate, 2008.
Ntarangwi, Mwenda. *East African Hip Hop: Youth Culture and Globalization*. Urbana: University of Illinois Press, 2009.
———. *The Street Is My Pulpit: Hip Hop and Christianity in Kenya*. Urbana: University of Illinois Press, 2016.
Nyabuga, George. "Things Fall Apart: What Troubles Hath Hip-Hop in Kenya?" In *Music, Performance, and African Identities*, edited by Toyin Falola and Tyler Fleming, 283–95. New York: Routledge, 2012.
Nyanzi, Stella. "Queering Queer Africa." In Matebeni, *Reclaiming Afrikan*, 65–68.
———. "When the State Produces Hate: Re-Thinking the Global Queer Movement Through Silence in The Gambia." In Tellis and Bala, *Global Trajectories of Queerness*, 179–93.
Nyeck, S. N., and Marc Epprecht, eds. *Sexual Diversity in Africa: Politics, Theory, Citizenship*. Montreal: McGill-Queen's University Press, 2013.
Nygren, Anders. *Agape and Eros*. London: SPCK, 1982.
Obadare, Ebenezer, and Wendy Willems, eds. *Civic Agency in Africa: Arts of Resistance in the Twenty-First Century*. London: James Currey, 2014.

Ocholla, Akinya Margareta. "The Kenyan LGBTI Social Movement—Context, Volunteerism, and Approaches to Campaigning." *Journal of Human Rights Practice* 3, no. 1 (2011): 93–104.

Oduyoye, Mercy Amba. "A Coming Home to Myself: The Childless Woman in the West African Space." In *Liberating Eschatology: Essays in Honor of Letty M. Russell*, edited by Margaret A. Farley and Serene Jones, 105–20. Louisville: Westminster John Knox Press, 1999.

———. "A Critique of Mbiti's View on Love and Marriage in Africa." In *Religious Plurality in Africa: Essays in Honour of John S. Mbiti*, edited by Jacob K. Olupona and Sulayman S. Nyang, 341–66. Berlin: Mouton de Gruyter, 1993.

———. *Introducing African Women's Theology*. Cleveland: Pilgrim Press, 2001.

Oduyoye, Mercy Amba, and Elizabeth Amoah. "The Christ for African Women." In *With Passion and Compassion: Third World Women Doing Theology*, edited by Mercy Amba Oduyoye and Virginia Fabella, 35–46. Maryknoll: Orbis Books, 1988.

Ombagi, Eddie. "Nairobi Is a Shot of Whisky: Queer (Ob)scenes in the City." *Journal of African Cultural Studies* (June 2018). https://www.tandfonline.com/doi/full/10.1080/13696815.2018.1484709.

Orobator, Agbonkhianmeghe E. *The Church as Family: African Ecclesiology in Its Social Context*. Nairobi: Paulines, 2000.

———. *Theology Brewed in an African Pot*. Maryknoll: Orbis Books, 2008.

Orsi, Robert A. *Between Heaven and Earth: The Religious Worlds People Make and the Scholars Who Study Them*. Princeton: Princeton University Press, 2004.

Otu, Kwame Edwin. "LGBT Human Rights Expeditions in Homophobic Safaris: Racialized Neoliberalism and Post-Traumatic White Disorder in the BBC's *The World's Worst Place to Be Gay*." *Critical Ethnic Studies* 3, no. 2 (2017): 126–50.

———. "Saints and Sinners: African Holocaust, 'Clandestine Countermemories,' and LGBT Visibility Politics in Postcolonial Africa." In *Being and Becoming: Gender, Culture, and Shifting Identity in Sub-Saharan Africa*, edited by Chinyere Ukpokolo, 195–216. Denver: Spears Media, 2016.

Oyěwùmí, Oyèrónkẹ́. *The Invention of Women: Making an African Sense of Western Gender Discourses*. Minneapolis: University of Minnesota Press, 1997.

Parratt, John. *Reinventing Christianity: African Theology Today*. Grand Rapids: Eerdmans, 1995.

Parsitau, Damaris. "Embodying Holiness: Gender, Sex, and Bodies in a Neo-Pentecostal Church in Kenya." In *Body Talk and Cultural Identity in the African World*, edited by Augustine Agwuele, 181–201. London: Equinox, 2015.

———. "Gospel Music in Africa." In *The Wiley-Blackwell Companion to African Religions*, edited by Elias K. Bongmba, 489–502. Malden, Mass.: Wiley-Blackwell, 2012.

———. "Prophets, Power, Authority, and the Kenyan State: Prophet David Owuor of the National Repentance and Holiness Ministry." In *Religious Freedom and Religious Pluralism in Africa: Prospects and Limitations*, edited by Pieter Coertzen, Christian M. Green, and Len Hansen, 233–56. Stellenbosch: SUN Media, 2016.

Parsitau, Damaris, and Philomena Njeri Mwaura. "God in the City: Pentecostalism as an Urban Phenomenon in Kenya." *Studia Historiae Ecclesiasticae* 36, no. 2 (2010): 95–112.

Phan, Peter C. "Roman Catholic Theology." In *The Oxford Handbook of Eschatology*, edited by Jerry L. Walls, 215–32. Oxford: Oxford University Press, 2008.

Phiri, Isabel A., Devaraksham Betty Govinden, and Sarojini Nadar. "Introduction." In *Her-Stories: Hidden Histories of Women of Faith in Africa*, edited by Isabel A. Phiri, Devaraksham Betty Govinden, and Sarojini Nadar, 1–13. Pietermaritzburg: Cluster, 2002.

Phiri, Lilly. "Born This Way: The Imago Dei in Men Who Love Other Men in Lusaka, Zambia." In *Christianity and Controversies over Homosexuality in Contemporary Africa*, edited by Ezra Chitando and Adriaan van Klinken, 157–70. London: Routledge, 2016.

Pinn, Anthony B. *Embodiment and the New Shape of Black Theological Thought*. New York: New York University Press, 2010.

Plummer, Ken. *Cosmopolitan Sexualities*. Cambridge: Polity Press, 2015.

———. *Intimate Citizenship: Private Decisions and Public Dialogue*. Seattle: University of Washington Press, 2003.

———. *Telling Sexual Stories: Power, Change, and Social Worlds*. London: Routledge, 1995.

Porter, Mary A. "Talking at the Margins: Kenyan Discourses on Homosexuality." In *Beyond the Lavender Lexicon: Authenticity, Imagination, and Appropriation in Lesbian and Gay Languages*, edited by William L. Leap, 133–54. Amsterdam: Gordon and Breach, 1995.

Puar, Jasbir K. *Terrorist Assemblages: Homonationalism in Queer Times*. Durham: Duke University Press, 2007.

Rao, Rahul. "Re-Membering Mwanga: Same-Sex Intimacy, Memory, and Belonging in Postcolonial Uganda." *Journal of Eastern African Studies* 9, no. 1 (2015): 1–19.

———. *Third World Protest: Between Home and the World*. Oxford: Oxford University Press, 2010.

Reid, Graeme. *Above the Skyline: Reverend Tsietsi Thandekiso and the Founding of an African Gay Church*. Johannesburg: UNISA Press, 2011.

Rooke, Alison. "Queer in the Field: On Emotions, Temporality, and Performativity in Ethnography." In *Queer Methods and Methodologies: Intersecting Queer Theories and Social Science Research*, edited by Catherine J. Nash and Kath Browne, 25–40. Farnham: Ashgate, 2010.

Sadgrove, Joanna, Robert M. Vanderbeck, Johan Andersson, Gill Valentine, and Kevin Ward. "Morality Plays and Money Matters: Towards a Situated Understanding of the Politics of Homosexuality in Uganda." *Journal of Modern African Studies* 50, no. 1 (2012): 103–29.

Sandfort, Theo, Fabienne Simenel, Kevin Mwachiro, and Vasu Reddy, eds. *Boldly Queer: African Perspectives on Same-Sex Sexuality and Gender Diversity*. The Hague: HIVOS, 2015.

Sandoval, Chela, and Guisela Latorre. "Chicana/o Artivism: Judy Baca's Digital Work with Youth of Color." In *Learning Race and Ethnicity: Youth and Digital Media*, edited by Anna Everett, 81–108. Cambridge: MIT Press, 2008.

Sartre, Jean-Paul. "Genocide." *New Left Review* 1, no. 48 (1968): 13–25.

Scott, James C. *Domination and the Arts of Resistance: Hidden Transcripts*. New Haven: Yale University Press, 1990.

Sedgwick, Eve Kosofsky. *Epistemology of the Closet*. Berkeley: University of California Press, 2008.

Senyonjo, Christopher. *In Defense of All God's Children: The Life and Ministry of Bishop Christopher Senyonjo*. New York: Morehouse, 2016.

Shankar, Shobana. "Civil Society and Religion." In *The Handbook of Civil Society in Africa*, edited by Ebenezer Obadare, 25–42. New York: Springer, 2013.

Shepherd, Gill. "Rank, Gender, and Homosexuality: Mombasa as a Key to Understanding Sexual Options." In *The Cultural Construction of Sexuality*, edited by Pat Caplan, 240–70. London: Tavistock, 1987.

Shulman, George. *American Prophecy: Race and Redemption in American Political Culture*. Minneapolis: University of Minnesota Press, 2008.

Simone, AbdouMaliq. *For the City Yet to Come: Changing African Life in Four Cities*. Durham: Duke University Press, 2004.

Simone, AbdouMaliq, and Edgar Pieterse. *New Urban Worlds: Inhabiting Dissonant Times*. Cambridge: Polity Press, 2017.

Sneed, Roger A. *Representations of Homosexuality: Black Liberation Theology and Cultural Criticism*. New York: Palgrave Macmillan, 2010.

Soyinka, Wole. *Of Africa*. New Haven: Yale University Press, 2012.

Spivak, Gayatri Chakravorty. "Can the Subaltern Speak?" In *Marxism and the Interpretation of Culture*, edited by Cary Nelson and Lawrence Grossberg, 271–313. Basingstoke: Macmillan, 1988.

Spronk, Rachel. "Media and the Therapeutic Ethos of Romantic Love in Middle-Class Nairibi." In *Love in Africa*, edited by Jennifer Cole and Lynn M. Thomas, 181–203. Chicago: University of Chicago Press, 2009.

———. "Sex, Sexuality, and Negotiating Africanness in Nairobi." *Africa* 79, no. 4 (2009): 500–519.

Spurlin, William J. *Imperialism Within the Margins: Queer Representation and the Politics of Culture in Southern Africa*. New York: Palgrave Macmillan, 2006.

Stinton, Diana, ed. *African Theology on the Way*. Minneapolis: Fortress Press, 2015.

Stone-Mediatore, Shari. *Reading Across Borders: Storytelling and Knowledges of Resistance*. New York: Palgrave Macmillan, 2003.

Stuart, Elizabeth, ed. *Religion Is a Queer Thing*. Cleveland: Pilgrim Press, 1997.

———. "Sacramental Flesh." In *Queer Theology: Rethinking the Western Body*, edited by Gerard Loughlin, 65–75. Malden, Mass.: Blackwell, 2007.

Talvacchia, Kathleen T., Michael F. Pettinger, and Mark Larrimore, eds. *Queer Christianities: Lived Religion in Transgressive Forms*. New York: New York University Press, 2015.

Tamale, Sylvia. "Researching and Theorising Sexualities in Africa." In *African Sexualities: A Reader*, edited by Sylvia Tamale, 11–36. Dakar: Pambazuka Press, 2011.

Tang, Patricia. "The Rapper as Modern Griot: Reclaiming Ancient Traditions." In *Hip Hop Africa: New African Music in a Globalizing World*, edited by Eric Charry, 79–91. Bloomington: Indiana University Press, 2012.

Tellis, Ashley, and Sruti Bala, eds. *The Global Trajectories of Queerness: Re-Thinking Same-Sex Politics in the Global South*. Leiden: Brill Rodopi, 2015.

Theophano, Teresa. "Pornographic Film and Video: Lesbian." In *The Queer Encyclopedia of Film and Television*, edited by Claude J. Summers, 237–39. San Francisco: Cleis Press, 2005.

Thomas, Lynn M., and Jennifer Cole. "Introduction: Thinking Through Love in Africa." In *Love in Africa*, edited by Jennifer Cole and Lynn M. Thomas, 1–30. Chicago: University of Chicago Press, 2009.

Thoreson, Ryan R. "Troubling the Waters of a 'Wave of Homophobia': Political Economies of Anti-Queer Animus in Sub-Saharan Africa." *Sexualities* 17, nos. 1–2 (2014): 23–42.

Togarasei, Lovemore, and Ezra Chitando. "'Beyond the Bible': Critical Reflections on the Contributions of Cultural and Postcolonial Studies on Same-Sex Relationships in Africa." *Journal of Gender and Religion in Africa* 17, no. 2 (2011): 109–25.

Tomlinson, Matt. *Ritual Textuality: Pattern and Motion in Performance*. Oxford: Oxford University Press, 2014.

Vaughan, Megan. *Curing Their Ills: Colonial Power and African Illness*. Cambridge: Polity Press, 1991.

———. "The Discovery of Suicide in Eastern and Southern Africa." *African Studies* 71, no. 2 (2012): 234–50.

Vengeyi, Obvious. "Zimbabwean Pentecostal Prophets: Rekindling the 'True and False Prophecy' Debate." In *Prophets, Profits, and the Bible in Zimbabwe*, edited by Ezra Chitando, Masiiwa Ragies Gunda, and Joachim Kügler, 29–54. Bamberg: University of Bamberg Press, 2013.

Vernallis, Carol. "Music Video's Second Aesthetic." In *The Oxford Handbook of New Audiovisual Aesthetics*, edited by John Richardson, Claudia Gorbman, and Carol Vernallis, 437–65. Oxford: Oxford University Press, 2013.

Wainaina, Binyavanga. *One Day I Will Write About This Place*. London: Granta Books, 2011.

Waites, Matthew. "Genocide and Global Queer Politics." *Journal of Genocide Research* 20, no. 1 (2018): 44–67.

Walls, Andrew F. *The Cross-Cultural Process in Christian History: Studies in the Transmission and Appropriation of Faith*. Maryknoll: Orbis Books, 2002.

Walls, Jerry L. "Introduction." In *The Oxford Handbook of Eschatology*, edited by Jerry L. Walls, 3–22. Oxford: Oxford University Press, 2008.

Ward, Kevin. "Marching or Stumbling Towards a Christian Ethic? Homosexuality and African Anglicanism." In *Other Voices, Other Worlds: The Global Church Speaks Out on Homosexuality*, edited by Terry Brown, 129–41. New York: Church Publishing, 2006.

Wariboko, Nimi. *The Charismatic City and the Public Resurgence of Religion: A Pentecostal Social Ethics of Cosmopolitan Urban Life*. New York: Palgrave Macmillan, 2014.

Warner, Michael. "Introduction." In *Fear of a Queer Planet: Queer Politics and Social Change*, edited by Michael Warner, vii–xxxi. Minneapolis: University of Minnesota Press, 1993.

———. "Publics and Counterpublics." *Public Culture* 14, no. 1 (2002): 49–90.

———. "Tongues Untied: Memories of a Pentecostal Boyhood." In *Que(e)rying Religion: A Critical Anthology*, edited by Gary D. Comstock and Susan E. Henking, 223–31. New York: Continuum, 1997.

Warner, R. Stephen. *A Church of Our Own: Disestablishment and Diversity in American Religion*. New Brunswick: Rutgers University Press, 2005.

West, Gerald. *The Stolen Bible: From Tool of Imperialism to African Icon*. Leiden: Brill, 2016.

———. "Towards an African Liberationist Queer Theological Pedagogy." *Journal of Theology for Southern Africa* 155 (July 2016): 216–24.

Westhelle, Vitor. "Liberation Theology." In *The Oxford Handbook of Eschatology*, edited by Jerry L. Walls, 311–27. Oxford: Oxford University Press, 2008.

Weston, Kath. "Get Thee to a Big City: Sexual Imaginary and the Great Gay Migration." *GLQ: A Journal of Lesbian and Gay Studies* 2, no. 3 (1995): 253–77.

Wilcox, Melissa M. *Coming Out in Christianity: Religion, Identity, and Community*. Bloomington: Indiana University Press, 2003.

———. "Outlaws or In-Laws? Queer Theory, LGBT Studies, and Religious Studies." *Journal of Homosexuality* 52, nos. 1–2 (2006): 73–100.

Willems, Wendy, and Ebenezer Obadare. "Introduction: African Resistance in an Age of Fractured Sovereignty." In Obadare and Willems, *Civic Agency in Africa*, 1–23.

Wilson, Erin K. "The Socio-Political Dynamics of Secularism and Epistemological Injustice in Global Justice Theory and Practice." *European Societies* 19, no. 5 (2017): 529–50.

Zabus, Chantal. *Out in Africa: Same-Sex Desire in Sub-Saharan Literatures and Cultures*. Suffolk: James Currey, 2013.

Index